the Federal Landscape

Gerald D. Nash

the

The University of Arizona Press
Tucson

Federal Landscape

An Economic History

Landscape

of the
Twentieth-
Century
West

To Marie

The University of Arizona Press
©1999 The Arizona Board of Regents
First printing
All rights reserved

∞ This book is printed on acid-free, archival-quality paper.
Manufactured in the United States of America
04 03 02 01 00 99   6 5 4 3 2 1

Library of Congress Cataloging-in-Publication Data

Nash, Gerald D.
  The federal landscape : an economic history of the twentieth-century
West / Gerald D. Nash
    p. cm. — (The modern American West)
  Includes bibliographical references (p.) and index.

  ISBN 0-8165-1863-7 (acid-free, archival-quality paper)
  ISBN 0-8165-1988-9 (pbk. : acid-free, archival-quality paper)
  1. West (U.S.)—Economic conditions—20th century. 2. Regional
planning—West (U.S.)—History—20th century. 3. Federal aid—West
(U.S.)—History—20th century. I. Title. II. Series.
  HC107.A17 N3714 1999
  330.978'032—dc21
                    99-6027
                    CIP

British Library Cataloguing-in-Publication Data
A catalogue record for this book is available from the British Library.

The Modern American West

Gerald D. Nash and Richard W. Etulain, Editors

Carl Abbott

The Metropolitan Frontier: Cities in the Modern American West

Richard W. Etulain

Re-imagining the Modern American West: A Century of Fiction, History, and Art

Gerald D. Nash

The Federal Landscape: An Economic History of the Twentieth-Century West

Contents

A nyone who flies across the United States coast to coast and looks at the ground below is bound to observe the vastness of the land. In the more humid regions, especially in the Midwest, the curious traveler sees a checkerboard pattern of small farms on rectangular plots of land. As the plane flies across the Mississippi River and above the arid trans-Mississippi West, the landscape changes and vast stretches of open lands, some seemingly uninhabited, appear, perhaps with ribbons of highways connecting small settlements. Then, suddenly, large desert cities loom, urban oases in the wilderness. Most airline pilots like to point out the mammoth dam developments in different regions of the West, along with expansive manmade lakes and waterways. Other interesting sites

Preface

include large stretches of land set aside for military purposes—test grounds, air force bases, or training camps. Striking also are the Indian reservations that seem to emerge from wilderness. As the plane finally lands on the Pacific coast, let us say in Seattle, Portland, the San Francisco Bay region, or southern California, our curious traveler is impressed by huge naval complexes and vast compounds dedicated to aerospace manufacturing or research and development on the ground below.

By this time our inquisitive traveler has formed the impression that this is a land that to a considerable extent has been formed by the federal government. It was the federal government that determined the pattern of farms in the humid regions, built the major roads and highways, and fostered the growth of the principal cities in the West. The federal government built the large dams and diverted important river systems throughout the West, determined the shape of the large military reservations and their environs, and forced Native Americans to occupy the reservations on which they can be found today. The government is largely responsible for the aerospace complexes and scientific research centers that became so important in the West during the second half of the twentieth century. In short, the federal government created a federal landscape in the West. The federal government may not have been the only influence on the shaping of the West in the twentieth century, but it must be considered the dominant force.

And therein lies a basic lesson. In the nineteenth century the West was largely developed by individual enterprise. At least that was the perception of the well-known historian Frederick Jackson Turner, who popularized the idea that the West fostered individualism on a moving frontier. Whether that perception was real or not is irrelevant; it was a conclusion embraced by millions of Americans and other people around the world. By contrast, the development of the West in the twentieth century was shaped by the federal government. In short, if the nineteenth-century West was the product of American individualism, then the twentieth-century West is the creation of the federal government.

But we need to place the economic growth of the West in a broad global and historical context. Historians and economists have long been interested in charting long waves or cycles of economic activity. In the first half of the twentieth century, various distinguished theorists—including

Wesley C. Mitchell in the United States and S. S. De Wolff, C. Van Gelderen, and A. Spiethoff in the Netherlands—developed suggestive hypotheses. Earlier, the German theoretician Wilhelm Abel had attracted a wide following. Indeed, the French founder of the Annales school, Fernand Braudel, largely followed the pioneering work of Abel in charting secular long waves in the economies of Early Modern Europe.[1]

Some of the most innovative work in this field was accomplished by the Russian economist Nicolae Kondratieff in the 1920s, while he was the director of the Institute of Business Cycles in Moscow. Some of his essays were translated into English in the 1930s and reached a wider audience. Kondratieff's objective was to determine why capitalism in industrial societies seemed to experience forty- to fifty-year swings and to experience crises within that time frame.

Kondratieff wrote about three long waves. The first extended from about 1787 to 1845 and was generated by steam engines and new sources of power. These developments stimulated puddling, new textile industries, and iron manufactures; gave rise to small factories; stimulated the growth of small towns; and transformed Great Britain into the first industrialized society. The second wave came between 1845 and 1890 when steamships and the development of Bessemer furnaces provided new technology. These innovations gave rise to the machine tool and steel industries. The large factories characteristic of this era required a large concentration of capital. Cities grew larger. The United States, Germany, and Great Britain were caught up in the wave. While the European nations expanded their markets overseas, the United States accelerated its westward movement. The third wave swept in from about 1890 to 1947. Electric light, alternating current, and the automobile were the dynamic technological inventions that spurred new industries such as chemicals, automobiles, and electrical engineering. This wave brought mass production, huge factories, finance capital, and cartels. The United States and Germany became the leaders of the third-wave economies, and their rivalries spurred on two world wars.

If Kondratieff's ideas are extrapolated, the fourth wave began sometime in the late 1960s, characterized by the further development of the transistor (first built in 1947) and especially by its adaptation in the computer chip (1971). This new technology created electronics industries, computers, telecommunications, and aerospace and service industries. It led to the creation of multinational corporations, a mix of small and large corporations, suburbanization of cities, and the development of entirely new postindustrial regions such as the American West. The United States and Japan were the leaders in developing these new economies. The cold war and the space race were outgrowths of these fourth-wave developments.

One wave did not necessarily follow closely on the heels of its predecessor. Often a twenty- to thirty-year hiatus developed between the peak of one wave and the start of another. These were usually periods reflecting some confusion and trial and error until entrepreneurs could adapt new technologies to stimulate economic change.

But Kondratieff went further than merely describing waves of societal development. As he developed his initial theories, he concluded that capitalist societies seemed to have a self-correcting mechanism that enabled them to survive and overcome periodic crises. Unfortunately, such a conclusion was totally out of step with the orthodox Marxist economic doctrines of the 1920s. It angered many of Kondratieff's colleagues, but most of all it infuriated the Soviet dictator, Joseph Stalin, who had Kondratieff arrested and sent to a labor camp in Siberia. There, according to Aleksander Solzhenitsyn's account in *The Gulag Archipelago,* Kondratieff died insane.[2]

In the later 1930s the eminent economist Joseph Schumpeter revised and amplified Kondratieff's theories. Schumpeter emphasized the central importance of technology and argued that the start of each wave was caused by new technological innovations, which in turn created new industries. Between 1785 and 1842 it was coal, iron, and steam; from 1842 to 1900 it was steel, railways, steamships, and machine tools. By the early twentieth century, automobiles, electrical goods, and chemicals were prime movers. Schumpeter challenged the classical tradition in economics and the Keynesians, who had largely ignored technological innovations. Moreover, Schumpeter emphasized the important role of entrepreneurs in undertaking innovation, thus defining the human dimension in development. It was the entrepreneurs who provided the key to economic change.[3]

After 1939, economists developed new interests and largely ignored Schumpeter and Kondratieff. Only in the 1980s, a period of economic transition, was interest in their theories revived as dynamic new inventions such as the computer chip were clearly vitalizing economies in developed nations such as the United States, Great Britain, and Japan. By the 1990s, economists were debating the nature of the long waves. They raised old and new questions. Does innovation really peak at intervals of about half a century? Do waves respond to crises of capital accumulation? What is the influence of technological change on business organization? What is the role of managerial expertise on corporate development, as emphasized by Alfred D. Chandler? Issues concerning waves of growth or the impact of technological innovation in the context of socioeconomic systems in the United States, Great Britain, France, Germany, and the Netherlands engaged the attention of a new generation of economists in the last two decades of the twentieth century.[4]

In an effort to combine the theories describing socioeconomic systems, economist Carlota Perez has suggested that capitalist systems contain two main subsystems, one technoeconomic, the other socioinstitutional. Long waves constitute modes of development shaped in response to a specific technological style understood as a paradigm for the most efficient system of production. Perez suggests a harmonic complementarity between technological style and the socioeconomic framework.[5]

The Kondratieff-Schumpeter cycles help to explain the successive waves of growth in the western United States. Since the eighteenth century, four such waves have affected the western economy. Between 1780 and 1860, when steam engines and power looms were generating what came to be known as the Industrial Revolution, the American West, still in the infancy of its economic development, was barely affected. The second wave's railroads, steamships, steel, and electricity inaugurated a new economic age, and these changes profoundly affected the American West, largely by integrating it into the national economy and ending its isolation. When the third wave's automobiles, aerospace engineering, and petrochemicals ushered in another era, the West grasped at this rare opportunity and became a pacesetter in developing the new technologies. The development that took place at that time also spawned the enormous growth of cities in the region. The fourth wave had a profound impact on the West because it eliminated time and distance, which for many years had defined the West as a region. The microchip stimulated the growth of Silicon Valley and its clones, fostered the reorganization of business enterprises, and stimulated a revamping of federal regulatory policies.

But waves of economic growth inspired by technology were not the only formative factors in the growth of the twentieth-century western economy. Major changes in global monetary conditions were also crucial, reflected either in the world's supplies of precious metals or in the monetary and fiscal policies of governments. These created price revolutions that stimulated entrepreneurial activity and provided a context for technological innovation. Such price movements were largely put in motion by the monetary and fiscal policies of the federal government as well as by markets. But price revolutions, like technology, are not abstract, impersonal forces that work themselves out automatically. Rather, they are fashioned by live men and women, often utilizing the machinery of government. The West might have followed very different historical patterns had the federal government not been the dominant influence guiding its growth. It could be argued that the decision to provide strong federal leadership to undertake the expansion of the western economy was a conscious effort by eastern America to develop the youngest part of the United States. In many ways this decision was bound up with Americans' perception of the West as a land of opportunity, a perception that had been popular in the nineteenth century and that had persisted for many years thereafter.

As the least densely populated region of the nation in 1900, the West still represented a tableau nouveau. In this thinly populated area, dreams and experiments could still be fulfilled, at least more successfully than in the older and more congested East. Thus, the federal government's decision to invest in the West represented an investment in the nation's future in fulfillment of American dreams at every level of society.[6]

This book tells the story of how an erstwhile hinterland became the most dynamic and most rapidly growing part of the United States over the course of a century. Although numerous studies have dealt with aspects of that growth, an overview has yet to be published. The prime purpose of this book is to provide such an overview, using a multidisciplinary analysis. We will examine the history of public policy; economic development; environmental issues; issues of race, class, and gender; and urban problems, among other issues. I hope that such a survey will show how the federal government fashioned the West in the course of the last one hundred years.

✤ In writing this synthesis I have profited in various ways from the XV work of numerous scholars. Among them I should mention Carl Abbott, Tom Alexander, Leonard Arrington, Mansel Blackford, Larry W. Burt, William R. Childs, Richard O. Davies, Lawrence B. De Graaf, Lyle Dorsett, Lynn Doti, Mark Foster, Art Gomez, Gene Gressley, Norris Hundley, Marilynn L. Johnson, Amy Kesselman, Lawrence Lee, Roger Lotchin, Richard Lowitt, Martin Melosi, Spenser Olin, Donald Pisani, Mark Rose, William D. Rowley, Carlos Schwantes, Larry Schweikart, and Quintard Taylor. I owe a special debt to Richard W. Etulain, whose suggestions and imaginative insights seem endless and whose wise advice and encouragement did a great deal to lead me to write and to complete this work. Our joint interest in western history has long been infectious. For special help with the accompanying map I am indebted to Mary Wyant and especially to Randy Wallace of the University of New Mexico's Map and Geographic Information Center (MAGIC) and to the Environmental Systems Research Institute in Redlands, California, for data. Melinda Conner contributed her very special editorial skills to improve the manuscript. If many individuals contributed to the making of the book, I am still responsible for the final product. Finally, I am immeasurably indebted to my wife, Marie, without whose help in so many different ways it would have been difficult to bring the volume to completion.

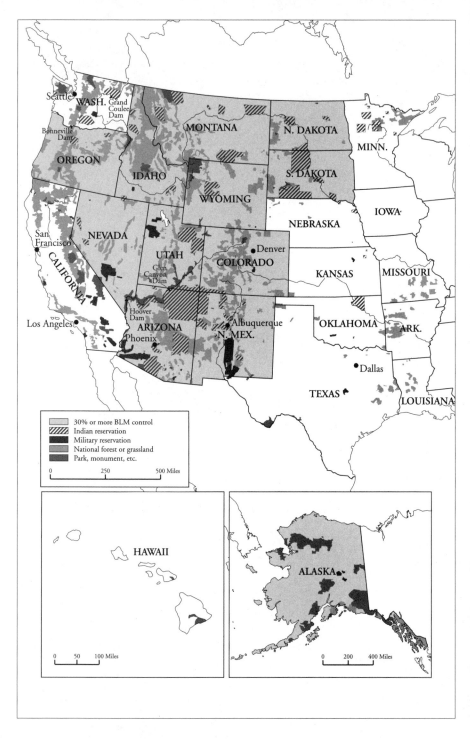

The Federal Landscape in the West. (Based on a map by Randy Wallace and Mary Wyant, with data from the Environmental Systems Research Institute, Redlands, California.)

the Federal Landscape

W all Street or Main Street? Wall Street or Pennsylvania Avenue? Westerners pondered these questions at the opening of the twentieth century as they looked forward to further development of their region. Local capital was not sufficient to finance economic growth. Private financiers, on the other hand, were hesitant to invest large sums except in industries likely to generate immediate profits, such as mining or railroads. Frederick Jackson Turner, a contemporary historian of the West, gave voice to a prevailing perception when he wrote in 1903 that, considering the semiarid nature of the trans-Mississippi West: "Here expensive irrigation works must be constructed, cooperative activity was demanded in utilization of the water supply, capital beyond the reach of the small farmer was required. In a word, the

A Colonial Landscape, 1900–1929

physiographic province itself decreed that the destiny of this new frontier should be social rather than individual."[1] When Turner expressed that view, the American West displayed many of the characteristics of a colonial economy. The population of the trans-Mississippi region was small by national standards—no more than ten million people, or about 12 percent of the national total. Most of the region's economy was based on the exploitation of natural resources once owned by the federal government but transferred over the years to private interests. The West had few manufactures of its own and largely depended on goods imported from the older Northeast. It was not in a prime position to participate fully in the third Kondratieff wave, which was characterized by industrialism, electricity, and the automobile. In many respects much of the West was still something of an economic hinterland.

Most important, the West lacked the investment capital needed for rapid economic development and self-sufficiency. If westerners could not attract enough private capitalists, they hoped to utilize their political influence in the nation's capital to secure needed money from the federal government. What was needed was a large investment in the infrastructure of the region—in transportation, in water projects, and perhaps in such service industries as tourism. Western rhetoric about individualism and self-reliance aside, the record reveals the region's primary reliance on the federal government to create the parameters of economic change. After all, in the nineteenth century the federal government had been a major source of funds for the building of the railroads and had provided land for agriculture. If Wall Street was reluctant to invest in the twentieth-century West, perhaps Pennsylvania Avenue would be more willing. With all the uncertainties of their position, westerners' desire to escape their colonial relationship amounted to a passion. Somehow, the necessary infrastructure had to be built.

Transportation was a key element in that infrastructure. Transportation would bring more people and provide the West with access to markets in the more populous East. It would lessen the geographic isolation that was still a reality for many portions of the West. The transcontinental railroads built between 1869 and 1887 had done much to lessen that isolation and to integrate the West into the national economy. Railroads had provided new markets for the products of western farms, ranches, and mines. An expanded transportation net promised even greater benefits; but without federal aid, expansion seemed unlikely.

One project Americans were pondering at the opening of the century was a link between the Atlantic and Pacific Oceans—perhaps a canal built somewhere in Central America. Already in the 1850s thousands of easterners looked longingly toward California and dreamed of a canal that would facilitate travel there. That dream did not disappear in succeeding years. In fact, the Clayton-Bulwer Treaty of 1850 gave the United States the right to build such a waterway, and by 1856 private investors had built a railroad across the Isthmus of Panama.

But a forty-mile-long canal was a daunting project, and for many years the United States did not take up the option to build it. Meanwhile, private enterprise found the task too difficult. Between 1870 and 1903 a French company had intermittently worked on the canal but found construction problems too difficult and costs too high. Finally forced into bankruptcy, the French company gave up. As the United States embarked on expansion in the Caribbean and the Pacific after the Spanish-American War of 1898, imperialists such as Theodore Roosevelt came to consider a canal a necessity for national defense. Military strategists such as Captain Alfred Thayer Mahan advised Roosevelt that the nation's one-ocean navy could be used more flexibly and quickly in both the Atlantic and the Pacific Oceans if a canal were built. Once Roosevelt was in the White House he vigorously prosecuted the canal project. He acquired the rights from the French company and from Colombia to build a waterway and soon thereafter secured congressional approval. The construction of the canal proved to be both more difficult and more expensive than expected ($165 million). By the time it was completed in 1914, Roosevelt was no longer in the White House.[2]

The Panama Canal had a significant economic impact on the West. It opened up vast new markets for western farmers, especially for bulky products such as wheat and timber. Large population centers in the Northeast and in Great Britain became more accessible. The Pacific coast fisheries secured new markets. The waterway stimulated trade with Asia as well and increased the volume of trade handled by West Coast ports. Westerners' dreams of future wealth were reflected in the Panama Exposition of 1915 in San Diego, which proudly displayed the products of the western states. A year later, San Francisco held the Panama-Pacific International Exposition to focus on the importance of that city in international trade. In a more symbolic sense, many westerners viewed the opening of the Panama Canal as a steppingstone to economic independence.[3]

If the Panama Canal was the culmination of many years of planning, the rapid growth in popularity of automobiles between 1900 and 1920 was an unforeseen technological development that further wove the West into the national economy. Like the railroads of the nineteenth century, autos accelerated the urbanization of the West. But where railroads had tended to foster the growth of large population centers, cars also affected medium and small communities and knit the West into a more cohesive market area, diminishing its colonial status. Automobiles also made the West more accessible to the rest of America, facilitating an increased volume of trade and commerce, and a growing tourist industry. Even more, they had a multiplier effect on the economy. Rather quickly, the growing number of cars led to popular demands for a whole network of new roads, including major arteries, feeder roads, and better local thoroughfares. As the road-building boom gathered momentum, it stimulated a wide range of auxiliary industries such as cement and asphalt. And once the new roads were built, they brought about a significant appreciation in real estate prices. Automobiles themselves virtually created a major new industry for the West, because America's oil was found mainly in California, Texas, Kansas, and Oklahoma. At the same time, cars directly stimulated the rise of new service industries such as gasoline stations and repair shops.

Another important economic impact of the automobile in the West was to alter retailing and lifestyles. Before 1900, a ten-mile road trip to town could take three hours or more. Automobiles could cover that distance in just a few minutes, and this new mobility changed the lifestyles of millions of people. Shopping trips to nearby towns on weekends soon became a favorite pastime.[4]

The many advantages of automobiles could not be realized without a good system of roads, however, and these required the combined efforts of federal and state governments. During the first two decades of the century, the nation's roads were in wretched condition, but it was not long before motorists and members of the farm lobby in Washington began to demand federal aid to build better thoroughfares. The Automobile Club of Southern California was one of the leaders of the Good Roads Movement in 1903. The National Grange was another early supporter. Farmers hoped that better feeder roads would enable them to get goods to market faster, more efficiently, and more cheaply.

Few people in 1900 believed that cross-country travel by car was feasible. But in 1908 Henry Ford built his first Model T, and in 1909 one of these cars successfully made the trip between New York and San Francisco in twenty-two days, proving that automobile travel between the two coasts was possible. The reports of these early pioneers about the abominable road conditions they encountered—including mud, ruts, and other impediments—did much to popularize the need for better highways. It also led to the organization of the Lincoln Highway Association, an umbrella group that advocated a coast-to-coast highway. To dramatize its cause, the association in 1912 sponsored an automobile race from New York City to San Francisco, with a fork to Los Angeles as well. The caravans that made the trek experienced many difficulties. But they succeeded in publicizing the need for a national road system. Their influence was reflected in the presidential campaign of 1912, when both major political parties took note of the issue.

Congress responded to the public's demands with the Highway Act of 1916, which created a framework for a national highway system. Under the law the national government agreed to match state funds on a 50–50 basis to facilitate delivery of the mails. Responding to the demands of farm groups, the measure gave special attention to the improvement of rural roads and the implementation of Rural Free Delivery, a service the federal government had established just a few years earlier. With this act, highways became an increasingly significant part of the federal landscape in the West.[5]

Less visible in the landscape but no less important was federal development of West Coast harbors. At the opening of the century these were not equipped to receive the large steamships that were beginning to dominate oceanic trade. Neither the cities nor the states had the financial ability to rebuild their ports. After intensive lobbying by westerners in Washington, Congress made substantial appropriations for deepening, expanding, and improving the harbors of San Diego, Long Beach,

San Francisco, Portland, and Seattle. The improvements enabled these ports to carry on an expanding trade with Japan and other Asian nations, especially after the opening of the Panama Canal. Harbors, too, were part of the federal landscape in the West.

✤ The rivers of the West also reflected a federal imprint. Since the nineteenth century the U.S. Army Corps of Engineers had been changing the course of many western rivers, from the Mississippi to the Sacramento, deepening and dredging them to maintain them as avenues of commerce. As in transportation, the federal government's role was central in developing the water resources of the West. Much of the area west of the Mississippi River was semiarid, with no more than five to ten inches of rainfall yearly. As famed geologist John Wesley Powell had predicted in the late nineteenth century, the West was not really suited for the eastern settlement pattern of self-sufficient farmers on 160-acre lots. At best, the land could be adapted to cattle grazing. In 1900 the federal government was allowing western stock raisers to graze their animals on federal lands free of charge. But many engineers were already dreaming of turning this great American desert into an American garden. That miracle could be accomplished by bringing water to the West: by building dams, developing irrigation, and reclaiming arid lands. Perhaps then the Jeffersonian dream of peopling the West with millions of self-sufficient farmers could be realized after all. Between 1900 and 1918 this movement to transform the West took on all the earmarks of a crusade. Brilliant engineers such as Elwood P. Mead, Frederick Newell, and George Chaffee were at the forefront of those preaching the new gospel. Many of these men and their followers were members of the National Irrigation Congress, an advocacy group that proposed extensive federal aid to further their goal. Much of the fervor of the movement was captured in the writings of a well-known popularizer named William E. Smythe, whose book *The Conquest of Arid America* (1905) aroused much discussion. In that work Smythe argued that the Jeffersonian dream of creating fertile lands for family farms could be realized in the West if only the federal government would support massive irrigation projects. The American frontier had not disappeared after all, despite what some contemporaries proclaimed.

Chapter 1

Various private developers did establish model irrigation projects. In California, George Chaffee, a Canadian engineer, established a new settlement near Riverside along the lower Colorado River. With the California Development Company, Chaffee built a series of canals that made the desert bloom. Somewhat grandiosely he designated the area the Imperial Valley. Eventually it became one of California's richest agricultural regions. It was clear, however, that if large stretches of the western landscape were to be made fruitful, only the vast resources of the federal government would suffice to remake nature.

The prospect of changing the western landscape had a wide appeal to Americans at the beginning of the century. The vision was as exciting as the conquest of the frontier had been for earlier generations. Had not the Louisiana Purchase more than doubled the territories of the United States in 1803? Similarly, one hundred years later the irrigation and reclamation of arid lands promised to expand the nation's arable stretches and to increase the wealth of millions of people. Perhaps the idea struck an especially responsive chord because of a widely held assumption, popularized by the historian Frederick Jackson Turner, that the western frontier had ceased to exist in 1890, leaving no new frontiers for Americans to conquer. But the irrigation movement promised to open vast new territories. Instead of pessimism, the irrigation movement promised optimism and a new frontier. Just as visions of outer space excited Americans at the end of the twentieth century, so the prospect of new lands stirred an earlier generation one hundred years before.

President Theodore Roosevelt enthusiastically embraced the irrigation ethic and used his considerable political skills to guide the appropriate federal legislation through Congress. Congressman Francis G. Newlands, the lone House member from Nevada, became an enthusiastic advocate of federal aid to irrigation. Newlands was a skilled lawyer with degrees from Yale and Columbia Law School. An easterner bred and born, he had moved to Nevada from California to manage the properties of his multimillionaire father-in-law, William Sharon. If the western economy was to be developed, Newlands believed, the sparse western population would have to increase. That could be achieved by increasing agricultural settlement in the newly irrigated arid lands. Roosevelt supported the Newlands Act of 1902, which provided federal funds to enable individuals to build irrigation works. The act granted 160 acres to persons who promised to irrigate the land within a five-year period. The act also created a Reclamation Fund, which received money from public land sales in sixteen western states that could be used to subsidize the building of irrigation works throughout the West.

Within a decade western congressmen succeeded in expanding the federal role in water development. In 1914 Congress created the Reclamation Service in the Department of the Interior to supervise federal dam and irrigation projects. In that mission the service's work at times paralleled that of the army engineers who had been engaged in such programs for decades. Together, the Reclamation Service and the Corps of Engineers greatly expanded the federal role in the remaking of the West.[6]

But the federal government did not try to remake all of the West for agriculture. It retained a portion of the land in its natural state to serve as a foundation for a nascent tourist industry. Until the opening of the twentieth century, touring was a pleasure usually enjoyed only by the wealthy. The average American wage earner had neither the leisure nor the income to marvel at the West's magnificent scenery. Times were changing rapidly, however. Industrialization was breeding an expanding and more affluent middle class able to afford vacations. And the automobile made western sites more accessible than they had been in previous years. At the same time, conservationists such as Theodore Roosevelt and his friend Gifford Pinchot advocated conserving scenic areas and forests. Their hope was to preserve at least a small portion of America's natural patrimony in the public domain.

During the first two decades of the twentieth century, the federal government carved out another federal landscape in the form of national monuments and national parks. President Theodore Roosevelt was one of the prime movers in this effort. Not only was he an avid outdoorsman who had spent many happy hours in the West, he was also steeped in its history and had written about it extensively. On one of his western trips in 1905 he visited the ancient Indian ruins at Mesa Verde, Colorado, which contain some of the most dramatic cliff dwellings in the region. Roosevelt was chagrined to find that the area was unkempt. Previous visitors had defaced priceless ruins and had littered the area with trash. On his return to Washington Roosevelt worked to provide federal protection for sites like Mesa Verde. After considerable negotiations he persuaded Congress to enact the National Monuments Act of 1905. This extended federal protection to important historic areas. In addition to protecting such sites from desecration, the act would enable them to serve as reminders of the nation's heritage. Conservationists hoped for a wider effort, however. Between 1905 and 1914 they pressed for the creation of national parks. In earlier years Congress had designated a few national parks, such as Yellowstone (1871), but the United States did not as yet have a national park system. Many westerners opposed placing large segments of the public domain in parks because it closed off such lands for private exploitation. By 1916, however, Congress had established a national park system and had created the National Park Service to administer it. Apart from conserving the region's majestic scenery, the national park system laid the foundation for a major new tourist industry in the West. Year by year the number of visitors to the parks increased. Park Service officials were quite ready to tie conservation of natural areas to economic practicality because it eased their efforts to secure congressional appropriations.[7]

Moreover, the West contained more than just natural wonders. It was also the home of well-established old cultures that appeared exotic to easterners. Native American tribes had inhabited the Great Plains and the Southwest for many centuries. Hispanic Americans had settled in California, New Mexico, Arizona, and Texas and had developed unique cultures there, some even before the founding of New England. They were among the oldest inhabitants of North America.

The federal landscape in the West expanded further with the establishment of new military installations that provided much-needed income to the region. Dozens of forts and supply depots scattered throughout the West significantly affected the economies of nearby towns and cities. On the Pacific coast, navy shipyards were an important local asset, greater even than the airfields the army and navy would create by the second decade of the twentieth century.

The relationship between San Diego and the navy provides a specific illustration of this point. When the navy undertook a cruise around the world in 1907 it stopped at the main ports on the Pacific coast. Unfortunately, most had extremely limited facilities and were unable to accommodate the large new capital ships of the Great White Fleet. What they lacked in such facilities, however, Californians made up in their enthusiasm in welcoming the navy. They realized quickly that naval establishments would provide a tremendous boost for the under-developed local economy. The only naval presence in San Diego at the time was a small coaling station established in 1898. But the visit of 1907 aroused Californians to visions of dollars: of dry docks, massive wharves, training stations, and ship-servicing facilities. The city's civic boosters, many of whom were active in the chamber of commerce, were mesmerized by the prospect. A greater naval presence would attract more people and new industries. It would also do wonders for the price of real estate. Up and down the Pacific coast, business people and civic officials in port cities determined to do their share to attract this lucrative indus-try. The United States was going to have a two-ocean navy, with one fleet stationed along the Atlantic coast and the other in the Pacific, and their cities would host the Pacific fleet. In the years between 1900 and 1914, California's U.S. senators, James D. Phelan from San Francisco and John D. Works from Los Angeles, worked tirelessly to secure new bases for their state.

Major changes in American foreign policy made their efforts particu-larly timely. With the outbreak of World War I in Europe, the Wilson administration became increasingly concerned about national security. Between 1906 and 1913 a wave of anti-Japanese feeling had swept Cal-ifornia, reflected in the San Francisco School Board crisis of 1906 (when the board had attempted to segregate Japanese schoolchildren) and the Alien Land Act of 1913 (which sought to prevent Japanese from owning land in the state). With America now in possession of territories in the Pacific, there was increasing concern about protecting Hawaii and the Philippines from the Japanese. Such considerations persuaded Congress in July 1916 to enact the Naval Preparedness Act, which envisaged a very substantial expansion of the navy. Although Senator Works had not yet secured passage of an amendment to station part of the navy on the Pacific coast, he had the solid support of the representatives from Cali-fornia, Oregon, Washington, Idaho, Nevada, Utah, and Arizona. West-erners were very conscious of the economic contributions that the military establishment could make to their colonial economy.

Chapter 1

After 1913 San Diego's city boosters entered the fierce competition among West Coast municipalities to attract naval installations. One of the prominent members of the chamber of commerce in 1913 was William Kettner, recently elected to the House of Representatives as a Democrat. Kettner formed important political alliances in the nation's capital. Among the important people he impressed were Secretary of the Navy Josephus Daniels and his personable assistant secretary, Franklin D. Roosevelt. Under Kettner's direction, both of them toured the San Diego area and went away charmed. San Diego was close to the Panama Canal, which was just about to open to international traffic. It was also near Mexico, which was just then in the throes of revolution. Only recently President Woodrow Wilson had sent General John J. Pershing into Mexico to find Pancho Villa, the rebel leader. San Diego was not far from the Mexican border should the administration contemplate other interventions in the future. In addition to touting the mild, pleasant climate, favored by high military officers and retirees, the San Diego city officials were extremely friendly toward the navy and very sensitive to its demands. As an additional inducement, the city indicated its willingness to donate large sections of land to the navy.

In Washington, Representative Kettner worked tirelessly to bring a greater naval presence to San Diego. One of his first successes came in 1913 when he secured a large appropriation for dredging of the harbor so that it could accommodate the large capital ships of the new American fleet. In 1914 he secured funds for a major expansion of the old coaling station to enable the facility to store fuel oil. Most new naval vessels operated on diesel fuel rather than coal. Kettner did not let up in his efforts. In 1915 he arranged for a visit by U.S. Navy ships to the Panama-Pacific Exposition in San Diego. The beauties of the area left a lasting impression on many of the visitors. At the same time Kettner prevailed on Congress to authorize a radio station for the navy in San Diego, at the time the largest such facility in the world.

America's entry into World War I did much to further Kettner's efforts. In 1917 the navy set up an advanced marine base near San Diego. The base was later known as Camp Pendleton, named after a contemporary marine colonel who was enchanted by the area. The navy also decided to establish a naval air station at North Island and expanded Fort Rosecrans at the entrance of the harbor. Meanwhile, between 1913 and 1917 the Corps of Engineers did extensive dredging in the harbor that greatly increased berthing spaces and anchorage areas. In fact, in 1918 Kettner succeeded in persuading the navy to designate San Diego as a mothball site for surplus destroyers. The federal landscape was as important under the ocean as it was above. One estimate suggests that between 1919 and 1929 one-third of San Diego's income came from naval expenditures. It was by far the largest industry in town.[8]

World War I further emphasized the importance of military expenditures in the West. The infusion of federal funds acted like a shot of adrenaline in the region. Unfortunately, the increased pace of activities lasted for only eighteen months. The abrupt cancellation of federal contracts in late 1918 had a devastating effect on the economy and contributed to the depression conditions during the next two years. But while it lasted, the war stimulated production in western natural resource industries such as agriculture, livestock, and mining, and in manufacturing as well, mainly shipbuilding and to a lesser extent aircraft manufacturing. Military expenditures did not expand as readily as they did in the East because the West was remote from the war in Europe. In various ways, however, the wartime activities of the federal government left a deep imprint on the region.

During the conflict American agriculture came under the direction of the U.S. Food Administration, headed by Herbert Hoover. In his efforts to increase production, Hoover offered generous subsidies to farmers while limiting civilian consumption. His task was to provide food for the armed forces and for America's allies while still allowing enough for the civilian population. Western farmers rose to the challenge. California grain, fruit, and vegetable production doubled and constituted one-third of all the food grown in the United States. Generous federal subsidies virtually created a large new cotton industry in California's Imperial Valley, and for the first time the state became one of the nation's major cotton producers. On the Great Plains, wheat farmers substantially expanded their acreage and harvested bumper crops. The Food Administration also paid generous subsidies to cattle growers, who increased their herds to feed the three million men in the American Expeditionary Force. To conserve meat, Hoover proclaimed meatless Fridays for civilians. That action benefited Pacific coast fishermen, who brought in record catches of tuna and sardines.

When the military draft created labor shortages, farmers resorted to emergency measures. Women pitched in and ably performed a wide range of jobs. In the Pacific Northwest they were crucial in bringing in the wartime fruit crops. They also planted victory gardens and developed innovative canning techniques. Temporary Mexican field workers also helped to alleviate the labor shortage. With the Mexican Revolution still creating unsettled conditions, thousands of Mexicans were eager for jobs in the United States. At least fifty thousand came to work on farms in California and the Southwest.

The federal government did much to stimulate the western mining industry during the war. If the nation's manufacturing industries in the East were to be mobilized, more minerals were required from the West. Most important was copper, mined in large quantities in Arizona, New Mexico, Utah, Montana, and other states. The enormous increase in minerals production was spurred by the high prices guaranteed by the War Industries Board. Federal subsidies also stimulated the mining of molybdenum, vanadium, and tungsten in Colorado. Once the war was over, private operators closed most of these mines because they were not profitable without federal subsidies.[9]

During the conflict the federal government even intruded on labor relations in the mines. In the summer of 1917, copper miners in Arizona and Montana went on strike to demand higher wages. The War Industries Board was mainly concerned with maximum production, however, and quickly suppressed the strike through the Department of Justice. The National Guard occupied Butte, Montana, and broke the strike there. Attorney General A. Mitchell Palmer was equally determined in Bisbee, Arizona. With his encouragement, local law enforcement officials rounded up twelve hundred strikers and their families and forcibly put them on a freight train, which took them out of the state. In September 1917 agents of the U.S. Department of Justice under Palmer's direction raided offices of the Industrial Workers of the World, a militant union, in Omaha, Tulsa, Spokane, and Seattle, and charged the union with obstructing the war effort and violating the Sedition Act of 1917. These actions effectively destroyed the union.

Federal efforts were similar in the Pacific Northwest lumber industry. The war created a great need for increased timber production. Wood was needed not only to build hundreds of new army camps but also to manufacture shipping boxes. The War Industries Board set very high price levels for lumber, stimulating a threefold production increase during the war. The temporary boom ended in 1919. Meanwhile, in July 1917 the federal government imposed its fiat on workers in the industry. That summer, lumber workers, organized by the American Federation of Labor and the Industrial Workers of the World, went on strike, demanding an eight-hour day and higher wages. But to avoid stoppages the National War Labor Board simply bypassed the unionized workers and organized a federally sponsored union, the Loyal Legion of Loggers and Lumbermen. The legion's more than 100,000 members, men and women, were guaranteed an eight-hour day in wartime.[10]

The federal government also stepped in to create wartime controls over the western oil industry. These were administered by the U.S. Fuel Administration, headed by Californian Mark Requa. He set high prices for oil and imposed rigid production and price controls on the industry. Much of western petroleum production was reserved for the U.S. Navy and for the military needs of the Allies.

Because the western states were still mainly in a colonial mode as producers of raw materials, it was in those spheres that the federal presence was most noticeable. It was certainly less evident in manufacturing. Yet shipbuilders and aircraft fabricators found government orders dominating their activities. Wartime contracts led to a veritable boom in shipbuilding on the Pacific coast. Shipyards hired more than 100,000 men and women, who worked for the navy as well as for private yards supervised by the Emergency Fleet Corporation, a federal agency. During the boom, which ended in late 1918, the federal government spent more than $1 billion for Pacific coast facilities. Shipyards in the Pacific Northwest delivered 497 ships worth $458 million. It was the most profitable era in the region's history up to that point.

San Francisco also enjoyed a shipbuilding boom. Most of the vessels crafted there were small, many of them wooden schooners intended to haul bulky materials through the Panama Canal, but some larger steel vessels were built there as well. The Emergency Fleet Corporation not only issued contracts for ships but also paid for the expansion of ship-building facilities. In a very real sense, parts of the waterfront belonged to the federal landscape. But in December 1918, as the Great War ended, the Emergency Fleet Corporation canceled almost all of its contracts, ending more than 90 percent of ship construction on the Pacific coast and contributing to large-scale unemployment. Without government contracts the West Coast shipbuilding industry could not compete with other shipyards able to turn out ships for less.[11]

Army and navy contracts did much to stimulate the fledgling aircraft industry on the Pacific coast. Most airplane manufacturers were still located in the East and Midwest, but federal largesse did lure some west-ward. One of the pioneers was Glenn Martin, whose shop in Santa Ana, California, was kept going by navy contracts. In 1916 Martin merged with the Wright Company and hired young Donald Douglas, who had been trained at the U.S. Naval Academy. America's entry into the war brought more navy contracts and led Martin to move to Cleveland, Ohio. But Douglas and Martin continued to collaborate and in 1918 produced one of the largest planes of the time, the MB-1 bomber, which they designed with James Kindelberger. In Burbank, California, two broth-ers, California natives Allen and Malcolm Loughead, operated a small shop building navy seaplanes. The brothers had begun their operations in 1916 in Santa Barbara, California, where they secured the services of Jack Northrop, a more experienced builder than they. After the United States entered the war, the brothers changed their name to Lockheed. Without federal contracts after 1919, their company failed, but they revived it in 1926, still dependent on military orders.

In Seattle, federal largesse did much to encourage the new aircraft-building venture founded by William E. Boeing, whose interest in fly-ing had been stimulated by his friend William Westerveldt, an engineer in the Naval Construction Corps at the Puget Sound Navy Yard. Together they experimented with various airplane designs and in 1916 built two seaplanes. The following year Boeing created the Boeing Company and benefited from an army order for trainers and a navy order for seaplanes. When his federal contracts were canceled in 1919, Boeing resorted to the manufacture of furniture for several years before new military orders in the 1920s helped him to continue with his aircraft manufacturing.[12]

American participation in World War I was of relatively short duration, and that limited the impact of the federal government on the western economy. At the time the influence seemed transitory. Its significance became more evident in later years. The generation that had lived through the war remembered its effect on the western economy. Only fifteen years later they held it up as a model for federal action during the Great Depression. The World War I experience had a very decided impact on the New Deal in the 1930s and soon thereafter on domestic mobilization for World War II. Nor were the potentials of federal investment in the West forgotten. Regardless of their rhetoric about individualism, westerners wanted federal investment to build the infrastructure of their economy. As Bernard De Voto, a shrewd observer of the West, remarked, because the twentieth-century West was born of industrialism, "the country had to be developed with the tools of the Industrial Revolution, and these cost money."[13]

Just how important the federal investment in the West was to the economy was dramatically demonstrated by the postwar depression, which began in 1919 when the Wilson administration abruptly canceled government war contracts. This thoughtless action brought on one of the nation's worst depressions, and it had serious effects in the West as well. Its immediate impact was to accentuate unemployment, especially in San Francisco and Seattle, where shipbuilding had been important. The action also had a devastating effect on western farmers and cattle raisers, who faced a sudden shrinkage of their markets just when many had gone into debt to buy new machinery for increasing production. Prices plunged for farm products and meat, for minerals, and for timber as demand slackened.

So serious was the agricultural depression in 1920–21 that farmers turned to the federal government in a desperate effort to stabilize the structure of their industry. A group of westerners in Congress organized the Farm Bloc, which lobbied for helpful legislation. That came in the form of the Packers and Stockyards Act of 1921, which provided for federal regulation of grain exchanges and for federal meat inspection. Both provisions were designed to equalize competition and raise prices. In 1921 Congress also revived the War Finance Corporation, a World War I agency, to make emergency loans to farmers and cattlemen and women.

Chapter 1

With a billion dollars to spend, the War Finance Corporation rescued many thousands from bankruptcy, particularly on the Great Plains and in the Southwest. As a more permanent measure, Congress in 1923 created a comprehensive federal bank system, the Federal Intermediate Credit Banks, to provide low-cost loans to farmers.[14]

The federal government continued to invest in the economic infrastructure of the West throughout the 1920s. It expanded its policy of making dry lands wet through irrigation, begun in the Newlands Act of 1902. In 1922 Secretary of Commerce Herbert Hoover negotiated the Colorado River Compact, under which the western states (but not Arizona) agreed to divide the waters of that mighty river. Four years later federal involvement in western water development became even more substantial when Congress authorized the construction of Boulder Dam in southern Nevada. Located near Las Vegas, the dam had two purposes: to provide electric power for Los Angeles and other cities in the Southwest, and to irrigate the dry lands of southern California. At the time, it was planned as the largest dam in the world.[15]

During the 1920s the federal government was also a dominant presence in developing the highway system of the West. The Highway Act of 1921 provided for a federal investment of more than a billion dollars for the construction of major roads. Under this law the federal government paid at least half of the cost, which it shared with the states. Between 1920 and 1932, federal grants-in-aid for highways doubled and contributed to the construction of 206,000 miles of roads.[16]

The federal landscape was also marked by the expansion of national parks in the 1920s. The national park system's dynamic director, Steve Mather, became acutely conscious of the need to expand tourism in the West now that automobile travel and new highways had made the parks more accessible. Mather was especially concerned about building campsites and picnic areas. He succeeded in drawing at least ten million visitors to the parks in the 1920s.

Thus, without fanfare, in the 1920s the federal government became increasingly active in bolstering the economic infrastructure of the West by substantial investments in water projects, the transportation net, and the tourist industry. Nevertheless, between 1900 and 1929 westerners were not able to diversify their economy sufficiently to end their colonial relationship with the older East. The West was still a purveyor of raw materials for the industrial Northeast, which garnered most of the profits. The prospects of equalizing this relationship seemed dim in 1929 without a massive influx of federal aid. That appeared unlikely at the time, given the West's small population and limited political influence in national politics. But quite unexpectedly, the Great Depression and World War II were to provide surprising new opportunities.

Chapter 1

D uring the 1930s lawmakers in the nation's capital
expanded the federal landscape in the West much more
rapidly than they had done in preceding years. Their immediate goal was economic recovery, of course. But President
Franklin D. Roosevelt and his secretary of the interior,
Harold L. Ickes, also had a special mission: to end the colonialism under which westerners (and southerners) had chafed
for many decades. Since the early years of the twentieth century, the West had sought greater economic diversification
and a higher degree of industrialization but without much
success. During the era of the New Deal, however, the federal
government provided not only plans but also vast amounts of
much-needed investment capital. New Dealers called for a
greater balance in the West among agriculture, the produc-

Changing the Federal
Landscape in the
Great Depression,
1929–1940

tion of raw materials, and manufacturing. And they were sensitive also to developing the human potential of people in the region, particularly Native Americans and Hispanics. Some New Dealers (such as Ickes and Henry Wallace), as well as a spate of bureaucrats (such as Undersecretary of the Interior Abe Fortas, director of the Bureau of Reclamation John C. Page, and administrator of the Bonneville Power Administration Paul Raver), fervently believed that the economic development of the West should be promoted primarily under federal auspices and with federal funds.

President Roosevelt articulated this vision early in his administration. In 1934 he said:

> Men and Nature must walk hand in hand. The throwing out of balance of the resources of nature throws out of balance the lives of men. We think of our land and water and human resources not as a static and sterile possession but as life-giving assets to be directed by wise provision for the future days. We seek to use our natural resources not as a thing apart but as something that is interwoven with industry, labor, finance, taxation, agriculture, homes, recreation, good citizenship. The . . . results of this process will have a greater influence on the future American standard of living than all the rest of our economies together.[1]

Secretary of the Interior Ickes was an even more vocal advocate of economic diversification. His department had direct supervision over the area west of the ninety-eighth meridian, which also contained most of the remaining public lands owned by the federal government. Ickes was aware that he had considerable power to direct the course of economic development in the West at a crucial juncture of its history, and no one ever accused Ickes of being bashful. Rather, he was a very outspoken and abrasive man, deeply committed to the causes in which he believed. "The development of the whole area west of the Mississippi," he declared, "had been somewhat neglected." The future of the West depended on greater "diversification and a wider use of its resources through the development of industries located close to the resources. No section of the Nation can prosper if it is treated like a colony, if its resources are pumped out of it and it is later left stranded. . . . I believe that by taking

Chapter 2

thought . . . and by working out a coordinated program for mining, industry and agriculture in the western states, the West will enter a new era of responsible progress." Although he saw a major role for the federal government and his department in this projected transformation, Ickes reiterated that he did not believe in the government "doing things for people which they can do themselves. But I believe strongly in the Government taking down the hurdles and barriers so that people can do things for themselves."[2]

Ickes was not alone in his quest. In Washington, D.C., Secretary of Agriculture Henry A. Wallace, farm experts such as M. L. Wilson and Rexford Tugwell, and a small army of idealistic young planners labored hard to transform their dreams into reality. Their goal was to create a more prosperous and more democratic West. A centerpiece of their program was the building of massive multipurpose dams throughout the West on the model of the Tennessee Valley Authority, which was created in 1933. These mammoth structures would provide electric power to support growing populations in western cities and stimulate a wide range of profitable new industrial enterprises. In addition, dams would expand the irrigated acreage of the West and would make dry deserts bloom. By creating new recreational areas, they would lay the foundations for tourist and service industries. The irrigated lands would be home to hundreds of thousands of prosperous, independent small farmers who would fulfill the nineteenth-century Jeffersonian dream of a sturdy yeomanry in the West, the true bedrock of American democracy. Theirs was a glorious vision of a twentieth-century federal landscape. In many ways the New Dealers shared the ideals of the proponents of the irrigation movement during the Progressive Era a generation earlier.

But they hoped to do more than merely develop the economic landscape of the West. They also believed that it was necessary to protect the region's remaining natural resources. They would repair and preserve areas that had already been ravaged by wasteful or thoughtless exploitation by private enterprise bent only on short-term economic gain. Since the federal government was the largest landlord west of the ninety-eighth meridian, the New Dealers saw a chance to preserve the region's natural bounty. Thus, New Deal administrators were concerned with soil conservation, with protecting forests on the national domain, and with controlling the exploitation of oil and minerals. And they expressed compassion for the oldest but poorest dwellers in the West, Native Americans and Hispanics.[3]

To a considerable extent, the perceptions of New Deal planners sprang from a Progressive belief, especially popular in the 1920s, that science, technology, and engineering would be the keys to the improvement of society. Herbert Hoover had been an apostle of this creed, but more in theory than in practice. New Dealers wanted to do better. If Nature revealed such "imperfections" as aridity and untamed rivers, then engineers could improve on the environment so that it would yield greater economic benefits. Such assumptions guided the Bureau of Reclamation in the 1930s and for some time thereafter. In their mission, the bureau and its directors reflected much of the same fervor as other New Dealers.

As they planned hundreds of new projects throughout the West in the 1930s, the bureau's administrators were also engaged in protecting and expanding their bureaucratic turf. For many other federal agencies were also active in western development, including the Department of Agriculture, the U.S. Army Corps of Engineers, the Forest Service, and the National Park Service. Ickes, in whose department the Bureau of Reclamation operated, was intensely jealous of any real or perceived threats to his authority. He viewed himself as the primary spokesman for the extension of the federal landscape in the West. He also had direct control over the General Land Office; the Grazing Service, which supervised millions of acres of federal grazing lands; and the Bureau of Mines, which dealt with mineral resources, including coal, oil, and gas.

Among the largest projects of the decade was Boulder Dam (after 1935, Hoover Dam) near Las Vegas. The project was begun at the behest of Californians who feared that Los Angeles could not grow without access to ample water and power. They assured themselves of the water, but they could not secure electric power without federal assistance. Although Congress authorized the dam in 1928, its construction took another seven years. It seemed the perfect project to "correct" nature. Its advocates were sure that it would regulate the erratic course of the Colorado River. It would also control floods and provide water for irrigation in California's dry Imperial Valley. Almost as a bonus, the dam created Lake Mead, the world's largest artificial lake, which was certain to become a major tourist attraction. Over a fifty-year period the dam could generate enough electric power to pay for its original cost.[4]

Elated by the success of Boulder Dam, Ickes and the Bureau of Reclamation pressed Congress for similar projects to develop the West—under their watchful eyes, of course. In 1935 they collaborated with the Metropolitan Water District of Southern California to build Parker Dam, about 150 miles south of the Boulder site. Its purpose was to store water for the district and to provide flood control and irrigation for central Arizona. That, it was hoped, would stimulate population growth and economic development in this still sparsely settled area. Half of the power generated by Parker Dam belonged to the Bureau of Reclamation. Like the bureau's other projects, the dam reflected a belief that humans should prevail over nature.[5]

On occasion the bureau was eager to alter mountains as well as rivers, as the Big Thompson Project in Colorado revealed. Ickes may not actually have said that one good dam deserves another, but in effect that came to be the policy of his department. No sooner was the Parker Dam construction under way than he was planning another major dam in Colorado. For the Big Thompson Project, Ickes literally had to move mountains and rivers. The complex enterprise provided for the diversion of about 300,000 acre-feet of Colorado River water yearly to irrigate eastern Colorado. Congress authorized the building program in 1937. It involved a thirteen-mile-long tunnel through mountains and an extensive chain of reservoirs. So many obstacles were in the way in the Rocky Mountain terrain that the Big Thompson Project took almost twenty years to finish. When the five power plants, storage reservoirs, and elaborate tunnels were finally completed, the Big Thompson proved to be an even larger and more expensive undertaking than Boulder Dam.[6]

Farther inland, Ickes embarked on the controversial Fort Peck Project to divert the Missouri River. Since 1933 the Corps of Engineers had urged construction of a dam to improve navigation on the Missouri River. In 1934 the Public Works Administration under Ickes provided extensive funding for such a plan and broadened its purpose to include irrigation development and the production of electric power as well. Since it also involved the removal of the Sioux Indians from their traditional homes, the Fort Peck Project had social and cultural as well as far-ranging economic impacts. The Corps of Engineers and the Bureau of Reclamation disagreed over many details of this complex operation. Despite their disagreements, however, the two agencies persisted and completed the dam by 1939. It was one of the world's largest earthen dams.[7]

Beginning in 1937, the Bureau of Reclamation cooperated with the state of California to underwrite the cost of the Central Valley Project. Its primary purpose was to transport some of the plentiful water in the northern part of California to the arid southern part of the state. This was to be done through a series of dams like the huge Shasta Dam, power plants, canals, and intricate systems of transmission lines. Although operations began in 1947, some of the elements of the system were not completed for another decade. Like other New Deal water ventures, the Central Valley Project had varied purposes. These included reclamation, irrigation, the generation of power, and the improvement of river navigation. The system irrigated more than two million acres and made new farmland available in the Central Valley. To a considerable extent, however, the beneficiaries of the enterprise were not small farmers but giant corporate farms, which were already dominating California agriculture. Its final cost of about $2.3 billion made the Central Valley Project one of the costliest of the Bureau of Reclamation's projects.[8]

The federal government left an indelible stamp on the Pacific Northwest with two huge projects: the Bonneville Dam and the Grand Coulee Dam. The Bonneville Dam was built near Portland, Oregon, by the Corps of Engineers. New Deal planners thought it seemed ideal because of its multiple purposes, all designed to focus on the economic development of a region that they considered seriously underdeveloped. The dam was designed to produce electric power, to develop irrigation, to improve navigation of the Columbia River, to expand tourism, and to attract manufacturing and other industries. Begun in 1933, Bonneville cost about $75 million. When completed in 1938 it produced 600,000 horsepower of electricity and created a 180-mile-long inland seaway to the Pacific to encourage shipping and trade. To protect spawning salmon that used the Columbia River, engineers built an elaborate system of fishways to allow the fish continued access to the ocean.[9]

The Grand Coulee Dam was built ninety-two miles northwest of Spokane, Washington, by the Bureau of Reclamation. Begun in 1934, it was virtually complete in 1941 and became a prime producer of power for the Pacific Northwest. During World War II the dam was essential in providing electricity for war industries. President Franklin D. Roosevelt always viewed it as the cornerstone of his administration's dam-building program and as a model project. When Roosevelt visited the construction site in 1937, he declared that the dam's cost would be "returned to the people of the United States many times over in the improvement of navigation and transportation, the cheapening of electric power, and the distribution of this power to hundreds of small communities within a great radius." New Dealers viewed the Grand Coulee Dam, which was planned to be larger than Boulder Dam, as a showcase of the potential of dam projects in regional economic development.[10]

In addition to literally moving rivers and mountains, New Dealers also attempted to restructure agriculture in the West. When Herbert Hoover and the Food Administration had urged farmers to strive for maximum production during World War I, the Great Plains were enjoying a series of years with adequate rainfall. Throughout the 1920s, many farmers planted wheat on lands that would have been better left fallow because in many seasons they received inadequate moisture. After 1929 came successive years of drought, and topsoil was replaced by dust as fierce winds swept over the area. The Plains experienced some of the worst weather in a century. Insufficient rainfall and debilitating insect infestations also contributed to the creation of the Dust Bowl. In one way or another, these blights brought economic ruin on hundreds of thousands of farmers. Personal tragedies rivaled sufferings noted in the Bible. At the same time, farmers in other parts of the country created market surpluses and contributed to the collapse of prices for wheat and other crops. Such conditions created the worst farm crisis in the American experience. On the Great Plains during the 1930s, at least 400,000 farm families lost everything they had.

In what amounted to a massive rescue effort, the Roosevelt administration attempted to aid the farmers caught in this debacle by restructuring the agricultural landscape of the West. President Roosevelt summarized the situation when he said that "the problem is one of arresting the decline of agricultural economy not adapted to the climatic conditions because of lack of information and understanding at the time of settlement, and of readjusting the economy in the light of later experience and of scientific information now available."[11]

Dozens of federal agencies now involved themselves in the everyday life of farmers. Most important were the Department of Agriculture and its subdivisions. Their specific activities in the overall effort varied. They carried out short-range plans to ameliorate the immediate crisis and also long-range programs for reorienting farming in the West. To deal with the situation at hand in the 1930s, the New Deal provided direct relief payments, created temporary government jobs, expanded federal farm credit and low-interest loans, and directly purchased farm surpluses. It also directed farmers to reduce the acreage they planted in return for subsidies. Long-range programs of the New Deal included the resettlement of farmers living on marginal land, extensive soil conservation and soil erosion control programs, the planting of millions of trees on the Great Plains to hold soil, and the unveiling of even more comprehensive plans for the future reorganization of western agriculture.

In view of the immediate emergency, with hundreds of thousands of western farmers destitute, several New Deal agencies made direct relief payments. The Federal Emergency Relief Administration (FERA) in 1934 and the Works Projects Administration (WPA) after 1935 created small work projects such as road repair or the painting or remodeling of public buildings. Although the federal wage often was no more than fifty dollars per month, it provided a bare subsistence for many who were otherwise near starvation. Such federal assistance served as a life preserver for those who had no other source of income.

One of the most popular programs in agricultural regions of the West was the Civilian Conservation Corps (CCC), a labor corps designed for young men (and a few women) between the ages of eighteen and twenty-five. Corps members lived in camps supervised by the army, where they received room and board and a dollar per day for their labor. They worked largely on outdoor projects involving soil conservation, reforestation, fire control in forests, and flood control and reclamation. The Department of Agriculture used the CCC to plant trees on the Great Plains, and the Soil Conservation Service employed CCC workers in many of its local programs. The Forest Service and the National Park Service also benefited from their work. One of the largest CCC endeavors in

1934 was planting a great shelterbelt of trees stretching from the Dakotas south to Texas. The CCC was popular in agricultural regions because farm boys were accustomed to outdoor work.

To slow the flood of farm failures, the U.S. Department of Agriculture (USDA) extended low-cost credit to millions of farmers in the West. In states such as Montana and North Dakota, at least half of the agricultural population lost their farms between 1933 and 1937. The rest faced foreclosure or bankruptcy. In 1933, to give recipients better service, the USDA consolidated most federal lending programs in the Farm Credit Administration. Within a year it extended more than $100 million in loans to drought-stricken farmers, often without requiring any security. Quite frankly, its goal was to prevent starvation and to enable farmers to survive one more year until conditions might improve. The Agricultural Adjustment Administration (AAA) purchased livestock in 1934 from cattle growers who had no other buyers but could not afford to feed the animals. The Federal Emergency Relief Administration was able to distribute some meat and grain to the needy. Unfortunately, it felt compelled to destroy some food in a desperate effort to prevent a further plunge in prices. The Surplus Marketing Administration bought edible food surpluses and distributed them to the poor, including those on Indian reservations. The Commodity Credit Corporation also bought surpluses, which it used for export or stored for future use.

Meanwhile, the Department of Agriculture made a major effort to reduce farm acreage. The AAA was the principal agency in charge of this program. It paid farmers just to let land lie fallow or to plant less than they had planned. When the U.S. Supreme Court declared the process unconstitutional, Congress enacted a somewhat similar law in 1938 under which the AAA could pay farmers not to plant crops in the cause of soil conservation, a goal that was approved by the courts. Moreover, when the consent of two-thirds of the producers of particular crops was secured through elections, the AAA could impose quotas on production and marketing in order to maintain price levels.

The USDA's long-range programs included the resettlement of poor farmers, many of whom were farm tenants, from marginal to more fertile lands. After 1937 the Resettlement Administration moved people to more promising properties, which it bought for them. Although it seemed workable in theory, the program was not very successful in practice. Transferring people from familiar areas to strange ones proved more difficult than expected.[12]

More successful were New Deal soil conservation programs to control erosion. For generations, wasteful farming practices had destroyed vegetation that once had held topsoil in place. When the winds roared over the Great Plains, as they did in the 1930s, they blew much of the topsoil away. Experts estimated that each year about 200,000 acres of topsoil was blown away, at least half of it on the Great Plains. Many of these lands had been rapidly denuded since 1914 by intensive cultivation. The Dust Bowl created by incessant storms in the early 1930s encompassed Nebraska, western Kansas, Oklahoma, the Texas Panhandle, eastern New Mexico, and eastern Colorado. To rejuvenate this depressed section of the West, the USDA in 1935 created the Soil Conservation Service and put Hugh Bennett, an eminent soil scientist, in charge. Bennett estimated that 322 million acres had been eroded by the winds and that another 50 million acres was at risk. The service attempted to cope with the dilemma in various ways. It built water storage facilities and conducted thousands of demonstration programs to educate farmers about improved farming practices. Other activities included distributing seeds to control erosion and encouraging the planting of sorghum and other drought-resistant crops. One of its major projects was the planting of trees on the Great Plains to hold soil in place.[13]

These were all stopgap measures to deal with the immediate emergency. But the New Dealers also developed long-range schemes. In looking to the future, they were convinced that only comprehensive planning at the federal level could solve the major economic problems of western agriculture. Some of these difficulties had been predicted as early as 1899 when John Wesley Powell, the great explorer of the Colorado River and the first director of the U.S. Geological Survey, warned against overcultivation of the Great Plains. Much of the land there, he accurately noted, was suitable only for grazing. As he said in 1899, "In the Western portion all dependence on rain will ultimately bring disaster to the people . . . [and] years will come of abundance and years will come of disaster, and between the two the people will be prosperous and unprosperous." A generation later, a similar refrain was elaborated by Secretary of Agriculture Henry A. Wallace in the 1930s. Wallace outlined his views in *New Frontiers,* a book in which he envisaged major changes in farming practices to ensure greater farm prosperity. "Obviously," Wallace wrote, "certain limits must be placed on competition and individualism. . . . If our civilization is to continue in its present complex basis, modern democracy must make rules . . . concerning harmonious relationships between prices, margins, profits and distribution of income."[14]

Wallace's views were reflected by thousands of government bureaucrats who issued innumerable publications during these years. They included engineers, agronomists, and soil experts who envisaged a restructured federal agricultural landscape in the West largely supervised by experts. Improved conservation policies, they firmly believed, could nurse worn-out lands back to health and so create a profitable new landscape that would provide good incomes for millions of people.

One of the New Deal planning agencies was the Great Plains Drought Area Committee, created by President Roosevelt in 1935 to develop a comprehensive plan for that region. After extensive study of the Great Plains, the committee made numerous recommendations for the restructuring of agriculture there. Chairman Morris L. Cooke, a distinguished engineer, and his colleagues suggested that instead of wheat farming or subsistence farming the government should help individuals take worn-out lands out of production and plant soil-conserving crops like buffalo grass. They also urged more emphasis on flood control, contour plowing to lessen erosion, and the planting of more trees to lessen wind damage. In its general recommendations the committee reflected Powell's opinion that farming practices appropriate in the humid East were not at all suitable for the semiarid West. If the committee's suggestions had been carried out, they would have substantially altered the agricultural map of the Great Plains. But members of Congress and their constituents were not prepared to have the government impose such far-reaching changes. Under the circumstances, President Roosevelt gingerly sidestepped the committee's recommendations.[15]

On publicly held lands, of course, the federal government had greater control. The public domain included millions of acres of grazing lands. New Dealers were more successful in reshaping grazing policies because they had considerable support from western stock growers, both men and women. Before the Great Depression, all public lands had been open to anyone wishing to use them for stock grazing free of charge. That had been the government's policy for more than a century, and it had resulted in serious deterioration of the rangelands. Such a generous practice seemed tenable when land appeared to be limitless, but by 1933 the public domain open for grazing had shrunk considerably and was in terrible condition. Of the 975 million acres of grazing lands in the United States, the federal government owned one-third. Conservationists, as well as many stock growers, favored some sort of federal control to protect the land that remained.

Under the leadership of Representative Edward Taylor from Colorado, Congress enacted the Taylor Grazing Act of 1934 to protect the remaining patrimony from overgrazing and soil depletion. According to its wording, the purpose of the act was "to stop injury to the public grazing lands by preventing overgrazing and soil deterioration." It was designed "to stabilize the livestock industry dependent on the public range." Henceforth, anyone seeking to use publicly owned grazing lands had to secure a permit and pay a very small fee. One-fourth of such fees was to be used for improvement of the range. The Department of the Interior also created hundreds of local grazing districts with advisory boards chosen by people in the industry. By 1936 the department was overseeing 142 million acres under these terms, including some supervised earlier by the Forest Service and the Bureau of Wildlife Management. Within six years, eleven million animals were feeding on federal rangelands.

The Taylor Grazing Act signified an end to the unrestrained use of natural resources in the West. As the distinguished western writer Wallace Stegner observed, "The historical process was complete; not only was the public domain virtually closed to settlement, but the remaining public land was assumed to be continuing federal property, income producing property to be managed according to principles of wide use for the benefit of the nation." In a larger sense, Ickes hoped that the new policy would help to stabilize the economy of the Great Basin. "We have reached the end of the pioneering period of go ahead and take," he said. "We are in an age of planning for the best of everything for all." As natural resources became scarcer, careful economic planning by the federal government would institute a new order.[16]

Chapter 2

The federal landscape was visible not only in farming and grazing lands but also in the western mining country. Of the various minerals produced in the region during the 1930s, silver was the biggest beneficiary of New Deal policies. Seven western states—Idaho, Montana, Colorado, Utah, Nevada, Arizona, and New Mexico—contained 95 percent of the nation's silver deposits. The silver lobby was a potent influence in Congress. Its members included the major beneficiaries of federal largesse, and they were not only small miners but large enterprises as well. In 1933 the market for silver was as depressed as the markets for most other industries. Nor was silver needed by governments around the globe that used silver in their currencies.

But the seven silver states and their allies were a powerful presence in the U.S. Senate. The silver lobby hoped to increase demand by establishing a federal silver purchase program. Led by Senators Burton K. Wheeler of Montana and Key Pittman of Nevada, they secured passage of the Silver Purchase Act of 1934, which obligated the federal government to buy nearly the entire silver output of the western mines. Under the act's provisions, the government agreed to buy silver until it reached one-fourth of the nation's monetary reserves at a limit of $1.29 an ounce. The market price of silver in 1933 was about 25 cents an ounce. Proponents of the measure hoped that the silver purchased under the provisions of the act would debase the value of the dollar and that the resulting inflation would lift the entire American economy out of depression. President Roosevelt in 1934 was in a mood to experiment with monetary policies. Unfortunately, the effort failed. Nevertheless, until 1938 the Treasury continued to buy silver at about 65 cents an ounce, a generous subsidy for western silver miners. Because silver was usually mined together with lead, zinc, and copper, the subsidy benefited all of the Rocky Mountain states. It provided employment for at least ten thousand people with more than fifty thousand dependents. After 1938 the silver purchase program shrank. But while it was in effect, western mines were an integral part of the federal landscape in the West. When the Treasury bought the entire silver output, it virtually nationalized the industry, in fact if not in theory.[17]

The federal landscape in the West also embraced about one-fifth of the region's forests, or about 134 million acres; the remaining four-fifths was

Changing the Federal Landscape

in private hands. Management of this patrimony was divided among several federal agencies. Most important was the Forest Service, which sold some of its trees but also carried out conservation and reforestation policies on its lands. In addition, the Department of the Interior supervised forests under its jurisdiction, mostly worn-out areas that Ickes hoped to rehabilitate. In fact, he purchased 224 million acres from private owners in the hope of rejuvenating the forests. The National Park Service also had some forestlands in its domain and strongly opposed private efforts to cut timber in national parks. Conflicts among these agencies often grew heated during the New Deal era, partly because they had different goals. The Forest Service had close ties to the lumber industry and was sensitive to timber needs of the economy. The Department of the Interior, on the other hand, favored centralized government control over western forests, largely to protect watersheds for its extensive dam-building program. The National Park Service, conscious of being the custodian of some of the most beautiful landscapes west of the ninety-eighth meridian, was concerned with fostering tourism in the West and maintaining the aesthetic qualities of forests.

During the New Deal years the federal government did much to foster forest preservation policies. President Roosevelt himself loved trees and took a personal interest in such programs. As a gentleman farmer on his estate at Hyde Park, New York, and as governor of that state, he had taken a keen interest in tree culture. His influence led Congress to allot ample funds to the Forest Service for reforestation and flood control. The agency supervised a conservation army. It utilized CCC and WPA workers by the thousands to plant trees throughout the West, to control water runoff, and to build new roads and trails, new campgrounds, and fire lookout towers. In its effort to help bolster the economy, the Forest Service adopted a sustained-yield management policy whereby timber was not only harvested but conserved and replenished as well.

New Deal forest policies were especially important in the Pacific Northwest. Montana, Idaho, Oregon, and Washington contained 55 percent of the nation's timber. And 96 percent of the national forests were in the western states (not including Alaska, which was still a territory). Some of the most divisive bureaucratic battles were fought in this region. Especially heated was the dispute over the Oregon and California Railroad Lands, an extensive tract in western Oregon. In 1937 Congress authorized the Department of the Interior to sell some of the timber there while also undertaking reforestation under a sustained-yield policy. Ickes was reluctant to sell any of the lands he administered. Another controversy arose in 1938 over a proposal to create Olympic National Park in Washington, where private lumber operators opposed reserving any timberlands. Eventually, the conflicting groups agreed to a compromise under which Congress created a smaller Olympic National Park than had originally been intended. Despite conflicting agendas, however, the Roosevelt administration succeeded in improving the management and care of the national forests.[18]

As might be expected, the restructuring of the economic conditions under which people in the federal landscape lived was more difficult than changing the use of natural resources. Nevertheless, the federal government tried to do just that during the New Deal, especially with respect to Native Americans living on reservations. It also exerted a significant influence on the economic welfare of Hispanics in the Southwest. Of the various influences affecting these people's lives, those emanating from the federal government played a major role. New Dealers hoped to lift them out of poverty, but those expectations were only partly met. It was easier for planners to articulate economic objectives than to carry them out. Cultural values often interfered with the best of plans.

Most policy planners in the 1930s agreed that the economic conditions of Native Americans were among the worst in the nation. Under the federal programs of the Indian Service under Commissioner John Collier, self-determination was to be the key to improvement. Such self-determination was to be political and cultural as well as economic. Collier was able to steer short-term relief programs into Indian country, but he was much less successful in establishing long-term self-sufficiency. Of the short-term programs, the CCC was the most popular because it provided temporary jobs with immediate cash income. The CCC projects involved road and fence construction, forest conservation, and soil erosion control on Indian lands. About seventy-seven thousand Native Americans were enrolled in the CCC. The outdoor work they performed was well adapted to reservation lifestyles. Moreover, enrollees could often continue to live at home while earning $35 to $40 per month, with extra allowances if they provided their own room and board. In addition, Social Security pensions provided subsistence payments, especially near reservations where jobs were few. Limited WPA and Public Works Administration (PWA) projects at times provided work for half of the men living on reservations. The New Deal's short-term programs did much to tide Native Americans over an excruciatingly difficult time.

Collier's long-term plans to restructure Indian economies were more difficult to achieve. One of his major hopes was to transform the Navajo economy by reducing the number of cattle and sheep on their reservation, which Collier considered to be overstocked. Such overstocking had accentuated erosion of Navajo grazing lands for decades. The Public Works Administration stood ready to reimburse owners of animals to be slaughtered. But to the Navajos, ownership of stock animals was both an ancient practice and a badge of social status. The federal stock reduction program thus aroused a great deal of opposition and even hatred for Collier and other federal officials who tried to impose the policy in the name of self-determination. The Navajos did reduce their herds of sheep and goats to some extent in the hope that they would receive more federal lands, yet the number of animals remaining was still greater than the carrying capacity of their range. And each year the number of animals increased faster than the Navajo population, placing greater pressures on the range. The issue remained unresolved in the 1930s.

The situation was different among the Pueblo tribes because smaller tracts of land were involved. Soil erosion programs carried out by the Soil Conservation Service had some success there. New Deal long-range economic programs did not change the economic landscape of Native America very much. But relief policies did much to ameliorate immediate suffering.[19]

New Deal planners were also eager to restructure the Hispanic landscape of New Mexico. Most New Dealers were easterners who had a rather romantic view of communal life in the small villages in the northern part of the state. That vision had been developed in the previous two decades by writers and artists who considered Hispanic village life an ideal alternative to the impersonal cities of industrial America. Writers such Mary Austin, Mabel Dodge Luhan, and Willa Cather, and artists such as John Sloan and the Taos school had fashioned a romantic aura for the Hispanic Southwest. Yet, from an economic perspective, their vision was utterly unreal. Hispanic farmers of northern New Mexico lived lives of increasing poverty, with little hope of improvement. Like other subsistence farmers in the West, they were enmeshed in a declining occupation. Each year it became more difficult to compete with large-scale or highly mechanized agriculture. In that respect their situation was hardly unique. What was distinctive was their sense of community, their cohesive social organization, their historical traditions, and their ethnic identity and pride. The challenge for many of these villagers was to balance the cultural advantages of village life with the economic drawbacks. Many of the younger people in the 1930s (and later) decided to leave the small communities to search for economic opportunities elsewhere.

In seeking to revive the village economies, the New Deal planners became involved in conflicting trends. To some extent the New Dealers were looking backward rather than forward, although they saw themselves as liberal reformers rather than reactionaries. During the 1930s they worked hard to have the federal government expand land ownership, to provide new jobs, to improve finances by extending credit, and to improve agricultural technology.

One purpose of the Department of Agriculture's program was to promote land reform. New Dealers hoped to return large areas of New Mexico's former Hispanic land grants to small Hispanic farmers. Unfortunately that policy clashed with Collier's program in the Indian Service to expand the land base for Navajos. That set the stage for a conflict over grazing areas between Native Americans and Hispanics. In 1934 Collier acquired 425,000 acres of eroded lands once included in Spanish land grants. The Land Division of the Indian Service bought the properties through a land retirement program of the Bureau of Agricultural Economics, using AAA funds. In 1935 Collier made an agreement with Hugh Bennett, the director of the Soil Conservation Service, to begin conservation work using CCC Indian workers. Both men were also concerned about the nearby Elephant Butte reservoir, a large federal project, because the eroding lands might send silt into the reservoir, which could impede its efficient operation.

But the Collier program aroused a strong reaction, both from Hispanic villages and from large, powerful stock growers in the state. Villages such as Peña Blanca, Española, and Cuba Valley sent protests to the Indian Service concerning the possible loss of their grazing lands. Senators Dennis Chavez and Carl Hatch from New Mexico quickly took up their cause. Federal and state officials were also worried about the removal of private lands from state tax rolls. Consequently, Chavez blocked all legislation to expand the Navajo reservation. In a temporary retreat, Collier formed the Rio Grande Advisory Commission with representatives from federal agencies seeking to resolve the dispute. Meanwhile, Chavez secured control over the lands in question and arranged for their transfer to the Resettlement Administration in the hope that they would be distributed to Hispanic villagers rather than to Navajos.

In this conflict the wily Chavez prevailed. Between 1935 and 1939 the Resettlement Administration extended generous loans to the poorest farmers while the Soil Conservation Service worked hard to restore the exhausted lands. The Soil Conservation Service also established demonstration projects for soil conservation and other efficient farming techniques in Taos and the upper Pecos Valley. But increasingly they found that villagers were suspicious of Anglos and hesitant to change their ways. They feared signing official papers and losing their language, their culture, and their social organization in the context of economic changes. Gradually it became clear to both the New Dealers and the villagers that the cultural dimension in economic restructuring was a major factor that could be an impediment to rapid economic change.[20]

The New Deal for Hispanics thus had a mixed record. Short-term relief programs such as the CCC and the WPA that provided cash incomes were very welcome, and the Social Security Act of 1935 proved to be a lifesaver for the impoverished population. More than one-third of the inhabitants of New Mexico received stipends, and the percentage in the villages was at least twice that. Such programs did not appear to require changes in their recipients' lifestyles. But the effort to restructure village economies was less successful. Meanwhile, a younger generation of Hispanics sought wage-paying jobs in both nearby and faraway places, leaving the villages poorer than before. The federal effort to restructure Hispanic communities foundered on cultural differences and market forces outside the region.

Chapter 2

✦ The New Deal had a significant economic impact on the West. It spurred modernization of the western economy by securing a greater balance between the natural resource economy and industrialization. This it achieved largely by substantial capital investment, especially in electric power. To contemporaries in the 1930s it appeared that the capital needed to develop the vast stretches of arid lands and to build an infrastructure for them was beyond the means of private investors. Later generations would question the wisdom of building giant dams as an essential part of this infrastructure, but it represented the best conventional wisdom of the time. The need for federal help had certainly been recognized since 1900, but during the New Deal it was institutionalized.

What did the New Deal do for the West? On a per capita basis, New Deal expenditures amounted to $399 per person in the nation. But in Nevada the federal government spent $1,499 per person. The average for the Rocky Mountain states was $716 per capita; and it was $536 per capita for the Pacific coast states and $424 per capita in the Great Plains. In other words, the western states received much greater benefits from federal largesse than any other part of the United States.[21]

The 1930s had been a dizzying time for westerners. The pace of change seemed much more rapid than that of the previous two decades. Such a judgment was relative, however, because World War II generated even greater disruptions and led to an even more prominent presence of the federal government in the West.

C ertainly President Roosevelt's economic policies during the Great Depression had done much to alleviate the suffering of millions of people. But the New Deal had not succeeded in bringing about substantial economic recovery, which proved to be elusive. Neither the recommendations of economic theorists such as John Maynard Keynes nor the carefully developed programs of economic planners such as the National Resources Planning Board had transformed the nation into the promised land of affluence. Neither Hoover nor Roosevelt had found the magic key to wealth. Nor could they foresee that federal involvement in promoting economic growth during World War II would do much to help the West ride the crest of the third Kondratieff wave, which had already affected other regions of the United States in preceding decades.

Expanding the Federal Landscape in World War II, 1940–1945

The New Deal had expanded the federal landscape in the West by its emphasis on the use of government as a positive force. But New Deal policies also laid a firm foundation for even greater federal involvement in the economy during World War II. It was ironic, indeed, that the prosperity Americans had vainly sought in peacetime during the 1930s was achieved through federal intervention in the war years of the 1940s.

That prosperity came into being not by design but through the exigencies of national mobilization. In this effort the West played a major role. As an underdeveloped region it was more open to experimentation than the older industrially developed regions of the East. Moreover, since much of the military action of World War II took place in the Pacific, the West was well positioned by dint of geographical proximity to become an important staging area. Because it was without elaborate economic infrastructures, the West did not require massive reconversion to war production but instead offered ample opportunities for the rapid development of new industries. During World War II the federal government transformed what had been largely a natural resource–oriented economy into one that was more diversified and could soon boast a limited industrial base.

The $60 billion spent in the West by the federal government between 1940 and 1945 dwarfed government expenditures during the New Deal. Congress authorized half of this huge amount (at the time) to be spent on war matériel. This was five times the value of all manufactures in the West in 1939! Federal agencies spent almost half of the $60 billion in California, which developed a major aircraft industry. Additional expenditures were made on building and maintaining military installations and for other war-related purposes. In 1930 the federal government spent $130 million in California; in 1945 government expenditures had increased to $8.5 billion. In its collaborative efforts with private enterprise, government set the parameters and goals. The government was the senior partner, and private enterprise the junior associate, in carrying out the mobilization of the western economy for war. The war effort included facilitating major shifts of population westward, a vast overhaul of selected sectors of the western economy, an enormous increase in the size and number of military establishments, and a reshaping of the physical and economic contours of western cities. As might be expected, the older sectors of the western economy were not as significantly affected by the war as the newer ones. Agriculture, mining, the oil industry, and electric power producers certainly increased their production during the conflict. But in the context of a century of change, they were not radically affected.

The federal government facilitated rapid capital formation through the private banking system. The function of private banks was not just to buy and sell war bonds. The Federal Reserve Board also authorized them to extend government-guaranteed loans to large-scale war contractors. Typically such loans allowed private corporations to retool and to expand their plants for war production. Initially, in the first months after Pearl Harbor, it was difficult for small subcontractors to convert to war manufactures because they were not included in the program. This gap in federal policy was quickly perceived by A. P. Giannini, the dynamic president of the Bank of America and the best-known banker in California and the West. He had pioneered branch banking in the 1920s and 1930s and was adept at influencing federal banking regulations. In 1942 Giannini organized an information service for small contractors to provide them with leads in securing federal contracts. His lobbying in Congress was also important in securing the passage of a 1942 law that allowed businesspeople to use government contracts as collateral for bank loans. Meanwhile, Mario Giannini, A. P.'s brother, was successful in persuading Congress to authorize creation of the Smaller War Plants Corporation, a new federal corporation whose sole task was to channel federal contracts to small businesses. A. P. Giannini was also instrumental in persuading the Federal Reserve Board to issue Regulation V, which greatly eased requirements for small contractors seeking bank loans. Among the small enterprises that took advantage of these federal inducements was Walt Disney Productions, which produced propaganda and army training films in wartime. In these varied ways, the federal government was directly involved in stimulating capital formation by the western banks.[1]

From 1940 to 1945 the federal government precipitated a major westward shift of the nation's population. The creation of new wartime jobs as a result of federal spending drew millions of people to the Pacific coast, including sizable numbers of racial and ethnic minorities. More than 200,000 African Americans came from the South, and increasing numbers of Mexicans were drawn across the border. Of the fifteen million men and women who served in the armed forces, perhaps as many as half were at one time stationed in the West. Many of those who traveled through the region on their way to the Pacific theater of operations returned to settle there in the postwar period. California gained one million newcomers between 1940 and 1945, and Washington and Oregon registered substantial increases as well. Western states of the interior, on the other hand, lost population. Many of their citizens went farther west to take lucrative jobs on the coast. Montana, the Dakotas, and Nebraska lost as much as 10 percent of their people.

Within California, population growth rates varied. The southern part of the state grew more rapidly than the north. More than 660,000 people poured into San Diego and Los Angeles. The Bay Area cities of San Francisco and Oakland gained in population as well. Aircraft factories and shipbuilding were important magnets to attract newcomers. In Portland and Seattle at least 100,000 openings in shipbuilding attracted people from all over the nation. This vast movement of people had immediate economic consequences. It created an enormous demand for housing, stimulated service industries of all kinds, and created profitable markets for agricultural and manufactured goods. The flood of people transformed an economy characterized by underemployment and underproduction, typical of the depression years, into one with full employment and maximum utilization of productive capacity.[2]

As a deliberate policy, the federal government, largely through the Defense Plant Corporation and the War Department, dispersed war production. The dispersal policy reflected a concern for national security and a willingness to locate manufactures in the interior West. Denver, for example, prospered as a center for ammunition and small ship production. The Las Vegas area was the site of the world's largest magnesium plant. Phoenix drew tire and parachute factories. Provo, Utah, became the location for the West's largest steel plant on the basis of its proximity to the West Coast. The federal government also built some of its largest supply depots and military training facilities in Utah. Wichita became a substantial aircraft-manufacturing center. Smaller communities throughout the West profited from thousands of subcontractors who worked for large enterprises on the Pacific coast. Within four short years the federal government altered the physical and economic landscape of the West.

The war provided a direct impetus to the expansion of manufacturing industries in the West, particularly aircraft fabrication, shipbuilding, and steel, aluminum, and magnesium production. Shipbuilding alone provided about 400,000 new jobs. Between 1919 and 1939 western shipyards did not build a single new ship because the industry was not competitive in peacetime. But during World War II they constructed almost half of all the merchant vessels made in the United States, or more than two thousand ships. The most spectacular feats of shipbuilding came from the yards of Henry J. Kaiser, a building contractor and industrialist from Oakland. Between 1920 and 1939 Kaiser had made a name for himself as a major road builder. He was also an important participant with the Six Companies, the consortium that built Hoover Dam between 1928 and 1935 and participated in erecting the San Francisco–Oakland Bay Bridge in 1937. In 1939 Kaiser began building merchant ships for the British government. Although he had no experience in building ships, he quickly applied the mass production and prefabrication methods he had used as a contractor to shipbuilding. Through such innovation he was able to build a ten-thousand-ton vessel in a matter of weeks, while it took eastern shipyards more than a year. As he received federal contracts and financing in 1941, he established major shipyards in Los Angeles, the San Francisco Bay area (Richmond), and Portland, employing more than 250,000 people around the clock. By providing health care, housing, and child care, he was also able to attract large numbers of women, who alleviated the critical labor shortage.

Shipbuilding stimulated other industries in the West. As Kaiser faced increasing problems in securing sufficient steel for his operations, he pressed the Defense Plant Corporation to provide him with funds to build new steel plants. Eastern steelmakers feared his competition and tried to block him. Despite their opposition, the Defense Plant Corporation provided Kaiser with the needed capital to build a steel plant in Fontana, California, fifty miles from Los Angeles. As a concession to the easterners, however, he was allowed to make only steel plates to supply his own shipyards.[3]

The federal government virtually created a new aircraft industry during the war years. To be sure, a number of aircraft manufacturers had operated in southern California since World War I, but in 1939 their total production, in profitable years, was not much more than 1,000 planes yearly. Between 1942 and 1945 they delivered about 40,000 planes yearly, although the engines were still manufactured in Detroit. The total amount of federal contracts in the West during the war years was about $29 billion, of which the California aircraft industry received a substantial portion. When President Roosevelt in 1940 called for the production of 50,000 planes per year, most of his contemporaries considered him unrealistic. But he energized the industry. Western plants built about 40 percent of the total aircraft produced in the United States, or about 120,000 planes. Douglas, Lockheed, and North American Aviation employed more than 200,000 people, with Boeing in Seattle hiring another 50,000; fully half of the employees were women.[4]

The mobilization program stimulated steel and other industries as well. In 1940 the largest steel fabrication facility in the West (owned by eastern capital) was the Colorado Fuel and Iron Company in Pueblo. A smaller plant was operated by the Columbia Steel Company in Provo. Since war manufactures required much larger steel production, President Roosevelt decided—after strenuous lobbying by Governor Herbert Maw and Senator Abe Murdock of Utah—that an expansion of the Utah facilities would be desirable. Of course, Utah's proximity to the West Coast and its location in the interior, assumed to be more secure from sabotage than sites right on the coast, were also considerations. The Defense Plant Corporation invested $200 million in a large new integrated steel plant in Provo and secured the services of the United States Steel Corporation to operate the facility. Known as the Geneva Works, the steel mill had the capacity to produce four million tons of steel annually and was invaluable in wartime. During the next four decades it also produced much smoke and smog for the Salt Lake Valley, an unfortunate manifestation of the federal landscape in Utah that was ultimately corrected.[5]

Wartime exigencies also fostered the creation of a federally owned aluminum industry in the West. Before 1940 the Aluminum Company of America was the sole supplier of the nation's limited aluminum needs. But once the manufacture of aircraft increased, the demand for aluminum, an important element of airframes, skyrocketed. Initially the company's officers were very reluctant to increase production because they feared that demand would shrink when peace returned. But the federal government, faced with a critical shortage of aluminum for the war effort, invested more than $200 million (through the Reconstruction Finance Corporation) to build six new aluminum plants in the West, which the Aluminum Company of America agreed to manage. Because the processing of aluminum required large amounts of electric power, the government built power plants in the Pacific Northwest not far from the Bonneville and Grand Coulee Dams. Four of the plants were in Washington, one was in Troutdale, Oregon, and another was in Torrance, California. Through such emergency programs the United States increased its aluminum output more than sevenfold, while the West gained a new industry as a result of large federal investment.[6]

On the sandy deserts of southern Nevada near the little town of Las Vegas, the Defense Plant Corporation built the world's largest magnesium plant. There was little peacetime demand for magnesium. Before 1940 only the Dow Chemical Company produced it, and only in small quantities. In wartime, however, the armed forces needed magnesium for firebombs and the manufacture of airplanes. The Defense Plant Corporation built a company town (Hendersonville) near Las Vegas to accommodate the fourteen thousand people who worked in the Basic Magnesium plant. The site was near needed deposits of pyrite, a mineral needed in the manufacturing process, and also close to cheap electric power from Hoover Dam. This huge factory produced all of the magnesium needed by the United States. Although the factory was closed in 1944, it became a tourist attraction during the second half of the twentieth century for millions of visitors to Las Vegas.[7]

Under federal direction, farmers accomplished prodigious feats in the World War II years. They fed not only American civilians but also the armed forces and the Allies overseas. And they were able to achieve record yields with a much smaller labor force than in peacetime through accelerated mechanization and the help of women and students. Moreover, nature was kind during the war years as rainfall in the West was above average. Western farmers produced two-thirds of the nation's wheat, half of its grains (corn, oats, and barley), and two-thirds of the fruits and vegetables. This was a very prosperous time for farmers; prices for farm goods increased, and the value of farms in many areas doubled due to rising land prices.

In the Pacific coast states and Texas, Mexican labor was important in harvesting the crops. As the chronic shortage of farm workers became more pronounced in 1941, growers appealed to the federal government for help. In response, the State Department negotiated the bracero agreement with Mexico in 1942. Under the terms of this treaty, Mexico recruited between 100,000 and 200,000 workers annually to help with American harvests or work on railroad track maintenance. Because Mexico had a very high rate of unemployment, the agreement was mutually beneficial. Working hours, wage scales, and housing conditions were carefully detailed in the treaty and were subject to inspection by Mexican consuls in the United States. The U.S. government transported the Mexican workers in special trains. Most lived in special camps and were urged by their government to send a portion of their earnings back home. In that way the Mexican government hoped to build up its currency reserves. Because the agreement was in the interest of both countries, it remained in effect until 1962.

Other minorities helped to ease the farm labor shortage too. Native Americans in the Southwest provided crucial help in that region. The abolition of New Deal agencies such as the WPA and the PWA had deprived them of the modest cash incomes they had earned during the depression, and they were eager to supplement what for most were still poverty-level earnings. African Americans came to the Texas Panhandle from the South to help with the cotton harvests, often working and living under unfavorable conditions.

Compared with the lean years of the depression, the war years provided a bonanza for cattle growers. Fully half of their annual beef production was used to feed the men and women of the armed forces. At the same time, civilians earning high wartime wages bought and ate twice as much meat as in the 1930s, creating a meat shortage. As demand exceeded supply and prices rose appreciably, the Roosevelt administration became increasingly concerned. In October 1942 the Office of Price Administration imposed price ceilings to control a flourishing black market in meat. As the situation worsened by 1943, the agency instituted wartime meat rationing. The system worked reasonably well during the conflict. Despite the federal controls, cattle growers expanded their herds, their ranches, and their profits.[8]

Mobilization was bound to affect the western mining industry. Federal policies reshaped mining operations in the West in various ways. One of the immediate issues to arise was the increased need for copper. To boost production the War Production Board established the Premium Price Plan, under which it paid very generous subsidies to mines that were marginal and not profitable in peacetime. But as Donald Nelson, chairman of the War Production Board, explained, national policy was mainly to encourage the import of copper and other needed minerals from countries outside the United States—such as Chile, Bolivia, and Peru—where production costs were much cheaper. That policy greatly upset the thousands of small miners in the West who had hoped to receive much higher prices than those allowed them by the Office of Price Administration. The federal policy thus forced small or less efficient mines to close (including all gold mines) while encouraging large and presumably more efficient operations, which were usually owned by multinational corporations with large investments overseas. Essentially, the framers of national mining policy assumed that the era of American self-sufficiency with regard to minerals was over, and that henceforth the United States would depend on foreign imports.[9]

To a considerable extent this was also true of the petroleum industry. During World War II the West still supplied more than half of the nation's oil requirements. But it was already apparent that the nation would soon become more dependent on the much cheaper crude oil from South America and the Middle East. That circumstance affected the landscape of the Southwest because thousands of small drillers found it more difficult to operate profitably in the face of foreign competition. During the war, however, the Petroleum Administration for War, headed by Secretary of the Interior Harold Ickes, succeeded through subsidies, rigid controls, and the import of Mexican oil to supply the petroleum needs of the armed forces while providing enough to keep everyone rolling on the home front. The Petroleum Administration for War was particularly successful in subsidizing refineries to produce one-hundred-octane aviation gasoline. This new product was urgently needed by the expanding air force, soon to total 300,000 planes, and the sophisticated airplane engines coming into use during these years required a high-octane product.

It was in the search for petroleum that the federal government significantly altered the landscape of Alaska. As by 1942 the demand for aviation fuel became more pressing, General Breton Somervell, chief of the army's supply corps, decided that oil refining in Alaska would help to alleviate the general shortage. In particular, he believed that a refinery at White Horse in the Yukon Territory of Canada would be important because under lend-lease agreements with the Soviet Union the United States was ferrying planes to Alaska from West Coast factories. General Somervell, who was not intimately acquainted with the geography of Alaska, gave his enthusiastic endorsement to the project. The first step was to build a highway across Alaska to transport the building materials needed to lay a pipeline. But such construction faced major obstacles, including mountains. Congress appropriated more than $200 million for the project, but progress was slow. It took four years to build the Alaska Highway, and the pipeline was still not finished at war's end. In 1945 the federal government sold the uncompleted pipeline for scrap, netting $700,000. In the long run the project was significant, however, because it speeded the building of a major highway between Alaska and the Pacific Northwest and greatly improved communication between the territory and the United States. Moreover, for better or worse, it opened visions of major oil pipelines in the future.[10]

Federal military installations and test sites also became a major industry during World War II. Certainly this was not an entirely new development; even in the nineteenth century military forts and supply bases were an important source of income for many western communities. Both the army and the navy had provided jobs and income. But World War II did much to expand the economic importance of the military in the region and to lay the foundation for what in the second half of the twentieth century came to be known as the military-industrial complex. Between 1940 and 1945 the western landscape was dotted with scores of training camps and major naval bases. Moreover, new geopolitical influences were at work in the nation. This was the first war in which the United States was engaged on a large scale in the Pacific, and the West served as a major way station and supply base for the Asian operations. Both the army and the navy built or expanded arsenals and supply depots in the West to serve the Pacific theater.

World War II was also the first American war in which air power played a crucial role. Scores of new air bases quickly became significant adjuncts to local western economies. Large testing areas for new weapons, usually although not always on public lands, also became familiar additions to the federal landscape. These facilities brought new jobs and new markets to scores of western communities. Such a military presence was especially important in areas whose economies were not diversified.

The size of the military presence in the West during World War II was unprecedented. In the 1930s the U.S. Army numbered no more than eighty thousand men and had fewer than one thousand planes. By 1945 about ten million men and women had served in the armed forces in the West at some time. More than one-fourth of the air force—including some 75,000 planes—was stationed in the West. The concentration of people and weapons had a profound effect on the economy. In four short years massive federal investment transformed a region that in 1939 had still been mired in depression into an affluent and diversified economy.[11]

The expansion of the military complex was closely related to federal sponsorship of science, which would become a major influence in the economic growth of the West after 1945. At the California Institute of Technology in Pasadena, federal money established what would one day be known as the Jet Propulsion Laboratory. The laboratory's design and manufacture of rockets and projectiles helped to lay the groundwork for new aerospace industries in southern California. At the University of California, federal money was important in establishing the cyclotron of Ernest O. Lawrence, which facilitated crucial nuclear research. In Los Alamos, New Mexico, the federal government constructed an entire new city devoted to the building of the atomic bomb under the direction of the brilliant J. Robert Oppenheimer. Through the Office of Research and Development, the federal government spent more than $2 billion on that project, which was administered by the University of California, providing new jobs for people in New Mexico and affecting the economy of this sparsely populated state. The federal facility in Hanford, Washington, employed some twenty thousand people to produce plutonium. In many ways the federal government made science an increasingly integral part of the western economy, contributing to its diversification.

Many of the economic activities generated by the war promoted rapid urbanization in the West. Directly or indirectly, federal expenditures made the cities the spearheads of economic change. San Diego, Los Angeles, Portland, Oregon, and Seattle grew significantly. Such growth was even more spectacular in the interior. Erstwhile towns before 1940 such as Tucson, Phoenix, El Paso, Albuquerque, and Las Vegas doubled the number of people in their environs. Like no other influence, federal spending built the cities of the West.[12]

✤ Viewed in a broad context, World War II ushered in a new era in western economic development so that it is possible to speak of the period before the war and the years thereafter. Essentially, the federal government promoted the restructuring of a natural resource–based colonial economy into a technologically oriented and service economy stimulated by massive federal expenditures. The federal government was the instrument that unleashed the entrepreneurial energies of millions of people who engineered the transformation in the course of the next half century.

The war brought economic diversification to the West. It stimulated the growth of manufacturing in the region as did no other single influence except the gold rush. It is true that some of the wartime industries ceased operations in 1945, but others remained. The aerospace complex of southern California expanded and prospered largely on the foundations laid during the war. The aluminum industry grew in the West in the postwar decades when the federal government sold its plants to private industry.

Some economists claim that wartime manufactures did not proliferate in the West after 1945. And it is true that industrial manufactures such as had characterized the East before 1940 were already on the decline in the 1950s when a new technologically oriented economy was already on the rise, buoyed by another Kondratieff wave. But westerners were attuned to the future, not the past. By the 1950s service industries were becoming more important in the economy. The emergence of major western financial institutions such as the Bank of America, the explosion of tourism, and the entertainment industry were harbingers of the new age, encouraged and abetted by federal policies.

Indeed, the westward population movement prompted by the federal government through its wartime job creation had a major impact. The enlarged population created major new markets, which provided a wide range of entrepreneurs with opportunities that simply had not existed before the war. Whether it was workers in war industries or men and women in the armed forces, the federal government acted as a great people mover speeding the westward progress of the U.S. population during the conflict.

Once the war was over, liberal federal housing policies accelerated urban growth, particularly in suburban neighborhoods, as cities' central cores were unable to cope with the sudden population increases. Federal housing policies and major new highways supported such expansion. In this process, too, the hand of the federal government was visible on the western landscape.

World War II created a symbiosis between the military establishment and entrepreneurs on local, state, and national levels. Soon this partnership became known as the military-industrial complex. Of course, such relationships had existed before 1940, but not on the same scale as in the second half of the century. The complex was another means by which the federal government invested vast sums not only to develop infrastructure but also to provide seed money for new, technically oriented industries. Whether this trend was desirable or undesirable is obviously open to debate. Perhaps many of these sums geared to research in weaponry could have been spent more fruitfully on social, educational, or cultural projects.

The military-industrial complex was closely related to a science-technology complex that the federal government brought into being during World War II. Before 1940 the federal government had spent little on scientific research and development in the West. When it granted such funds at all, they were concentrated in the East. But wartime government policies established the foundation for large-scale government-supported science facilities in federal laboratories and in universities. This was a new characteristic of the western economy after 1945.

It must be noted also that the economic growth inspired by the war did much to change the self-image of westerners concerning their place in the American economy. Before 1940 many westerners believed that economic opportunities in the West had come to an end. President Roosevelt himself in 1935 had expressed the belief that the frontier had ceased to exist and that further growth in the West was unlikely. But World War II changed that perception. Mobilization and full employment revealed hitherto unsuspected strengths in the western economy. Attitudes toward economic growth are a major factor in the rise and fall of nations. By the end of the war the pessimism of the 1930s had given way to an unbounded optimism. A new federal landscape was in sight, characterized by affluence and unlimited opportunity. But such hopes became enmeshed in cold war ideology after 1945.

The years between 1945 and 1960 were characterized by unparalleled peacetime affluence and growth. In many ways the trans-Mississippi West was a showcase for robust national prosperity. The West and the South had become the fastest growing sections in the United States. Before World War II these two regions had lagged behind the Northeast in their industrial development, but they caught up in the postwar era. This rapid growth was not entirely due to market forces. Rather, the development was engineered by the federal government, which had even more profound effects on the national economy during these years than it had during the New Deal and World War II.

Reconverting the West, 1945–1960

One major influence that produced the change was federal fiscal policy developed by Washington economic planners and politicians. During the war, President Roosevelt and James F. Byrnes, the director of the Office of War Mobilization and Reconversion, had expressed a widely held fear that once the conflict was over, the dreaded depression might reappear. Roosevelt remembered well that this was exactly what had happened after World War I. The demobilization of fifteen million men and women in the armed forces was bound to flood the job market. To forestall a possible debacle, the federal government had to take preventive action. That was the conventional wisdom of the day. It was based on the best thinking of many economists, including the famed British theorist John Maynard Keynes, who had won a large following in the United States. In particular, Professor Paul Samuelson of the Massachusetts Institute of Technology, author of the most widely used basic economics textbook in American colleges and universities during the 1950s, popularized Keynes's view that government needed to take an active role in maintaining economic stability. That could be accomplished by large-scale government spending when private-capital spending seemed to lag.

By the end of the war a widespread consensus had developed in Congress, in both political parties, to support that position. The result was the Employment Act of 1946, which institutionalized the view that government was responsible for maintaining maximum employment. Whenever unemployment increased to high levels, the federal government was to undertake deficit spending, or pump priming, to rejuvenate the economy. The new economic theory was particularly favorable to the West, which traditionally had suffered from a shortage of capital. Now the federal government was obligated by law to take up the slack. To develop this policy the act created the President's Council of Economic Advisers and the Joint Congressional Economic Committee. Between 1946 and 1960 these bodies were actively engaged in promoting high levels of employment and affluence throughout the nation. But the West continued to be a favored beneficiary of federal largesse, receiving more in federal funds than it paid in taxes.

Congress also increased the purchasing power of Americans. The decade before 1941, it will be recalled, was one of economic deprivation. Although the war years brought full employment and higher incomes, consumer goods were in short supply, creating much pent-up demand. But civilians and soldiers alike had to delay their gratification. In 1944 Congress increased the purchasing power of members of the armed forces with the G.I. Bill of 1944, by which the government paid most of the costs of a college or vocational education for veterans and paid them stipends for living expenses while they were in school. The sponsors of the bill were hopeful that it would cushion the transition from war to peace.

In a sense, the G.I. Bill was the domestic part of a worldwide program of reconstruction on which the United States embarked in the decade after 1945. The Marshall Plan was the foreign component; under it, the United States gave $13 billion to European nations to use in the reconstruction of war-torn areas. At the same time Congress also appropriated large sums for General Douglas MacArthur to use for restoring the economy of Japan and other selected nations in Asia. World War II promoted a decided Pacific tilt that benefited the western economy. The nation's new foreign policy provided western farmers and cattle growers with lucrative new markets.

Congress also bolstered western prosperity by enacting a liberal program to dispose of federally owned wartime plants. In a very real sense, this constituted another subsidy for the West. When it sold federal properties to private interests, the Defense Plant Corporation usually received only about ten cents on every dollar of their cost. At the same time, generous amortization policies accomplished the same objective for facilities in which private business interests had made investments. The United States Steel Corporation, for example, benefited by purchasing the Geneva Steel Works in Provo for a fraction of its cost. Henry J. Kaiser bought the steel plants at Fontana at similar bargain prices. The six aluminum plants that the Defense Plant Corporation had built in the Pacific Northwest were bought by private interests under similarly generous conditions. The Defense Plant Corporation found it more difficult to find buyers for the Basic Magnesium operation near Las Vegas. Ultimately it divided the plant into smaller units for use by chemical manufacturers. The underlying purpose of this federal program was to ease the transition to a peacetime economy while providing a special impetus to western growth.[1]

Other government programs hastened technological changes that helped to transform the West. In addition to television and jet engines, air-conditioning had a substantial influence on western growth in this period. Federal policies did much to hasten its acceptance.

Although air-conditioning was one of the most important inventions of the twentieth century, western historians have largely ignored its impact. Indeed, in 1979 *Time* correspondent Frank Trippett scolded academicians for their neglect of the economic, social, and cultural influences of air-conditioning. "Scholars have been aware of the social implications of the automobile and television," he wrote, but for some reason have avoided "charting and diagnosing all the changes brought about by air conditioning." The historian Ray Arsenault has suggested that such neglect could have been a reaction against environmental determinism as it was espoused by academics such as Walter Prescott Webb and Ellsworth Huntington earlier in the century, both of whom may have oversimplified the direct relationships between climate and culture. Climate may not be the only key to an understanding of the West, but it certainly cannot be ignored. Would the growth of Phoenix, Tucson, Las Vegas, or Los Angeles have been as rapid had it not been for air cooling?[2]

Certainly this was not the first time that cold air affected the course of western history. In the decade after the Civil War, several pioneers in the field of refrigeration revolutionized parts of the western economy with the development of the railroad refrigerator car, which greatly enlarged markets for western fruit and vegetable growers as well as cattle growers. The refrigerator car provided the foundation for California's fruit and vegetable industry.

Between 1945 and 1960 cold air again had a significant impact on the western economy. The preeminent pioneer in air-conditioning was Willis Haviland Carrier. In the decade before World War I, he was active in installing air-cooling systems in southern textile and tobacco factories. By the 1920s Carrier had placed his machines in moving-picture theaters and railroad trains. During the 1930s he expanded by selling air-conditioning systems for residential and office buildings. Both houses of Congress as well as the White House bought air conditioners during that decade. When Henry J. Kaiser in 1945 announced his plan to build thousands of new family homes in the West, he promised that they would be air-conditioned. In 1950, air cooling was still something of a novelty, however; only 5 percent of homes had a cooling system.[3]

Air-conditioning became common in the 1950s. In 1951 Carrier introduced a low-cost window unit and set off a boom. By 1960 more than 20 percent of homes in the West—50 percent in Arizona and Nevada—had air-conditioning. These percentages increased significantly during the next decade. Westerners also demanded air-conditioning in their cars. In 1939 the Packard Motor Car Company became the first auto maker to offer factory air-conditioning. World War II intervened, but by the 1950s most car manufacturers were offering it as an option. By 1960 about 20 percent of all cars in the United States had air-conditioning. But in the desert areas of the Southwest, more than 80 percent of automobile buyers requested it. At the same time government offices and schools and universities installed systems. For westerners born in the second half of the twentieth century, cooled air was a fact of life, a requirement for civilized living. Millions of newcomers to the West were enticed by the controlled climate, whereas in previous years many had been deterred by extremes of heat.

Federal policies endorsed air-conditioned living. Beginning in 1950 the Internal Revenue Service offered special tax deductions, allowances, and tax credits for homeowners who installed air-conditioning. When physicians prescribed air-conditioning as a medical necessity, for example, the Internal Revenue Service was willing to extend additional benefits. Under the prodding of the Federal Housing Administration (FHA), mortgage companies actually penalized customers who did not have air-conditioning in areas with hot climates. In 1959 the National Weather Service began issuing a "discomfort" index, a composite of heat and humidity that represented subtle government support for climate control and the air-conditioning industry.[4]

The rapid adoption of air-conditioning in this period was especially pronounced in hot desert cities like Phoenix, Tucson, and Las Vegas. Not only did air-conditioning become a new industry in the West, it also affected western lifestyles and hastened the pace of life. Some observers even believed that it affected sexual behavior and contributed to the increased birthrate. Certainly it affected the architecture of the burgeoning cities. It also had a major impact on western population growth by encouraging in-migration. Its influence was even broader, for as a contemporary noted: "It has had beneficial health effects, reducing infant mortality, prolonging the lives of patients with heart disease and respiratory disorders, improving conditions under which surgery is performed. . . . The humble air conditioner has been a powerful influence in circulating people as well as air."[5] In short, air-conditioning was a vital part of western industrial growth.

Affluence during the postwar years was also stimulated by demographic trends, especially the baby boom. These years saw a dramatic rise in the birthrate as returning veterans started new families. This factor contributed to a virtual doubling of the West's urban population between 1940 and 1960 as western cities came to hold 16 percent of the national population. At the same time, improving medical care lengthened life spans so that the percentage of the population over sixty-five years of age increased. Many hoped to spend their retirement years in warm climates of the South or West. The federal Social Security system made such dreams possible. The net result of these trends was a rapidly growing population in the West, a higher percentage of affluent consumers, and increased in-migration.[6]

The affluence spawned by the federal government was further accelerated by economic mobilization occasioned by the cold war and the war in Korea (1950–53). As relations between the United States and the Soviet Union worsened, the federal government spent increasing sums on national security. For the first time in its history the United States maintained a large military establishment in peacetime. As I describe in the following chapter, a significant portion of the federal funds allotted to national defense was spent in the West.

The cold war and air-conditioning shaped the broad context of western growth. In addition, the federal government spent ever larger sums to alleviate the shortage of water in the arid West so that it could support the growing population. That investment was made through an intensive dam-building program that dwarfed the programs of the pre–World War II years. Through the combination of deficit spending, the disposal of surplus war plants, the G.I. Bill, cold war expenditures, federal housing policies, the encouragement of air-conditioning, and water-development programs, the hand of the federal government created an increasingly impressive imprint on the western landscape.

Sleepy pre–World War II communities like Tucson, Phoenix, El Paso, Albuquerque, Reno, Boise, and Las Vegas became metropolitan areas almost overnight. Los Angeles, Portland, Seattle, San Diego, and Denver found themselves with millions of new residents. New technologies had a great impact in accelerating the pace of change in these cities, but it was federal policies that facilitated the enormous construction boom, the expansion of suburbs, and the building of new roads, highways, and airports. Federal housing policies also encouraged the building of new shopping centers and special retirement communities. In just fifteen years the economic, physical, and cultural topography of the West changed more than it had in the previous half century.[7]

The federal government did much to engineer the housing boom between 1945 and 1960. Of course, federal land policies in the nineteenth century had determined the checkerboard land patterns in the Midwest. In the twentieth century that influence continued, but in more indirect and subtle ways. The G.I. Bill allowed veterans to make low down payments on homes for their growing families, with federal backing. Affordable financing for young families was also available from the Veterans Administration (VA) and the FHA. The popular ranch-style house of the 1950s was the twentieth-century version of the 160-acre nineteenth-century homestead. The large number of people moving from rural to urban areas found ample land available for housing, and it was still relatively inexpensive. The frontier for farmland may have shrunk by 1890, but a frontier for mass-produced single-family houses was just opening up in 1945. The federal government supplied the massive credit that private developers, unaided, could not have provided. In 1956, for example, myriad federal agencies provided about $700 million in credit to home owners.

Many builders in the West took advantage of these federal programs. Among the first to do so was Henry J. Kaiser. He had built housing for workers at Hoover Dam in the 1930s and for shipyard workers in Portland during World War II. Kaiser believed that if private developers could not provide housing with federal help, the government would have to do it entirely on its own. Just two days after VJ Day, he formed a partnership with Fritz Burns, another West Coast developer, to build Panorama City in North Hollywood, California. Although the homes were not entirely prefabricated, Kaiser's factories supplied the cement, gypsum, gravel, and aluminum that went into them. Together the two men built ten thousand houses, backed by more than $50 million in federal loans.[8]

Throughout the West, other aggressive developers took up the challenge. With the backing of federal loans, Del Webb, John F. Long, Ralph Staggs, and David Murdock virtually rebuilt Tucson and Phoenix. Marriner and George Eccles used their extensive government contacts to secure substantial FHA loans to build single-family houses in Utah, a state with the highest level of home ownership in the nation. In Ogden, Utah, the Ogden Commercial Security Bank bought Washington Terrace from the government, a tract of thirteen hundred houses initially built by the federal government for government workers during the war. In many western towns and cities, the great majority of homes were built with guaranteed federal loans. Rapid City, South Dakota, was typical. The Rapid City National Bank used FHA-insured loans for 84 percent of the mortgages it issued in the city.[9]

Federal programs also provided a framework for retirement communities, another new type of neighborhood in western suburbs. With the adoption of the Social Security system in 1935, the federal government assured retirees of a stable minimal income. Taken together with federal housing programs sponsored by the FHA and the VA, government policies provided an incentive for private developers to establish housing clusters for people over fifty-five years of age, usually in areas with warm or moderate climates. The more-affluent seniors flocked to upscale communities such as Leisure World in Laguna Beach, California, and Sun City in Arizona. Those with more modest incomes moved into federally subsidized apartment complexes in cities, or to trailer courts or manufactured housing complexes in places such as Yuma, Arizona.[10]

Through its lending policies the federal government also had a role in shaping the skylines of western cities. Until the post–World War II decade few western cities had high-rise buildings in their downtown areas. But during the postwar years, developers, with federal encouragement, built high-rise towers, changing the largely horizontal landscapes of earlier years. That was strikingly true of Los Angeles, where the Union Bank and Bank of America buildings constructed in the 1950s introduced the new styles. Similarly, the Mile High Center in Denver reflected the new architectural direction of the urban West.

The Housing Act of 1949 visibly increased the federal influence on housing in the West. In what eventually proved to be faulty judgment, the FHA and other federal agencies built housing complexes for those with modest incomes. These projects seemed rational in theory but were often nonfunctional in practice. Many of them quickly deteriorated and became centers for crime and drug traffic. The inner-city slums they eventually became also formed a part of the federal landscape in the West.[11]

The rebuilding of the West included business clusters in the suburbs that sprouted as industrial parks between 1945 and 1960. In many ways these areas could have been designated federal business parks, because a large number of the enterprises there operated with federal contracts and received a large share of their income from the federal government. The Stanford Industrial Park in Palo Alto was among the first successful ventures of this type. It was the brainchild of Stanford provost Louis Terman, who had headed the radar development project at the Massachusetts Institute of Technology during the war years and had been impressed by the efficacy of partnerships between the federal government and research universities. He was convinced that such partnerships could achieve brilliant results in peacetime as well, particularly in spearheading regional economic development in the West.

Largely due to his influence, in 1946 Stanford University sponsored the establishment of the Stanford Research Institute to stimulate western economic conversion. The institute conducted a wide range of research programs for businesses. Then, in 1951, it attracted the first tenants for the Stanford Industrial Park and invited light manufacturing companies, especially in newer fields such as electronics, to locate there. The first tenant was Varian Associates, a company engaged with microwave technology. Soon Eastman Kodak, Hewlett-Packard, the missile division of Lockheed Aircraft, and Syntex, a pioneering pharmaceutical company, joined them. In 1950 the park had seven tenants; in 1962 it had forty-five, employing eleven thousand people. By that time fifty university-affiliated industrial parks had been built throughout the United States, boasting not only new industries but also closer networks made up of universities, businesses, and government. With the Korean War as an added stimulant, the Department of Defense and NASA awarded contracts that accounted for one-half to three-fifths of sales in the new technology-oriented industries. In 1951 the U.S. Census reported twenty electronics firms in California's Santa Clara Valley adjacent to the Stanford Research Institute. In 1960 there were more than one hundred.

The architecture of these industrial parks reflected the increasingly close relationship between the government and universities and research laboratories. The industries, nestled in parklike settings, blended into suburban neighborhoods. Designed like college campuses, they were set in horizontal low-rise buildings surrounded by greenery. That physical aspect was designed to attract a workforce with a high proportion of professionals and people with technical skills who preferred to work in an informal environment that encouraged interaction of people and ideas. Such industrial parks in the 1950s were in a real sense outgrowths of the federal landscape.[12]

In addition to urban construction the federal government did much to alter roads and highways in the West. President Eisenhower had long been interested in roads. As early as 1919 he had led a convoy of military vehicles on a coast-to-coast trek to dramatize the importance of good highways to national security. Twenty-five years later, his early impressions were strongly reinforced by his experiences in leading American forces down the autobahns of the Nazi Reich during World War II.

Eisenhower saw his administration as an especially propitious time for inaugurating a national highway program for the United States. The Korean War was followed by an economic slump. A highway-building program would both help to revive the economy and improve national defense. The result was the Highway Act of 1956, which created an interstate system that was to connect forty-two state capitals, which contained 90 percent of the nation's population. Most westerners favored the measure because it promised to link isolated areas to population centers. The act also provided special funds for road building on federal properties such as Indian reservations, national parks, and Forest Service lands. These provisions promised to open up the interior West and expand the growing tourist industry.[13]

Indian tribes in the Southwest had special hopes for the Highway Act. Navajo chairman Paul Jones noted in 1957 that he hoped the measure would lessen his people's isolation and would bring more jobs to the reservation. New roads might help efforts to develop oil and natural gas resources on the reservation and increase the flow of tourists. At the time, the unemployment rate among the Navajos was 50 percent. When Secretary of the Interior Stewart L. Udall ultimately dedicated Highway 89, one of the thoroughfares completed under the act, he took note of the situation and declared that "the Navajo Indians have remained isolated because of the lack of passable roads. We look forward to a generation of all American travelers discovering the unparalleled scenic beauties and colorful history of America's first settlers."[14]

Federal highways became the arteries that allowed exploitation of the West's mineral wealth, especially uranium. In the 1950s the federal government became the major influence behind the discovery and production of the metal, which was needed to manufacture plutonium for atomic bombs. Under the Atomic Energy Act of 1946, the Atomic Energy Commission (AEC) was in charge of the nation's nuclear program, with a monopoly on the production of uranium and the manufacture of atomic weapons. In the United States, uranium was found in Colorado, Utah, New Mexico, and on the Navajo reservation in Arizona. Canada and the Belgian Congo also had deposits. In the 1950s the AEC's purchasing program created an artificial mining boom in the West.

The government had gained some experience with the production of uranium during World War II. In 1942 the War Department had authorized the Vanadium Company of America to purchase uranium, a by-product of vanadium mined in Colorado. The Reconstruction Finance Corporation constructed five vanadium-processing plants in the Four Corners area of New Mexico. A year later, as research on the atomic bomb accelerated, the Metals Reserve Corporation, another federal entity, contracted with the Union Mines Company to explore for uranium. When the AEC began buying uranium in 1946, it thus drew on several years of experience.

In 1949, as the cold war accelerated, the AEC stepped up its uranium-purchasing program. The Soviet Union's development of a hydrogen bomb in that year persuaded Congress to increase the pace of atomic development activities. By 1955 the commission was spending more than $52 million annually for uranium production. That included the building of twelve hundred miles of access roads into mining areas and the construction of nine ore-processing mills. Between 1946 and 1971, when the uranium program ended, the commission spent $2.9 billion and bought 348 million tons of the ore. All of this money was spent in western states.

Some prospectors profited mightily from this federal largesse. In the Four Corners region, 795 miners operated with virtually guaranteed profits. The most famous of these prospectors was Charlie Steen, a trained engineer whose Mia Vida mine near Moab, Utah, made him a millionaire. Small, sleepy towns like Moab greatly increased their populations during the boom. Like most mining rushes, however, this one was short-lived. When the AEC suspended its uranium-purchasing program in 1971, with extensive stockpiles, the boom collapsed.[15]

Such was not the case with natural gas, however. Until 1945 most oil producers considered natural gas a worthless by-product of petroleum and viewed it as a nuisance. But then pipeline technology that allowed the transportation of oil and gas over thousands of miles was perfected. Suddenly, major markets for natural gas grew in the West and all around the nation. The rebuilding of the West between 1945 and 1960 and the spectacular growth of its population created new markets for cheap and efficient sources of energy. Natural gas was not just more economical than oil; it also burned more cleanly than oil or coal and thus was less polluting. Thus, innovative technologies and expanding markets combined to create a new industry. The greatest demand for gas was in the rapidly growing western cities, but large metropolitan areas in the Midwest and Northeast also provided millions of customers. Among the producers of natural gas, Texas, New Mexico, Louisiana, and Oklahoma became the leaders.

The federal government was deeply involved in the rise of the natural gas industry in the West. Under the Natural Gas Act of 1938, the Federal Power Commission received the authority to determine prices for gas sent across state boundaries. That authority was largely dormant until 1945 because gas was not an important source of energy. But the situation changed dramatically between 1945 and 1960 as natural gas became the heating and cooling fuel of choice in western suburbs. Gas also provided energy for enterprises such as copper mines in Arizona and federal military installations throughout the West. Unfortunately, heavy-handed federal regulation tended to limit expansion of the industry. In *Phillips Petroleum Company* v. *Wisconsin* (1954), a landmark case, the U.S. Supreme Court greatly broadened the jurisdiction of the Federal Power Commission by instructing it to regulate prices of all sales of gas in interstate commerce. That meant that the commission would set the precise rates for thousands of producers. The decision created a regulatory nightmare, which producers tried to overcome by confining production to intrastate sales as much as possible to escape federal jurisdiction. Although total production still increased after 1954, it was far less than it would have been without the federal overregulation that clearly shaped the dimensions of the natural gas industry, located almost exclusively in the West.

Gas and oil spring from the same sources in the ground, but in the postwar federal landscape they were an odd couple. While the Federal Power Commission exercised minute regulation over gas, the federal government did much less to control oil. The demand for gasoline increased enormously during the postwar years, largely because the suburbanized West depended on a vast number of automobiles. Between 1945 and 1959 domestic oil production increased by 50 percent, from 1.7 billion barrels to 2.6 billion. As prices for crude oil doubled in these years, they spurred nonwartime prosperity in the industry for the first time since the Great Depression.[16]

Federal policies shaped the pattern of domestic oil production, particularly in their great emphasis on foreign imports and on offshore drilling under the ocean floor. The grant of federally owned tidelands to the states was one of the most heated issues of the postwar decade. The controversy began in 1937 when Secretary of the Interior Harold Ickes openly challenged state ownership of tidal lands along the Gulf and Pacific coasts. In 1945 President Harry Truman issued an executive order proclaiming offshore lands to be federal property. That action raised such a furor that it brought the issue into national politics. Democrats favored retaining federal ownership, while Republicans urged grants to the states. When President Dwight Eisenhower was elected in 1952, he and the Republican Congress quickly moved to pass the Submerged Lands Act of 1953, which granted the coastal states full rights over submerged lands within the three-mile limit. That measure did much to direct the oil industry to ocean drilling and enriched coastal states such as California. The federal government retained its ownership of the land beyond the three-mile limit, yet this grant was one of the most generous transfers of federal property to the states in more than a century.[17]

Eisenhower clearly stated his views on the role of the federal government in power development in the West in 1952:

> The whole hog method is not the way to develop Western resources. These resources cannot be effectively developed without regard for local interests and local knowledge of local needs by bureaucrats 3000 miles away in the nation's capital. Nor can it be done by the states alone. All have a share in the task. We need river basin development to the highest degree, but not at the expense of accepting super government in which the people in the region have no voice. . . . We want this to be done through partnership . . . bringing in the federal government not as a boss, not as your dictator, but as a friendly partner, ready to help out and get its long nose out of your business as quickly as that can be accomplished.[18]

The issue of federal dam building came up after Eisenhower entered the White House and became enmeshed in the dispute over Hell's Canyon in Idaho. The Bureau of Reclamation proposed to build a multipurpose dam at Hell's Canyon on the Snake River. Many local citizens viewed this as the beginning of a more comprehensive federal dam-building program in the area, and that alarmed advocates of private ownership. Subsequently, President Eisenhower decided that since the Idaho Power Company, a private utility, was willing to develop the dam, the federal government should withdraw, and in 1953 he announced his decision to let the Idaho Power Company build the dam and develop power at Hell's Canyon.[19]

Throughout much of the West the federal government extended the national parks under its control and in the process expanded the federal landscape. Although the National Park Service was primarily concerned with preserving the nation's wilderness environment, it was also actively involved in promoting tourism. Economic interest groups, on the other hand—whether lumber producers, miners, oil drillers, cattle growers, or dam builders—sought to keep their access to lands that came to be off-limits to them as the Park Service expanded the national parks. The issues after 1945 were hardly new. The dispute over Hetch Hetchy in 1913 had caused such conflicts in Theodore Roosevelt's time, and similar disagreements had arisen in every presidential administration.

But national parks and tourist attractions became more important during the postwar years than they had been during the first half of the century. Increasingly, city and suburban dwellers living in artificial environments sought relief from the pressures of everyday life in contacts with nature. Automobiles and the growing highway net provided their link to natural areas.

Moreover, the national parks and monuments were an important part of the cultural landscape of the West. In the minds of many Americans they represented an important part of the nation's past. Tourists might flock to Disneyland to enter a realm of fantasy; or they might visit Las Vegas to lose themselves in another kind of imaginary world that included self-indulgence, gambling, and hoped-for sudden wealth. But the national parks in the West, in fact or myth, represented the old America, a simpler, unchanging, innocent land where, at least in imagination, time stood still.

The battles over national parks surfaced in the late 1940s when the National Park Service proposed enlarging Jackson Hole National Monument in Wyoming and Grand Teton National Park. Early in 1947 a number of western congressmen had proposed that various parts of the national park system be opened to lumbering and mineral exploitation. They argued that the transfer of federal property to private interests was very much in keeping with the American system of private enterprise. The leader in the House of Representatives was Congressman Frank Barrett of Wyoming. His goal was to prevent any enlargement of Grand Teton National Park and to limit the size of the Jackson Hole National

Monument. Intense political squabbling led to a compromise arrangement in 1949 that President Truman supported.

At the time, lumber interests looked askance at National Park Service efforts to expand Olympic National Park in the state of Washington and managed to secure the support of Senator Harry P. Cain and Congressman Henry Jackson, both of Washington. The struggle between conservationists and lumber interests continued between 1947 and 1948. In the end, the preservationists were successful in preventing extensive logging in this, one of the largest national parks in the Pacific Northwest.[20]

The fiercest battle during this period raged over the Bureau of Reclamation's plans to build new dams at Dinosaur National Monument. The conflict pitted business interests on one side and preservationists on the other. In January 1949 President Truman asked Congress to increase appropriations for the improvement of national parks. His opponents charged that the parks were stifling private enterprise and were an example of creeping socialism. Truman patiently bided his time, but the issue resurfaced in debates over the Upper Colorado Basin project. The Bureau of Reclamation had made development plans for the arid river valley that would affect at least six states. Among other things, it planned to build a series of dams and irrigation projects. But the question of whether private developers rather than agencies of the federal government should be allowed to develop the valley aroused heated debate within and outside of Congress. The central problem was that the Upper Colorado Basin project would inundate at least a dozen units of the national park system. Eventually the struggle became focused on the battle over Dinosaur National Monument.

Dinosaur National Monument lies at the junction of the Yampa and Green Rivers near the Colorado-Utah boundary. The canyons in the area seemed especially attractive to the officials in the Bureau of Reclamation as potential sites for new dams. But the monument is the site of many dinosaur fossils and since 1915 had attracted tourists in steady numbers. During the New Deal, CCC workers had developed visitor facilities in the nearby town of Vernal, Utah. By 1945 the Park Service was eager to develop more recreation sites there, but many of the local residents in eastern Utah were in favor of dam construction. The old issue of economic gains versus ecological and aesthetic values clearly emerged during this controversy. The Bureau of Reclamation claimed that the dam and the lake it would create would bring in many tourists. Preservationists argued that to leave the area in its natural state was to preserve the unadorned beauty of a unique area. As an official of the Sierra Club said:

> Aesthetic values existing in outstanding scenic areas of the West are greater than the values to be received from water development of every stream and the production of the last kilowatt of electrical energy. . . . It is our high belief that government and the people of the nation should never undertake so to state the issue in terms of the dollar, unless the day should come when the nation is so reduced in spirit that it must live on bread alone.

Arthur Carhart, another preservationist, put it more bluntly when he noted that "what happens [to the national parks] determines how long we live as a nation."

The preservationists organized in a crisis atmosphere. They created an emergency committee to save Dinosaur National Monument that attracted the attention of well-known writer Bernard De Voto. Their opponents included local cattle growers and potash producers. In general, the combatants were western economic interest groups arrayed against eastern preservationists. In addition, various government agencies were also at odds with each other on this issue. The Bureau of Reclamation was determined to build more dams, while the National Park Service opposed the projects as intruding on its domain. In view of the divisiveness of the controversy, Secretary of the Interior Oscar Chapman sought a compromise, suggesting an alternative site for the dams: Glen Canyon in Arizona. The National Park Service was allowed to keep Dinosaur National Monument but had to reduce its size. The Bureau of Reclamation was not permitted to build the proposed dams. Six years later, during the Eisenhower administration, Secretary of the Interior Douglas McKay authorized the building of Glen Canyon Dam, with the very reluctant agreement of the Sierra Club because this project also destroyed a majestic natural site.[21]

The conflicts between economic interests and conservationists continued throughout the administration of Dwight Eisenhower. In 1954 Eisenhower appointed Douglas McKay as his secretary of the interior. McKay, a Chevrolet dealer from Oregon, was not very adept in public relations. From the beginning, his enemies tagged him as "Giveaway McKay," although his record was one of seeking to find a compromise among conflicting pressures. McKay actually proved to be a friend of the national parks. After touring the entire park system he declared himself its staunch defender. He opposed the entry of loggers into Olympic National Park. He also refused to authorize the building of Glacier View Dam in Montana. In 1954 he denied Washington governor Arthur Langlie's request for a ski lift in Mount Rainier National Park. And he turned down an army request to acquire all of the Wichita Wildlife Refuge in Oklahoma. As a general policy he favored expansion of the national parks and wilderness areas. It was under his direction in 1955 that the national park system developed its Mission 66 program to prepare the parks to receive eighty million visitors yearly by 1966.[22]

In 1997, forty years after the Glen Canyon Dam was built, David Brower of the Sierra Club expressed his great regret at giving his assent to the Glen Canyon Dam. "That dam destroyed one of the most magnificent places on earth," he said, "in order to have flat water recreation." For forty years, Brower said, he had felt guilty about dropping his opposition to the Glen Canyon Dam as part of the trade-off that prevented the destruction of Dinosaur National Monument: "I was in a position to stop it, but we softened, and Glen Canyon dam was built."[23]

But the economic considerations of varied interest groups in the area were also strong. By the 1990s about 400,000 boats were being launched on Lake Powell every year, providing the local economy with considerable income. Among the beneficiaries was the Navajo Nation, for the nearby town of Page, Arizona, provided a significant number of jobs for tribal members. Before Glen Canyon formed Lake Powell, Rainbow Bridge National Monument attracted no more than a few hundred visitors yearly, who usually arrived on foot or by mule. With a boat dock nearby, the 290-foot-high natural arch attracted 325,000 people in 1996. The Glen Canyon project clearly placed the conflict between aesthetic considerations and economic interests, between easterners and westerners, in stark relief. Yet the issue was hardly dead.

As a solution to alleged silting, evaporation, and other environmental problems caused by the dam, Brower proposed draining Lake Powell. If that were done, the flooded scenery of Glen Canyon would be recovered

Chapter 4

and a wild-river habitat for fish could be restored. The executive board of the Sierra Club unanimously endorsed that plan in 1997. Critics responded that draining the lake would create a host of new environmental problems, including air pollution and land-dried salt. The Navajo Nation was strongly opposed because about twelve hundred members of the tribe had jobs at the electricity plant and related coal mine. Nevertheless, a congressional committee headed by Representative James V. Hansen (Rep., Utah) held hearings on the issue during the week of September 23, 1997. As early as 1981, novelist Edward Abbey, in *The Monkey Wrench Gang,* urged destruction of western dams. Now it seems quite likely that environmentalists will continue to press the issue in the twenty-first century.[24]

The conflict between national park enthusiasts and those favoring economic development has flared up again and again—for instance, in the controversy over the Grand Staircase–Escalante National Monument in Utah. In 1996 President Bill Clinton declared this new national monument of 1.7 million acres despite a great deal of opposition from ranchers who were angered by the withdrawal of lands they had hoped to buy from the federal government. One year later, however, some of that opposition had diminished as the monument attracted more than twenty thousand tourists in the first year of its existence. Since federal regulations to curb coal mining and drilling for oil and gas have become more stringent, tourism has surged to become Utah's most important source of income.[25]

Geologists estimate that the lands included in the monument contain eleven billion tons of coal. "It's un-American to lock these places up," declared Roger Holland, a city councilman in Kanab. "You're taking food out of children's mouths . . . and we're doing it again and again across the West." And the Utah school lands trust agency filed suit against the federal government to challenge creation of the national monument, arguing that royalties from coal mining would provide the schools with $1 billion of royalties from coal over the next fifty years.[26]

The controversy in Utah laid bare problems of increasing poverty in rural areas such as southern Utah. While the Wasatch front boomed with electronics industries, ranchers in the south were facing the prospect of losing their lands. Federal policies and global conditions have combined to create this unhappy situation. Among these policies are trade treaties that accelerated the import of cheap beef from South America and Australia, depressing beef prices in the United States. The deregulation of electric utilities has caused difficulties for small coal-fired plants in the area, which have found it difficult to compete with cheaper hydroelectric producers. The influx of aging baby boomers fleeing congested cities is often not profitable because they demand local services but do not create many new jobs or bring significant new investment capital. And more stringent federal environmental regulations restrict coal, oil, and gas exploitation; ranching; and timber harvests. Despite many changing conditions, the federal government is still a major force shaping the landscape of the West.

✤ Between 1945 and 1960 the federal government was a major architect of the western tourist industry. Although in some years Congress was niggardly in its appropriations for the National Park Service, general policy during these years was to expand the system and promote tourism. Essentially, the government was reshaping nature in the West to fit more closely into the affluent lifestyles that Americans developed in this era. The explosion of tourism was directly related to the special economic conditions of the 1950s, an era of unprecedented affluence. Many Americans enjoyed rising personal and family incomes that brought them into the middle class. With larger incomes, working-class people could now afford vacations. Shorter workweeks, paid vacations, and an increase in the number of retired persons reflected these trends.

Major technological improvements—including air-conditioning and jet planes—and lesser improvements such as mobile homes, campers, and new motels accelerated the westward flow. Most important, perhaps, was the great increase in highways, not only connecting population centers but also linking these to hitherto remote areas. National Park Service statistics revealed that by 1960, 85 percent of park visitors came by car, usually from urban areas.

Looking back from 1960 to 1945, it becomes apparent that the West rode the crest of a Kondratieff wave, stimulated by new technologies and federal monetary and fiscal policies. Technological innovations such as air-conditioning, television, jets, and electrical appliances; new pharmaceutical drugs like penicillin and the polio vaccine; industrial chemicals such as DDT; and transistors such as those used in radios fostered an economic boom. Governmental policies provided the institutional framework for this expansion. Heavy federal expenditures built an infrastructure so that the technologies could flourish. The federal government constructed dams to provide electric power and water to stimulate the growth of cities in the West; it built the highways and airports to provide an intricate transportation network; it supplied financing for a massive housing effort; and it expanded national parks to provide recreation for the teeming city dwellers of the West, and the nation. But the dams, highways, and parks were only a few of the visible elements of the federal landscape in the West. Another significant feature, not as apparent, was the military installations that dotted the West.

P erhaps the most striking addition to the federal landscape in the West during the second half of the twentieth century was the military-industrial complex that came
to play a dominant role in the region's economy. Military
installations had been important in the frontier West as well,
of course. During the nineteenth century, army forts and
navy shipyards had served as major stimuli to economic
growth in sparsely populated areas. Their importance did
not diminish in the four decades before World War II,
when a succession of new naval installations on the Pacific
coast, as well as airfields there and inland, came to dot many
western states. The economic importance of these installations was profound.

The Military-Industrial Complex in the Cold War, 1945–1960

But there was a very important contrast between the prewar and postwar periods. Before 1945 the United States had never supported a large standing military establishment in peacetime. Americans had fought their wars and then demobilized as quickly as possible. But in the era of the cold war, the nation maintained very large standing military forces. And when American foreign policy after 1941 became increasingly concerned with the Pacific rim, and America became enmeshed in vicious wars in Korea and Vietnam, military installations rapidly proliferated in the western states as they had not done in earlier periods. The size and scale of the new federal establishments were unprecedented. Congress poured more than $100 billion into western installations between 1945 and 1973, in addition to the large amounts it was already expending for dams, highways, and other components of the economic infrastructure.

Unlike earlier installations, this new military complex was spread far and wide over the landscape. It included large military bases, supply depots, and shipyards maintained by the army, navy, and air force. These bases were important economic assets not only in heavily populated states like California but also in smaller western communities in Idaho, Nevada, Utah, Wyoming, Montana, and the Dakotas. In some years the bases were the most important contributors to their respective states' incomes. After 1945 the federal government established major science research centers in California, Washington, New Mexico, Colorado, Nevada, and other western states. The military-industrial complex also spread its influence through the myriad contracts signed with tens of thousands of business firms throughout the West. More than in previous years, federal contracts also reached into universities, which became an important arm of the complex. As James Killian, the first presidential science adviser (for President Eisenhower), wrote nostalgically of the 1950s, there was an "enlightened spirit of partnership between Defense and the universities. . . . The academic institutions responded by inventing novel ways to serve government. . . . It was a golden era in government."[1] In addition, federal agencies such as the Atomic Energy Commission, the Department of Defense, and the National Aeronautics and Space Administration conducted research and development directly on projects related to national security. The military-industrial complex was the West's biggest business in the cold war years. And it grew, often in unexpected ways.

Chapter 5

The complex was neither a well-organized entity nor a planned conspiracy between government and industry. Rather, it was an amorphous conglomeration of private and public people. It included government officials, corporate executives, contractors and suppliers, legislators, workers in defense plants, union workers, and university scientists and research organizations. It extended also to the landlords and store owners who catered to customers from military bases.[2]

In view of the intricacy and size of the complex, it was inevitable that the people involved in it would establish personal relationships and networks. Members of the armed forces invariably had close contacts with arms suppliers and manufacturers. Such relationships were not really new. In the 1880s and 1890s, retired admirals and officers of lesser rank were often employed by shipbuilders, while army officers frequently found jobs in mining, banking, or other enterprises they had protected in earlier years. Such relationships were neither unusual nor unexpected. What was striking after 1945, however, was the size and scale of such networks and their influence in the western economy. When Congress investigated such contacts for the years between 1959 and 1969, it found 2,072 high-ranking retired military officers on the payrolls of one hundred leading defense contractors, a threefold increase over the previous decade.[3]

Why was the military-industrial complex particularly attracted to the West? No simple explanation suffices because various influences were at work. As a region economically less developed than the industrialized East, the West provided an inviting milieu for technological innovation and experimentation. As in the nineteenth century, there was still abundant cheap land and open space, especially significant factors at a time when air and missile power were becoming more important. Favorable Pacific coast climates added to the attractiveness of the leisure-oriented lifestyles that had become popular in the affluent society. Important also were the activities of aggressive local boosters throughout the West who labored energetically to attract new federal installations. Chambers of commerce, military officers, corporate executives, and congressional leaders in the West simply tried harder than their eastern counterparts to solicit federal largesse.

Military spending rather than market conditions determined the locations of high-tech industries. In the last analysis, federal spending created a new economic infrastructure as it brought massive new investment in technology; new plants; a wide range of industries; a greatly expanded workforce; new roads, water, and sewage systems; and new schools. The federal government did much to build the new cities of the West that housed the military-industrial establishment. Military spending raised per capita incomes and brought them into the range of those in the industrialized East. It served as both an accelerator for new industries and a people mover. It financed the influx of new population and created new labor pools of talented, highly skilled people. The federal government financed their move from other regions and often paid for their housing and resettlement. Newcomers came to work in electronics, aerospace, communications, and computers. Government-financed research and development was essential in these fields and guaranteed markets for emerging industries.

Much of the settlement and development of open spaces in the West during the cold war years was accomplished by the federal government rather than by private enterprise. Western business elites took advantage of the multiplicity of federal programs to stimulate further growth for private profit. The process was a prime illustration of the interplay between technological innovation during the crest of a Kondratieff cycle and the stimulation of entrepreneurship in a Schumpeterian mode.

The broader influence of this military buildup on American society was then, and is now, the subject of considerable dispute. Easterners argued that it transferred huge amounts of federal investments out of the older industrial regions. The federal government spent funds collected from taxpayers all across the nation in disproportionate amounts in the West. That had been true since the opening of the century. More serious was the question of whether money spent for national defense could have been used to greater advantage for domestic programs such as education, housing in inner cities, pollution control, and social services. Economist Arthur R. Burns concluded that by 1970 the military-industrial complex was promoting excessive government spending, thereby creating a large national debt that was passed on to future generations. The high rate of federal spending also encouraged waste and fueled inflation. It diverted resources from civilian needs and warped American higher education. By luring professors into defense-related research and development, the government distorted college curricula and glamorized the training of a generation of technocrats oriented to government service.

Perhaps the most surprising criticism of the complex came from President Eisenhower. In his farewell address to the nation in 1960 he said:

> Until the latest of our world conflicts the United States had no armaments industry. But now . . . we have been compelled to create a permanent armaments industry of vast proportions. Added to this, 3½ million men and women are directly engaged in the defense establishment. We annually spend on military security more than the net income of all United States corporations. This conjunction of an immense military establishment and a large arms industry is new to the American experience. . . . We must never let the weight of this combination endanger our liberties or democratic processes.[4]

The military influence on the western economy was revealed in at least four ways. First, and most visible on the federal landscape, were federal military installations, including training camps and training grounds for the army, airfields, naval facilities, supply depots, and test ranges. Second were the thousands of defense contracts that tied tens of thousands of primary and subcontractors to federal agencies such as the AEC, the DOD, NASA, and others. Third were the major science laboratories such as Lawrence Livermore, Los Alamos, and Richland. Fourth was university research, which was increasingly tied to military-oriented subjects through contracts.

Military installations were an important source of income for many communities in the West. According to economist Roger Bolton, military procurement and DOD payrolls provided at least 25 percent of the income from out-of-state sources in California, Washington, Hawaii, Alaska, Utah, and Colorado. Nevada, Arizona, New Mexico, Kansas, Oklahoma, and Texas received only slightly less. Between 1950 and 1980, federal spending was relatively stable except for steep increases during the Korean and Vietnam Wars.

The military's effect on the federal landscape in the West was perhaps most clearly visible in Colorado Springs, where many scenic areas seemed to be overwhelmed by a military presence. Army camps, training bases, airfields, the Air Force Academy, and the North American Air Defense Command (NORAD) in Cheyenne Mountain were just a few of the installations that transformed a sleepy resort village into a military city.

In fact, Colorado Springs reached this stage of being a model military city after extensive federal investment. By 1985 this community of about 200,000 people included 35,000 members of the military and 7,300 federal civilian employees. In addition, about 20,000 military retirees lived in the area. The total military payroll amounted to about $507 million annually in 1985, about half of all federal military expenditures in Colorado.

Colorado Springs had unlikely beginnings as a federal military city. It had been founded in the late nineteenth century by a small group of boosters that included Charles Tutt and Spencer Penrose, two men who had amassed fortunes in mining and railroading. Eager to establish a resort for the wealthy with a British Victorian ambiance, Tutt built the luxurious Broadmoor Hotel, which served for the next four decades as the centerpiece of the town.

With the outbreak of World War II, Tutt and fellow boosters saw an opportunity to broaden the economic base of the town with federal funds. They could offer the military cheap land and wide-open spaces. That proved to be a special boon just after Pearl Harbor, when the armed forces were desperately seeking to build army and air bases as quickly as possible. When in January 1942 local boosters offered thirty-five thousand acres of free land, the army agreed to establish Camp Carson and Peterson Army Air Base. The government spent $30 million to construct 1,650 buildings at Camp Carson to accommodate thirty thousand troops. The camp generated an annual payroll of at least $60 million. Meanwhile, Tutt used the Broadmoor Hotel to wine and dine the generals and other military brass who came along with the barracks and training grounds. Although the federal government briefly closed the camp in 1945, it was quickly reactivated and became an essential part of Colorado Springs.

The cold war did much to expand the federal military establishment in Colorado Springs. During World War II the nation's air strategy had been primarily offensive. After 1945, however, the strategy became defensive and required many more military bases. A fear of strategic bombers and nuclear missiles launched from land or sea led the air force to focus on radar and communications systems as well as jet interceptors. With that goal it created NORAD in 1950 to coordinate its widely dispersed fighter bases. Placing such a center on the East or West Coast would have made it too vulnerable. A location in the interior of the country was absolutely essential. As more than a hundred cities courted the air force in an effort to secure the headquarters of NORAD, the Colorado Springs Chamber of Commerce mounted its most intensive campaign ever. Thayer Tutt, the genial owner of the Broadmoor Hotel, was also the chairman of the chamber's Military Affairs Committee. He personally invited General Ennis Whitehead, newly appointed commander of NORAD, to visit Colorado Springs in 1951 before he toured other possible locations. As another member of the committee remembered, "He [Whitehead] looked it over and said he thought it an ideal location for the headquarters." The eager city also offered Peterson Air Force Field (which in 1945 the federal government had donated to the city) and promised to build a thousand housing units for air force personnel. This construction was possible because the Defense Housing Act provided up to 90 percent of the cost through FHA funds. When Canada agreed to cooperate in establishing NORAD in 1957, Colorado Springs succeeded in obtaining one of the most desirable military installations in the United States. In effect, whether directly or indirectly, the federal government footed virtually the entire cost of this installation, which forever changed the landscape of Colorado Springs.[5]

Similar intensive lobbying led the air force to establish its new service academy in Colorado Springs. When the air force gained its independence from the army in 1947, it sought its own training school. In 1948 General Hoyt Vandenberg, the air force chief of staff, announced plans for the new institution. Joe Reich, a member of the Colorado Springs Chamber of Commerce, read the announcement in a newspaper while he was sitting in a barber's chair. According to his recollection, the prospect excited him so much that he quickly ran across the street to the office of the chamber's president to spread the news. Within weeks the chamber began a lobbying effort and allotted $10,000 to mount a campaign to attract the academy. Thayer Tutt spearheaded the effort, but the competition was very tough. The air force was considering 528 potential sites in forty-five states. Tutt hoped that his personal acquaintance with Dwight Eisenhower and air force secretary Harold Talbott might be helpful. He also knew General Hubert Harmon, who had already been selected as the first superintendent of the Air Force Academy.

The air force wanted at least fifteen thousand acres for the academy. A parcel of land that Tutt secured just north of his hotel proved to be too small, but then he found a large plot of inexpensive land a few miles farther north of his establishment. By adroit lobbying in the Colorado legislature, Tutt secured $1 million from the state to finance the purchase. Meanwhile, the selection process proved to be agonizing. Even President Eisenhower did not want to have a hand in it because inevitably there would be a large number of disappointed suitors. Finally, on June 24, 1954, Secretary Talbott announced that he had selected Colorado Springs as the site for the academy. The air force then spent another $375 million to buy more land and $250 million to build the academy and related facilities. It quickly became one of the major industries of Colorado Springs.[6]

The local economy also received a tremendous boost from Fort Carson, a basic training facility for the army. The army placed the fort on a standby basis between 1945 and 1950 but activated it during the Korean War. Afterward the Defense Department considered closing the fort but decided instead to maintain it on a smaller scale. The Cuban missile crisis in 1961 led the air force to activate two divisions, one of which was stationed at Fort (upgraded) Carson. A site selection committee considered various locations before making the final recommendation for Colorado Springs. As the camp's official history notes, Major General Heintges, a member of that committee, "looked over the reservation and was impressed. The next morning, unable to sleep, he rose early at the Broadmoor Hotel and took a walk. In the beauty of the Colorado morning, he decided that Carson should remain open."[7]

The extensive communications installations in the NORAD head-quarters in Colorado Springs also affected the landscapes of other western states. To service the facilities at Cheyenne Mountain, the air force established the Strategic Air Command in Omaha, Nebraska. In addition, it built strings of silos in Montana and the Dakotas to house intercontinental ballistic missiles. In fact, one of Montana's main industries was Malstrom Air Force Base in Great Falls, which was the coordinating center for the missiles. Between 1957 and 1970 the air force also altered the landscape of Alaska by building long lines of radar stations to serve both NORAD and the Strategic Air Command. These new installations required thousands of new workers, many of whom lived in Fairbanks or Anchorage, stimulating the growth of these cities. Federal influence went farther, however. Once the radar stations were built, the federal government also provided a new infrastructure in the form of highways and airports, the port of Valdez, and even additional rail connections. The boom in Alaska began in 1952 as federal spending reached $200 million annually. The government maintained such investment levels for the next three decades. More than 20 percent of the employed population in Anchorage and Fairbanks worked for the federal government. If the indirect economic effects of such federal expenditures are considered, about half of Alaska's residents received federal money in some form.[8]

The Pacific tilt of American diplomacy also had a profound effect on the landscapes of the interior western states. The federal government was the largest employer in Utah. Although that may at first seem puzzling, it can be readily explained by geographic conditions in the context of transportation networks in the second half of the twentieth century. Ogden had excellent rail connections. Salt Lake City was equidistant from major Pacific coast ports such as Seattle, San Francisco, Los Angeles, and San Diego. Particularly in an age of jets, Utah was an ideal location for government supply bases and repair installations. In 1945 Utah had six such bases, employing about ten thousand people. As the cold war heated up in the 1950s, the number of employees grew to twenty-two thousand by 1956, with an annual payroll of $282 million. Half worked at Hill Air Force Base, Utah's largest employer.[9]

The Military-Industrial Complex

On the Pacific coast, the navy was one of the largest contributors to the economy throughout much of the twentieth century. Navy shipyards, of course, had been a significant economic presence ever since the establishment of the Mare Island shipyard in San Francisco Bay in 1854. That influence was greatly expanded when in 1919 the navy transferred fully half of the fleet to the Pacific, with headquarters in San Diego. In direct and indirect ways, the navy contributed 30 percent or more to that city's income. Such a major economic asset was bound to arouse the envy of other coastal cities, which also wanted, and received, a share of the federal largesse. The navy was eager to please as many as possible. In the 1920s, therefore, the navy began large-scale expansion of its facilities in San Francisco, Portland, and Seattle, creating landscapes similar to those in San Diego. In the latter city, as many as 200,000 people received some form of income from federal sources in 1960. San Diego's landscape was dominated by federal establishments, and hundreds of businesses concentrated on serving the navy and its employees. As Roger Lotchin has noted, visitors to San Diego might marvel at the majestic natural harbor, but they were also confronted with military hospitals, dry docks, anchorage sites, docking areas, warehouses, mothballed ships, ammunition depots, and barrack ships.[10]

Military contracts determined the contours of many western cities. Contracts bound important segments of the private economy to the federal government, creating an increasingly complex web. They created a new kind of economic federalism, one that could not have been foreseen by the framers of the Constitution. This unprecedented situation was well described in 1965 by H. L. Nieburg:

Government has become the economy's largest buyer and consumer. The government contract . . . has become an increasingly important device for intervention in public affairs, not only to procure goods and services, but to achieve a variety of explicit or inadvertent policy ends, allocati[ng] natural resources, organizing human effort, stimulating economic activity, and distributing status and power. The government contract has risen to its present prominence as a social management tool since World War II.

Instead of a free enterprise system, the United States was moving to a . . . government subsidized private profit system . . . which resembles traditional private profit enterprise and the corporate state of fascism.[11]

After 1950 most federal contracts were in the new high-tech industries, emphasizing research and development, missiles, computers, communications, and electronics. California, Washington, Kansas, Utah, Colorado, and New Mexico were among the major recipients of federal contracts in these fields. Silicon Valley in California could not have grown as rapidly as it did without federal contracts. But high-tech clones soon arose throughout the West in such spots as Colorado Springs, Phoenix, Austin, Salt Lake City, and Albuquerque. IBM went to Austin in 1966, followed by Advanced Micro Devices, Intel, and Motorola. Phoenix welcomed Motorola as early as 1948 and attracted other contractors such as General Electric, Sperry Rand, Airresearch, Honeywell, IBM, Intel, and National Semiconductor within a decade. Thiokol near Salt Lake City became another magnet.[12]

Los Angeles became the hub of federal contractors. A curious traveler approaching the city from the air could view miles of seemingly faceless buildings clustering around Los Angeles International Airport. Once on the ground, a visitor found the large aggregation of buildings in the federal landscape looming even larger. To be sure, the Santa Monica Mountains and Beverly Hills provided a backdrop, but the large square structures and rows of buildings along Highway 405 on the way to Orange County through Inglewood, Torrance, and Long Beach created a landscape that one observer dubbed Aerospace Valley. This area contained the highest concentration of high-tech weapons manufacturers in the world.

In this landscape were concentrated some of the federal government's biggest contractors: Rockwell International, Northrop, TRW, Hughes, McDonnell-Douglas, Lockheed, and Litton. These companies in the Los Angeles enclave garnered at least one-fourth of all prime aerospace contracts in the United States and more than half of all those awarded in California. They accounted for 8 percent of the region's employment.

Their payrolls generated significant sums for a wide range of service industries in California.

Airplane manufacturing had its beginnings in the Los Angeles area between World Wars I and II. It was during these years that pioneers like Glenn Martin, Donald Douglas, the Lockheed brothers, Dutch Kindelberger of North American Aviation, Jack Northrop, and Howard Hughes began their small-scale operations. They located there not so much because of the mild climate as because of the availability of cheap land. Moreover, the area had a good supply of labor, much of it not unionized. These were attractive features for early manufacturers. None of the companies could have survived without federal orders, however, although at times these were sporadic. The Lockheed brothers, we have noted, received their first order from the navy in 1916 for two flying boats. Thereafter their factory remained in operation only because of large army orders, even during the depression of the 1930s. In 1938 Lockheed also received sizable orders from the British, including one for 250 reconnaissance planes for the Royal Air Force. That required considerable expansion, to almost twenty-five hundred employees. The Lockheeds moved many of their operations into the as yet unpopulated San Fernando Valley. Douglas and North American found room for expansion in west Los Angeles. North American came there from the East in 1935 when Kindelberger secured an army order for 100 training planes. He set up shop on a bean field that the city and county of Los Angeles granted him in their effort to attract more industry. Jack Northrop manufactured mostly military planes in the 1920s and 1930s and remained in Los Angeles for the same reasons as the others: cheap land, mild climate, and a skilled labor force.

World War II did much to broaden the federal landscape in the Los Angeles area. Lockheed expanded into the San Fernando Valley, Hughes moved to Culver City, and Douglas, Northrop, and North American all established themselves in the western reaches near the ocean and the Los Angeles Airport (LAX). The gradual clustering of these companies was not accidental. It was the result of very active boosterism by civic leaders and the chamber of commerce, who were eager to attract new industries, particularly if much of the cost was underwritten by the federal government. Probably the most ardent civic booster was Harry Chandler, publisher of the *Los Angeles Times* from 1900 to 1940. As one of the largest land speculators in southern California, his interest in attracting new industries was not entirely selfless. As early as 1919 Chandler sent Bill Henry, his sports columnist, to Cleveland to work in Glenn Martin's aircraft factory and to become acquainted with this new industry. In Cleveland, Henry met the young Donald Douglas, whom Chandler financed with a $15,000 loan so that Douglas could fill a $120,000 navy contract for three torpedo planes. Chandler not only provided the money but also leased land he owned on Wilshire Boulevard in Los Angeles to Douglas. Cheap land, as in the nineteenth century, still proved to be a major attraction of the West in the twentieth century.

During the World War II years the federal government took over the site of the future LAX, which was not opened to commercial traffic until 1946. The federal government had paid for development of the site in 1937 and 1939. It served as the main delivery base for the thousands of aircraft that came off the assembly lines in nearby buildings. LAX reflected the strategic partnership between the War and Navy Departments and private airplane companies.[13]

The federal imprint was also very visible in Seattle after many decades of federal contracting with the Boeing Company. Tourists who arrived in the area to contemplate the beauties of Mount Rainier and other natural sites could not help but stumble on the vast complex of hangars, warehouses, and offices that made up the giant Boeing complex. As the largest employer in the city, Boeing was the lifeblood of Seattle, the dominant force in its economy into the 1980s, in good times as well as bad. At the end of World War II, Boeing employed 40,000 people; in 1980, 60,000; in 1990, 100,000. Of all the major aircraft companies in the United States, Boeing was the only one that also manufactured commercial aircraft.

The depression years of the 1930s were difficult for the Boeing Company, although it began to benefit when the U.S. Army Air Corps shifted its military air strategy from an emphasis on fighter planes to larger bombers. By 1934 Boeing had developed a prototype bomber, the B-1, which would later become the B-17, the dominant bomber in the European theater during World War II. Boeing increasingly shifted to the production of large, four-engine aircraft during the 1930s and by 1939 had completed the B-29, a superbomber. Before the year was out, Boeing had received a sheaf of federal contracts. In 1939 Boeing employed 4,000 people; during the war years that number increased tenfold just at the company's main Seattle plant. The cold war ensured Boeing's prosperity. The company's experience with jet engines proved to be valuable for the military as well as for commercial airplanes. By 1954 fully half of the employees engaged in manufacturing in Seattle worked for Boeing. In 1967, at the height of the Vietnam War, Boeing employed 150,000 people.

But there were always ups and downs in the delivery cycle, especially during 1968–69 and in 1971 when the company was forced to lay off large numbers of workers. Increasing commercial sales in the 1970s helped to offset the vagaries of military contracts. Between 1980 and 1990, however, Boeing prospered as a leading defense contractor, with annual sales exceeding $6 billion. Boeing probably could have secured even more contracts, but the Pentagon tended to issue contracts to financially troubled companies such as General Dynamics (for the TFX in 1962), Lockheed (for the C5B in 1982), and McDonnell-Douglas (for the KC-10 in 1976). These contracts, Pentagon critics contended, were corporate welfare—government subsidies to preserve ailing companies.

Boeing reoriented itself to defense in a big way in 1980, when military sales accounted for half of its total revenues but 70 percent of its total profits. The manufacture of helicopters, command aircraft, missile and space systems, electronics, and research and development accounted for much of this business. In 1982 Boeing employed about 10 percent of the total workforce in Seattle, half as many as in 1968. Until 1990 Boeing was the kingpin of the Seattle economy, garnering 72 percent of defense contracts in the Puget Sound area, or $2.6 billion. Since then, Microsoft and high-tech electronics, computers, and medical equipment firms have broadened the economic base.

Federal involvement in providing Seattle residents with jobs transcended Boeing. The Puget Sound Naval Shipyard employed about eleven thousand people annually in the 1950–90 period. A major Trident submarine base provided jobs for another seven thousand. Federal influence extended even further than that, however. Boeing's military contracts spurred the growth of educational institutions in the region. Many of the engineers employed by Boeing were graduates of the University of Washington or other area colleges, such as the University of Puget Sound, Seattle University, and Pacific Lutheran University. As early as 1917 Boeing donated a wind tunnel to the University of Washington, while the university established a chair in aeronautics. The university worked with Boeing to make the Pacific Northwest one of several centers of aeronautical talent and research.[14]

In an effort to spread federal largesse, the Department of Defense in 1952 decided to transfer some of Boeing's operations to the interior of the West. During World War II Boeing had established a satellite manufacturing plant in Wichita, Kansas. During the cold war the Pentagon revived the enterprise. In 1957, thirty-five thousand employees labored there to produce B-52 bombers. Even in the late stages of the cold war, in 1985, Boeing in Wichita still had as many as twenty thousand employees. They were divided between the Boeing Airplane Company and Boeing Computer Services. These two ventures were the largest single employers in Kansas. In 1979, Boeing bought the old government-owned plant for the bargain price of $44.7 million.

Federal contracts also dominated the economy of Utah. The shift in production from aircraft to rockets and missiles in the 1950s created an entire new industry. The Thiokol Corporation was a prominent presence. Missile production became the most important single component in the Utah economy, far ahead of tourism and the rising ski industry.[15]

Federal contracts also formed a major component of the economy of Colorado. By the 1960s congestion, rising land prices, and increasing labor costs in California, as well as the declining quality of life in California's Silicon Valley, led many high-tech companies there to search for less expensive locations for expansion elsewhere. Colorado Springs, already boasting a large concentration of military establishments and active civic boosters, beckoned. In addition to the attractive surroundings, Colorado Springs offered a very accessible and flexible labor force. Many of the spouses of military personnel stationed there were available for part-time or full-time work as markets fluctuated. Members of minorities in the armed forces—a higher percentage in the military than in the civilian population—were eager to take advantage of less discriminatory hiring practices after the 1960s. And some of the enlisted personnel who were mustered out were glad to take jobs in high-tech companies in an area that offered a pleasant lifestyle.

Of the largest federal contractors in Colorado Springs, Kaman Sciences and Hewlett-Packard were pioneers, arriving in 1957 and 1962, respectively. Relatively cheap land was still a great attraction then. By the 1970s, however, the city's boosters had become aware that relying on military installations could be unhealthy for the economy, and they made increasing efforts to recruit high-tech companies. Nevertheless, most of the companies had military connections. Enterprises that established branches in Colorado Springs included Honeywell, United Technologies, and Ford Microelectronics. These firms sold much of their output to the Defense Department. Moreover, most of their labor force came from the military. Fort Carson still had twenty thousand military personnel, plus their twenty-seven thousand family members and another thirty thousand retirees or related family members in the area.

President Reagan's emphasis on increasing American military forces in the 1980s benefited Colorado Springs. In 1982 the Pentagon awarded the Consolidated Space Operation Center, the U.S. Space Command, and the SDI National Test Bed Facility to the city. The importance of NORAD had declined by 1978, and its functions were transferred to Omaha and to Langley Field in Virginia. But space defense functions were expanded in Colorado Springs during the 1980s. That meant new federal contracts for at least thirty major subcontractors, such as IBM, Hughes Aircraft, Ford Aerospace, Honeywell, and TRW. Defense contracts in 1986 totaled $186 million. The local economy grew from 105,800 nonmilitary jobs in 1980 to 142,000 in 1985 while the rest of Colorado was depressed and suffering from a severe energy slump. In 1986 the three military bases accounted for 30 percent of the city's workforce, with an annual payroll of $884 million. Military expenditures accounted for fully half of the city's annual $4 billion economy.[16]

Chapter 5

The federal landscape in the West after World War II was also characterized by federal science facilities engaged in research and development of weapons and related projects. These installations had a profound economic impact on the areas in which they were located. Among the largest between 1950 and 1980 were the Los Alamos National Laboratory and the Sandia Corporation in New Mexico; the Hanford, Washington, plant that produced plutonium; the Lawrence Livermore Laboratory in California, which was concerned with H-bombs; Rocky Flats in Denver, which manufactured triggers for thermonuclear devices; White Sands Missile Range in New Mexico, which tested missiles; the Nevada Test Site near Las Vegas, which managed atomic tests; and the Jet Propulsion Laboratory in Pasadena. During these years the federal government usually hired private contractors to operate these laboratories. The University of California managed Lawrence Livermore and Los Alamos, Western Electric supervised Sandia, and various companies operated Rocky Flats. In establishing these centers the federal government created new cities in the image of company towns, with distinctive company cultures. The many thousands of people who worked in these communities were wholly dependent on the federal government not only for their incomes but also for their entire lifestyles.

Research and development activities during the cold war years bound western universities ever tighter to federal agencies. Between 1945 and the present, most of the universities in the West held federal contracts that involved a significant proportion of their science faculties and students. In fact, government insistence on the need for engineering talent led to the establishment of engineering centers on the campuses of the University of California and the University of Colorado at Colorado Springs, and expansion of facilities at Rice University, the California Institute of Technology, the University of New Mexico, the University of Washington, the University of Utah, and the University of Texas. An increasing amount of these institutions' budgets during these years came from federal agencies. This was true throughout the United States, but especially in the West. Protesters began to appear in the 1960s, but the relationship persisted. As Senator Daniel Patrick Moynihan noted in 1980, university faculties and administrators were only too willing to allow themselves to be co-opted into the military-industrial complex.[17]

The Military-Industrial Complex

Just how the relationship grew was well illustrated by federal involvement with research in rocketry. After World War I, Robert Millikan, a distinguished physicist at the California Institute of Technology, became eager to develop the new science of aeronautics. With a small grant from the Guggenheim Foundation, he succeeded in bringing Theodore von Karman, one of the world's great pioneers in that specialty, to the institute in 1929 to work on rockets. Von Karman operated on a small scale until 1943, when he received funds from the U.S. Army that helped to establish the Jet Propulsion Laboratory. The initial connection between the army and rockets was made by General Henry "Hap" Arnold, who had served as commander of March Field (near San Bernardino, California) between 1931 and 1936. During these years he developed a close friendship with Donald Douglas, who kept him abreast of developments in aircraft manufactures. He also became close to Millikan, whom he had known since World War I, and learned about the development of cosmic rays. Millikan introduced Arnold to von Karman. Arnold was impressed, and in 1936 he appointed von Karman to the army's Board of Ordnance as a consultant on the aerodynamic characteristics of supersonic projectiles. By 1935 the army was contributing $3 million to the laboratory for work on long-range jet-propelled missiles.

Immediately after World War II the Army Air Corps acted on Arnold's recommendation (he was now chief of staff) to develop missiles rather than airplanes. In 1946 the air corps awarded a contract to Convair in San Diego to develop an intercontinental ballistic missile (ICBM). Younger officers in the air force were committed to missile development, while older veterans like General Curtis LeMay favored aircraft. The Pentagon established a Strategic Missile Evaluation Committee, which included some of the best technical minds of the time, among them John von Neumann, a brilliant mathematician, and Edward Teller, developer of the H-bomb. In February 1954 this committee recommended building an intercontinental ballistic missile with an H-bomb warhead. The air force accepted the recommendation. President Eisenhower approved federal financing of this program, headquartered in Inglewood, California. By 1958, much of the program was being managed by TRW, which supervised 220 other prime contractors and thousands of subcontractors. Big companies such as Boeing, North American Aviation, General Dynamics, and United Aircraft became part of the complex project. By 1955 the ICBM program had helped to create a massive community of scientists in southern California. Airframe manufacturers increased their share of missile sales from 23.5 percent in 1956 to 74.5 percent just five years later. Apart from missile development, for good or ill the federal government had created one of the greatest concentrations of scientific and engineering talent in the world. Essential to the venture were the colleges and universities in the area, which provided a continuous flow of scientific talent into the aerospace complex. UCLA, the California Institute of Technology, the University of Southern California, Harvey Mudd College, and the California State Universities at Fullerton and Long Beach supplied much of the talent, and federal contracts provided an increasing percentage of their annual budgets after 1955.[18]

Between 1950 and 1963 southern California developed 661,000 new jobs in manufacturing. Of these, 146,000 were in aerospace fields and 146,000 were in electrical equipment for aircraft, and 90 percent of these jobs were defense related. More than 50 percent of the new jobs in southern California were involved with national security. In 1948, a total of 201,000 workers labored under Pentagon contracts. By 1963 the number had grown to more than 250,000. Defense spending accounted for 17 percent of California's income. Altogether, the federal government spent a minimum of $50 billion in Los Angeles County during the cold war. In some years 70 percent of the workforce worked in defense projects. Not surprisingly, those California counties that were most heavily involved with defense work registered the largest population increases in the 1950s, including Los Angeles, San Diego, Orange, and Santa Clara Counties.

In Utah, federal money came primarily through government installations. By 1965, however, Utah had received $4.2 billion in initial defense contracts, a gain of 1,700 percent since the Korean War. The largest contractor in the state was the Thiokol Corporation, which brought at least fifty thousand new jobs. By this time fully one-third of Utah's personal incomes depended on defense.[19]

✤ An overview reveals that between 1945 and 1965 the federal government spent 62 percent of its national budget, or $776 billion, on national security. One-fourth of the military and civilian employees involved in these jobs lived in thirteen western states containing only 16 percent of the nation's population. Companies in these states received one-third of all prime military contracts, half of research and development contracts, and two-thirds of all missile awards to private companies. In addition, NASA contracts in the Far West between 1961 and 1965 alone totaled $5.3 billion, or 48 percent of NASA expenditures. More than 90 percent of federal research and development contracts and half of its science grants were awarded by defense agencies. California received more contracts than any other state, and Utah boasted the largest percentage of income from defense installations. Truly, the West became the nation's military bastion. Without the cold war, the economic history of the West in the second half of the twentieth century would have been very different indeed.

Assessment of the economic impact of the military-industrial complex has given rise to an extensive literature, including thousands of books and articles. Although they vary in detail, these fall into three main categories. One group of critics concluded that the military-industrial complex retarded the nation's economic progress by distorting the allocation of economic resources and wasting human resources. Among the active writers on these themes was Seymour Melman. In a number of books, Melman concluded that scientific talent was drawn away from civilian to military industries, that the rate of economic growth was actually slowed by devoting so much of the national product to arms production, that such spending led to the gross neglect of environmental problems, and that universities were co-opted into focusing on short-term military projects rather than long-term basic research. Murray Weidenbaum added the caveat that technology transfer from military to civilian uses is highly unlikely.

Another group sidestepped these major themes and instead emphasized the importance of greater efficiency in the workings of the military-industrial complex. Former secretary of defense Robert McNamara argued that computers and new economic theories of cost-benefit analysis made it possible to lessen waste. This group analyzed the military-industrial complex in terms of function rather than service. Known as systems analysis, McNamara's argument was that the military-industrial complex functioned efficiently while allowing the administration to engage in a wide range of domestic programs. In other words, the complex did not drain funds from other urgent national priorities.[20]

A third group was committed to multilateral disarmament, which would make funds currently spent on defense available for domestic expenditures. Murray Weidenbaum was a strong advocate of such a policy. He argued that the savings that would come from the reduction of defense expenditures could be shifted to the civilian sector.[21]

The western states were the great beneficiaries of the increased federal expenditures for research and development during the cold war years. The money spent on such projects was a staggering 1,600 times the amount spent in the pre–World War II era. Three federal agencies—the DOD, NASA, and the AEC—spent 90 percent of this money, amounting to about 15 percent of the national budget. Some defenders of research and development have argued that it was the nation's best source of long-term industrial growth and that its benefits far outweighed its costs. John H. Rubel, one of McNamara's associates, espoused this view. Not all economists approved of this assumption. Robert Solo argued that research and development might not be the key to technological growth and might even hamper the economy. By measuring output per man-hour, the GNP, and the number of patents filed, Solo demonstrated that there was no positive correlation between the rate of economic growth and the level of research and development expenditures. That may be, he argued, because there was increasingly less spillover from military to civilian economies.[22]

This brief analysis only hints at some of the complexities that need to be considered in evaluating the impact of the military-industrial complex on the economy of the West. But our primary concern is with drawing some practical conclusions from the morass of evidence. From the short-term perspective, what was the influence of the complex on the western economy? It directed an increased flow of federal funds to the West; it accelerated the flow of population westward, including valuable skilled scientific and professional talent; and it created a wide range of new jobs. Between 1946 and 1965 the government spent $776 billion for defense, and the West garnered at least $250 billion of that. After NASA began operations in 1961, it spent at least $1 billion annually in the West. In the mountain states, most grant money went to military installations, although after 1965 there, too, industries received a larger share of the federal monies. California, which already had an airframe industry and a strong university system that was strictly oriented to research and development, received $67 billion in prime defense contracts between 1951 and 1965. Between 1946 and 1965, defense expenditures generated $28 billion in wages and salaries in California alone. When other military expenditures are included, the total is $73.5 billion, or about 10.9 percent of all personal income in California. About 661,000 new jobs were created, more than 60 percent of them in aerospace fields. During the same period, between 201,000 and 523,000 employers were involved in defense activities. The numbers fluctuated yearly. Economist Roger Bolton concluded that from 1951 to 1962, defense spending accounted for 17.2 percent of California's personal income and between 20 and 27 percent of the state's growth in income from sources outside the state.[23]

The military-industrial complex certainly accelerated population growth. Los Angeles County had the highest growth rate in the United States, adding 117,100 people between 1950 and 1960; 146,000 new jobs in the aircraft industry were created between 1950 and 1955, and 900,000 people came as a result. Without such spending, California's growth would have proceeded at one-third the rate that was registered. The complex was thus in large part responsible for the enormous economic and demographic changes that took place in Montana, Wyoming, Colorado, New Mexico, Arizona, Utah, Nevada, California, Washington, Alaska, and Hawaii during the cold war years.

The twentieth-century development of the West has been profoundly affected by the military stance of the United States. World War II, the cold war, the Korean War, and the Vietnam War were major influences. Indeed, the Soviet dictator Joseph Stalin can be considered a prime mover of the rapid growth of the western economy, especially in the cold war era. Through military installations, contracts, federal science laboratories, and contracts with universities, the federal government left a deep imprint on the region's history. Without the influence of the military-industrial complex, the history of the West during this century would have been very different. The complex was not a conspiracy foisted on an unwilling populace. It was a product of what westerners, and Americans, wanted. Clearly, they could have directed their energies in other directions. But then, the same could be said of citizens of the Roman Empire in its heyday. And after 1960, other forces were at work shaping the contours of the West.

T he years from 1960 to 1973 were a period of transition for the West. Although not clearly evident at the time, the Kondratieff wave that had begun in the late nineteenth century was nearing its end. A new wave was just beginning to form, prompted by the development of the computer chip in 1971. It took another twenty years for entrepreneurs to develop commercial applications for the chip that would have wide-reaching effects on the economy of the West.

By 1960 the urban pattern of the West was well established. The rapidly expanding western cities held more than 80 percent of the western population. Phoenix, Tucson, Albuquerque, Denver, Salt Lake City, and Las Vegas were truly oases, urban clusters in what not very long ago had been a

A Period of Transition, 1960–1973

western wilderness. And the Pacific coast cities of San Diego, Los Angeles, Portland, and Seattle also grew significantly during these years. This urban culture was both cause and effect of the more diversified economy of the region that was emerging by 1960, an economy in which high-tech and service industries were supplementing agriculture and natural resource extraction. Perhaps not intentionally, these industries employed an increasingly higher percentage of women and contributed to the feminization of the workforce. Between 1960 and 1973 federal policies continued to promote rapid urban growth in the West and high-tech industries, especially those related to national security.

But this period also witnessed an increasing concern with the quality, not just the quantity, of growth. The unbridled optimism of the post–World War II era gave way to a more pessimistic, or at least more cautious and critical, view of western growth. Certainly the Vietnam War, growing concerns for the environment, and a critical assessment of the weaknesses of American society contributed to this more tentative mood. After 1960 this changing outlook began to affect the federal landscape in the West. It brought an end to large-scale dam building because water was now needed less for agriculture than for the teeming millions living in cities. The new outlook also affected the exploitation of natural resources, especially coal, gas, and oil, when such extraction collided with concerns for the environment. Meanwhile, the civil rights movement of the 1950s began to influence federal policies concerning the economic welfare of minorities in the West: Indians, Hispanics, and African Americans, the human capital of the region. In this sea of change, one constant remained. Now more than ever, the federal government still shaped the contours of the West, still acted as the dominant force in its growth and development.

These years saw the development of the "Sunbelt" cities of the South and West, a designation first used in 1969 by Kevin Phillips, a journalist who described the fastest growing cities in the nation along a band stretching from the South to the Pacific coast. Another widely read writer, Kirkpatrick Sale, focused on the emergence of increasing western economic strength during these years. From his perspective, western growth resulted from a shift of economic and political power from East to West as the latter challenged the older, traditional industries of the former. Here was a transformation of the American landscape, a westward tilt, as the West was finally beginning to play a major role in the nation's economic life.

To a considerable extent, the federal government engineered this shift and facilitated the growth of the Sunbelt cities, and that did not go unnoticed in the rest of the nation. A contemporary observer noted: "The fact that the North continues to send money into the Sunbelt states through the Federal government, a prime the pump philosophy that has redistributed wealth under the Federal system from the richer states to the poorer ones, may contain the seeds of a regionally divisive issue."[1] An analysis of federal expenditures and tax collections revealed that the Sunbelt cities received billions of dollars more from the federal government than they had paid in taxes. These expenditures promoted the flow of wealth from East to West. Federal tax revenues combined with federal spending on public works, defense contracts, salaries, grants-in-aid, and retirement programs in 1975 resulted in a surplus of $10.6 billion for the mountain and Pacific states. Altogether, fourteen Sunbelt states received $13 billion more from federal coffers than they paid in taxes. Some contemporary observers wondered whether the prosperity of the Sunbelt cities was a direct result of the decline of the Northeast. Whether or not such a view was valid, the conflict over the distribution of public funds was real.

Between 1970 and 1974, Sunbelt cities accounted for an astounding 93 percent of the nation's metropolitan growth. In the period from 1940 to 1974 the South and West gained 52 million people, compared with 35 million for the rest of the country. The attractiveness of warm climates, new jobs, the expansion of military facilities, the construction of retirement centers, and the rise of new information-processing industries were the drawing cards. The growing population relied for income on the myriad service industries it had spawned. Service industries came to be the dominant source of income for forty-eight of the ninety-nine Standard Economic Areas in the West. By comparison, in the East only seven of sixty-seven Standard Economic Areas reflected such dependence.[2]

Federal housing policies did much to boost the growth of the Sunbelt cities. The lending policies of the Federal Housing Administration and the Veterans Administration facilitated the purchase of single-family homes by modest income earners who could not have qualified for private mortgages. Retirees in the Sunbelt depended on Social Security and, after 1965, on Medicare. Universities in the Sunbelt found their budgets increasingly dependent on grants from the National Science Foundation and the Pentagon. Their students benefited from the Student Loan Acts of 1965 and 1966, which provided them with grants and loans. From young to old, inhabitants of the Sunbelt became increasingly dependent on federal largesse.[3]

With the reshaping of western cities, the federal government also did much to reshape the western economy. Because the West did not have a substantial manufacturing infrastructure like that of the East before 1940, it was more flexible and open to new economic developments such as electronics and information processing, research and development, and the service industries. One contemporary noted that the invention of the microchip in 1971 was as significant in affecting the western economy as electricity had been a century before. Agriculture and mining still flourished, but these industries had a less dominant role in the trans-Mississippi area than they had in previous years. No longer was the West the colonial supplier of raw materials to the East. Now it played a pace-setting role in the national economy. This is not to say that the old colonial relationship between West and East had disappeared; but it was definitely fading.

The most striking reflection of the new western economy during the 1960s was the rise of Silicon Valley, which was in many ways a child of the federal government. The designation "Silicon Valley" came from Don Hoeffler, the editor of *Microelectronic News,* who coined the phrase in 1971 to designate an area between Palo Alto and San Jose, California, about ten miles wide and thirty miles long. In this conclave, high-tech companies grew rapidly between 1960 and 1974. The growth had actually begun in 1951, when the Stanford Research Institute first attracted high-tech firms to the region. By 1980 three thousand electronics firms had settled in the valley, employing 264,000 people. Many well-known names and logos dotted the area, including Hewlett-Packard, Xerox, Lockheed, and IBM. In these years their emphasis was on semiconductors, aerospace systems, communications equipment, and microelectronics. A substantial part of their income came from the federal government, which gave them fully half of all federal research and development funds in

1965. Essentially, the government was lord of the valley and the creator of this new federal landscape.[4]

The urbanization of the West changed priorities in the use of water. As the West's scarcest resource, water was no longer primarily needed for agricultural expansion. Moreover, the Jeffersonian ideal of a nation of small-scale independent farmers, however desirable in theory, was becoming less realistic by the middle of the twentieth century. Consequently, the federal policy of building dams throughout the West appeared less timely than it had in previous years.

Between 1960 and 1973 the conservation of water and other natural resources became a pressing public issue for a growing number of environmental groups. As the idealization of the family farm waned, the emotions the image had tapped and the idealism it had stimulated were transmuted into a passionate desire to preserve the nation's and the West's natural environment. As the Empty West became the Crowded West, questions arose regarding land use, increasing pollution of air and water, and the rapid destruction of resources such as water, minerals, and timber. Not unbridled economic growth but quality of growth became the important public issue.

The assumption that quality of growth, not quantity, should receive greater emphasis was reflected in Congress during Lyndon B. Johnson's presidency. The Air Quality Acts of 1965 and 1967 made federal grants available to local agencies for controlling air pollution. The Water Quality Act of 1965, the Clean Water Restoration Act of 1966, and the Solid Waste Disposal Act of 1965 provided for water purification and the development of sewage treatment programs. Such efforts became known as the New Environmentalism during the 1960s, and they generated new laws to protect the natural environment. These included the National Environmental Protection Act, passed in 1970 during the Nixon administration, which created the Environmental Protection Agency (EPA), a new government department whose primary concern was reflected in its title. Working together with the Council of Environmental Quality, the EPA would make recommendations on needed measures to protect the nation's natural heritage. Other laws regulated toxic chemicals, pesticides, and the dumping of dangerous wastes in the oceans and elsewhere. Environmental impact statements were now required for the building of highways, airports, bridges, dams, and nuclear plants. Viewed in their entirety, these various measures introduced environmental concerns into economic decision making.

Despite the continued rhetoric of politicians idealizing the small farmer in the West, federal farm policies continued to encourage large-scale corporate agriculture in the name of economic efficiency. Agribusiness was the dominant form of farming in the irrigated areas of California, Arizona, Colorado, Utah, and some sections of the Great Plains. As the number of farms—and farmers—decreased, the size of farms increased. Giant landholding companies such as the Southern Pacific, the Tejon Ranch, the Irvine Company, and Tenneco owned millions of acres in the West. The federal government bolstered their operations through a maze of subsidies, some for special crops, others for reclamation, and some for crop storage programs. Nor did the Department of the Interior enforce a 160-acre limit on the distribution of new lands made available by federal irrigation projects. In these years food was also an important tool in American cold war policies and a vital instrument of U.S. diplomacy. Federal agencies preferred to deal with large rather than small farmers because the former could provide the vast quantities that the United States shipped around the world. Nevertheless, the movement to decrease federal subsidies grew during these years. In 1970 President Richard Nixon recommended a decrease in federal farm subsidies but met strong opposition in Congress.[5]

The diversification of the western economy in the 1960s and the growth of environmental groups such as the Sierra Club and the Wilderness Society heightened the opposition to the construction of large dams. In contrast to the perceptions of many Americans in the first half of the century, who saw dams as saviors of western economic growth, dams were now viewed as despoilers of the environment. A complex of reasons lay behind this shift in attitude. One consideration lay in changing developments in the field of economics. In the 1950s, economic theorists were developing the field of cost-benefit analysis, of measuring economic benefits against their costs. By 1960 the field was sufficiently well advanced that economists were applying their hypotheses to thousands of specific projects, including the economic benefits of dams. Increasingly they came to the conclusion that the costs of some dams were too high for the benefits they brought.

In analyzing a succession of projects under the aegis of the Bureau of Reclamation, for example, the Water Resources Council in 1969 criticized the cost-benefit ratios as being much too high. Acting on the council's recommendation, President Nixon in 1970 impounded funds for the first stage of the Central Arizona Project. Attitude changes such as this one reflected the shift of water use from agriculture to the cities. A proposal offered in Congress for a similar project in Utah failed to secure approval as well. Instead, lawmakers now favored projects for municipal and industrial uses, which usually required less water than was needed for farming. Although the Central Arizona Project received congressional approval in 1968, it was the last of the big dam-building programs in the twentieth-century West.

Bureaucratic infighting also hindered the dam-building program in the West. The Corps of Engineers often resented the projects of the Bureau of Reclamation, charging that the bureau was trespassing on its domain. The National Park Service was frequently concerned about both agencies imposing their policies on parks under its direction and lessening its authority. Such struggles characterized the building of Glen Canyon Dam in the 1960s after environmental groups had prevented the flooding of Dinosaur National Monument. But the turf battles never ceased, and they seemed to grow more heated as larger amounts of federal dollars were at stake. In addition, environmental groups supported now one, now another of these agencies, leading to further acrimonious strife.[6]

By the mid-1960s the opposition to dams was crystallizing. One of the most eloquent spokesmen for the environmental position was Wallace Stegner, an important novelist who sought to pierce what he called the myths of the western dam. Stegner agreed that the West could not have achieved the economic development and productivity it had attained by 1965 without some of the large dam projects in the region. But increasingly, he stressed, the benefits brought by dams seemed to be diminishing. Projects such as Echo Park, Glen Canyon, Marble Canyon, and Rampart on the Yukon aroused opposition for that reason. The destruction of scenery and wildlife and the declining economic efficiency raised increasingly serious concerns. As the need for water in irrigated agriculture declined, only the power head produced by dams was important, and such power could be produced by alternative means. Moreover, economic analyses revealed that dams could waste as much water as they saved. On the Colorado River, which already had a number of dams, additional structures such as Marble and Bridge Canyons threatened to spread the water surface and lead to evaporation of as much as six feet of water annually. Glen Canyon Dam already revealed bank storage absorption of water into porous rock along the shores of Lake Powell, leading to increased silting.

Moreover, by the mid-1960s the Bureau of Reclamation had already built on many of the best dam sites in the West. The bureau hoped to survive by proposing ever greater and more grandiose projects. But in many cases private power companies offered more modest and more efficient alternatives. Some of these involved the production of power from local gas or coal. It appeared that the increasing size and complexity of dam projects was leading to diminishing economic returns.[7]

Oil was a promising alternative source of energy, but it also involved environmental problems. These were dramatized by a major oil spill off Santa Barbara, California, in 1969. Perhaps the most important effect of this ecological disaster was its dramatization of the need for greater corporate responsibility for protection of the environment. Beginning in 1963 the federal government granted offshore oil-drilling leases for 625 wells between Los Angeles and Santa Barbara beyond the three-mile limit. No problems arose until May 1968, when environmentalists noted a few oil slicks along the coast near Santa Barbara. That in itself was worrisome. But then on January 29, 1969, Union Oil Company's well number A-21 blew wide open and leaked 235,000 gallons of oil into the relatively pristine ocean along the California coast. Even worse, the spill created an oil slick 800 miles long and covered 5 miles of beach in the area, devastating the marine fauna. By early March even the beaches in San Diego were covered with the oil. More than thirty-five hundred birds died, choked by petroleum and its residues. Union Oil's workers were not able to plug the runaway well until March. Then the slow cleanup began.[8]

The Santa Barbara oil spill shocked the nation and led Congress to enact the National Environmental Policy Act of 1969, designed to prevent such disasters in the future. Although the spill probably did not result in permanent long-term damage, it forced oil companies to bear a greater responsibility for protection of the environment. And it demonstrated some of the perils and expenses of drilling for offshore oil.

With the enormous growth of western cities in the 1960s creating unprecedented demands for power and petroleum, some energy companies turned to coal to satisfy expanding markets. Many western states contained low-sulfur coal deposits that offered certain advantages in the energy situation of the 1960s. Low-sulfur coal was usually near the surface on coal-bearing lands. That allowed for strip mining, which was much cheaper than the underground mining necessary in the East. Moreover, with its low sulfur content, such coal burned more cleanly and was somewhat less air polluting than high-sulfur coal. During these years most of the major oil companies bought extensive tracts of low-sulfur coal on the Colorado Plateau, in the Four Corners area of New Mexico, in Utah, and in Wyoming. Under the oil companies' influence, Congress in 1958 amended the Minerals Leasing Act of 1920 to allow an increase in the size of coal lease tracts to 15,360 acres. Conoco, Humble Oil Company, Atlantic Richfield, Kerr-McGee, and the Sun Oil Company became important in western coal mining. Some ravaged the lands; others restored it to almost its original condition. The increased mining activities created new boomtowns such as Farmington, New Mexico, and Durango, Colorado. Denver between 1965 and 1973 became the biggest energy center in the West and a regional capital for most of the big oil companies. At the height of the boom Denver housed about two thousand energy companies, which employed approximately twenty-eight thousand people.[9]

One of the greatest beneficiaries of the boom was Wyoming, where coal production in the 1960s more than tripled. For a few years in the 1960s Gillette and Rock Springs profited from the escalating demand for power. Passage of the Clean Air Act of 1970 gave another boost to coal mining in Wyoming because the coal there had a low sulfur content. The Environmental Protection Agency was requiring lower sulfur emissions from coal-burning power plants than were required before. In 1971 the Bureau of Reclamation undertook the North Central Power Study, a master plan to develop water and coal in the West to produce 400 billion kilowatts of electricity yearly, but Secretary of the Interior Rogers Morton tabled the proposal. The Arab oil embargo of 1973 gave a further boost to the Wyoming coal mines. Between 1970 and 1975 they tripled their production again. Indeed, by the end of the decade Wyoming was the nation's fourth largest coal-producing state, with an output of 71.5 million tons in 1979. But then the boom collapsed. The concentration of coal-fired plants in the West created major air pollution problems even when burning low-sulfur coal. Air pollution became increasingly serious in the Four Corners and drifted over the Grand Canyon and into Glen Canyon, Zion, and Bryce Canyon National Parks.

As oil prices dropped in the 1980s and coal became more expensive because of environmental costs, the coal-mining boom in much of the West collapsed, leaving ghost towns such as Gillette and a host of social and environmental problems in its wake. These too came to be part of the federal landscape in the West, perhaps victims of the failed national energy policy or, more accurately, the absence of a coherent, well-defined national energy policy.[10]

Clearly, the years between 1960 and 1973 were a transition era in which increasing concerns about the environment challenged policies advocating uncontrolled growth. The federal government struggled to develop a balance between economic benefits, on the one hand, and the costs of greater environmental protection, on the other. These concerns were reflected in the rash of legislation during the Johnson administration, which tried to control pollution. The new laws did not put the issues to rest, but they did reflect serious efforts by government, business, and environmentalists to cope with an increasingly fragile environment.

Greater sensitivity to the environment was also accompanied by a greater awareness of the economic deprivation of minorities. Native Americans, Hispanics, and African Americans were among the poorest citizens in the West. Although the civil rights movement of the 1950s focused on involving minorities in the political process, by the 1960s the Johnson administration was also seeking to encourage their economic development. Johnson planned to establish greater economic self-sufficiency on reservations, just as the New Deal had tried to do, and to expand job opportunities in cities as well as rural areas. Hopes were high, although many expectations had not yet been met by 1973.

Among the Native American tribes in the West, the Navajos—the largest nation, with 200,000 people—seemed to be especially suitable for economic development. Their reservation held many natural riches. Estimates made in 1973 concluded that the reservation contained 11 million barrels of oil, 4.5 million cubic feet of natural gas, and 11 million tons of coal. Yet these brought in paltry revenues, only about $8.5 million annually from leases. Geologists estimated that the total coal reserves might be as great as 2.5 billion tons, and that probably another 100 million barrels of oil and 23 billion cubic feet of gas could be extracted. Between 1960 and 1973 the Navajo Nation signed several coal and oil leases that netted it only very modest sums. The Bureau of Indian Affairs (BIA) gave very little constructive advice to the tribes in negotiating or signing such leases, and the Navajos' income was far less than it would have been if they had employed a staff of shrewd attorneys. In one oil field leased to the Amoco Corporation, for example, the company did not account for production from 1.3 million acres between 1971 and 1982. Many of the coal leases signed with the BIA's approval in the 1950s and 1960s provided for royalties of 15 to 38 cents per ton when foreign buyers of the coal were paying $70 per ton. Such experiences led the Indian tribes in 1975 to organize the Council of Energy Resources, a sort of Indian OPEC. The council was a consortium of all Native American tribes in the West who had energy resources. It created a unified policy and gave advice for securing greater returns. Thus, for example, the council advised the Laguna Pueblo in New Mexico to negotiate on a grant of pipeline rights for $1.5 million instead of the $191,000 first offered.[11]

Efforts by the federal government to provide jobs for minorities were not very successful, either. The Navajos tried very hard to participate in the construction of Glen Canyon Dam when it began in 1956. For the next seven years Page, Arizona, became a boomtown. Its population spurted to six thousand, of whom half were construction workers. But Navajos held fewer than a thousand of these jobs. In any case, most of the workers spent their salaries outside the reservation, so their incomes had little impact on the Navajo economy. Once the power plant at Black Mesa near Page was completed, it required few employees and had a very modest economic effect on the surrounding region. The plant's major effects were in the consuming region, not in the area where the power was generated. It took several decades for the Glen Canyon Dam to provide the Navajos with economic benefits, which included not only coal mining but also, and more important, the income brought by tourists visiting Page and nearby Lake Powell.[12]

A broader effort by the federal government to promote economic development among Native Americans came in efforts to establish manufacturing enterprises and job-training programs on the reservations. Unfortunately, the Bureau of Indian Affairs had little experience in this sphere and was a very poor guide in leading the tribes into a postindustrial phase. Most of the training programs were sponsored by the Economic Development Administration, the Small Business Administration, and the BIA, and less often by the Office of Economic Opportunity. Among the attractions of reservations for outside investors were the absence of federal, state, and local taxes and the plentiful labor force. For the tribes, this was a strange new world. A few of the ventures were successful, but most quickly succumbed to lack of capital or lack of managerial experience.

In Arizona, the Parker Textile Company started operations in 1964 with loans from federal agencies and the Arizona tribes. It closed after eight months because the distance from profitable markets made it very hard to be competitive. More successful was the Pima Indian Industrial Park, where the Barron Container Corporation established itself in 1968 to manufacture Styrofoam cups. The Small Business Administration financed this facility, which was located about twenty-five miles from Phoenix and employed fifty-one people. The largest reservation plant in the state was established in 1968 at Fort Defiance by the General Dynamics Corporation. It operated successfully in these years with 224 people manufacturing electronic components.

New Mexico boasted a number of reservation enterprises. The largest was the Fairchild Semi-Conductor plant, established in 1964 near the Navajo reservation at Shiprock, which manufactured silicon transistors and employed as many as 1,100 people in 1969. The BIA spent more than $3 million on job-training programs there, while the Navajos contributed $844,000 to build the facility. Many unresolved conflicts led to its closure by 1980. Less successful was the Firestead Lumber Company at Santo Domingo Pueblo, which processed wood for furniture. The plant operated on and off between 1960 and 1969 before it finally closed. The Burnell Company established itself at Laguna Pueblo in 1961 after the tribe offered an incentive of $500,000. It operated with sixty people in the 1960s.[13]

On the Great Plains, the Wright-McGill Company began to manufacture fishing tackle at Wounded Knee, South Dakota, in 1961. The BIA provided on-the-job training for about 160 people. The company encountered problems with its workers as cultural values clashed with disciplined work procedures. But the major difficulties emanated from stiff competition from the Japanese, which eventually led to the demise of the business in 1970. Fort Peck Tribal Industries in Poplar in northeast Montana, which hired Assiniboine and Sioux, reconditioned carbines for the air force. Despite support from the Small Business Administration, the Office of Economic Opportunity, and the Bureau of Indian Affairs, the business experienced serious operational problems with its 118 employees and began large layoffs in 1971. Similarly, the Big Horn Carpet Mills established itself in the Crow Industrial Park in Hardin, Montana, amid high hopes in 1968. By 1971, serious management problems by non-Indian managers had undercut successful operation.

The record of Indian participation in businesses in the Pacific Northwest was more encouraging. The Suntex Veneer Company in Spokane, Washington, opened in 1966 with 289 employees, of whom 91 were Indians, and it prospered. Similarly, Textronix in Beaverton, Oregon, started in 1969 to manufacture oscilloscopes successfully with an Indian staff. In general, large companies provided discipline and management expertise and performed better than small entrepreneurs.

This period also saw the creation of some modestly successful tribal enterprises. The largest was the Navajo Forest Product Industry in New Mexico, which had 433 Indian employees, including some in managerial positions. A smaller operation was the Kah-Neefa Resort in Warm Springs, Oregon, which employed 32 people. The Mescalero Apaches built the Inn of the Mountain Gods in Ruidoso, New Mexico. Tourism was beginning to become a profitable industry, and the inn provided employment for about eighty tribal members. Indians were increasingly aware of the need to take the responsibility for their economic growth into their own hands. The point was well made by Logan Koopee, vice-chairman of the Hopi Tribal Council, in 1968 when he said: "We need to create jobs in our respective reservations. Opportunity for more employment needs to be made available to our people. The single most important thing the BIA can do for us is to train our children for a specific worthwhile job and then make sure that the jobs are available to them."[14]

But the tribal economies of this period were plagued with serious problems. One was the lack of service industries on the reservations. Even when Indian workers had good jobs with disposable incomes, they usually spent at least 80 percent of their income off the reservation. Thus, the jobs did not have a multiplier effect in stimulating other economic activity on the reservation. The income went to outsiders.

Another problem was reminiscent of Third World economies. By the 1960s the birthrate on reservations was higher than the national average. The percentage of people entering the job market was steadily outdistancing the rate of job creation. That contributed to a high rate of unemployment and a low standard of living. Most reservations could not support even their existing populations adequately because the agricultural potential of the lands around them was so limited.

Even by 1972 federal agencies were not much help in increasing Native Americans' income from leasing their natural resource properties. The Navajos, for example, still received relatively paltry sums from their coal leases. The private owners of the Black Mesa coal mine on the Navajo reservation and the Navajo Generating Station earned $22,944,000 in 1972. Their royalty payments to the Navajo Nation were $17.8 million. When they originally signed the agreement, the Navajos hoped that the project would have a multiplier effect—that it would bring new jobs, raise incomes, and attract investments. But these hopes were not fulfilled.

In 1972 the tribe contracted with the Peabody Coal Company to sell 455 million tons of coal at the rate of 13 million tons a year for thirty-five years. Peabody Coal was expected to receive an estimated $750 million for the coal; the Navajos would earn $76 million. The mines did provide jobs. Ninety percent of the mine laborers were Navajos, but these men spent 67 percent of their incomes off the reservation. Thus the Navajos derived very little economic benefit from their natural wealth. The mines did not provide many jobs, and they added little to tribal income. Nor did they result in massive new investments. Meanwhile, Navajos were losing their natural resources in the bargain. In short, resource development did not do as much to promote Navajo economic development as the federal government had hoped in encouraging exploitation of the mines. Furthermore, the BIA and the Bureau of Reclamation often followed their own bureaucratic interests rather than focusing primarily on the welfare of the Navajos.[15]

Federal encouragement of timber development was somewhat more successful during this period. Fourteen sawmills were operating near reservations by 1974. That was in marked contrast to 1960, when only two sawmills operated. The Economic Development Administration made a very active effort during the 1960s to enable tribes to utilize their timber resources by extending capital, job training, and managerial expertise. These enterprises provided good jobs and needed incomes. Unfortunately, the BIA continued to oversee the leasing of Native American timberlands to outsiders, with little benefit to the tribes.[16]

Between 1960 and 1973 the federal government remained the dominant influence on the Indian economy, and federal agencies continued to be the largest employer. The income the tribes received from their leases was relatively small compared with federal welfare benefits. In 1969, for example, tribal income from leases was only $2.4 million, and tribal enterprises brought in between $10 and $12 million. In comparison, the Navajos alone received approximately ten times as much in welfare benefits. In addition to being the largest employer, the federal government provided most of the capital invested in Indian enterprises, operated most of the job-training programs, and supplied 90 percent of social welfare payments. Yet the Indian standard of living did not rise appreciably in these years. The flurry of activity did heighten Native Americans' consciousness of the importance of economic development and the need to develop economic and managerial skills to heighten self-reliance and to chart their own course, but a long and difficult road lay ahead. Compared with 1900, however, their progress was very slow.[17]

One sign of the changing economy on the reservations was the decline of trading posts, once a major link in the barter economy. By 1945 the transition to a cash economy was well under way, although pawning valuables was still a way of life at most Indian trading posts. In the 1960s, young activist Native Americans became increasingly hostile to the Indian traders and encouraged the Office of Economic Opportunity to bring legal suits for charging excessive interest and pursuing unfair trading practices. In 1972 the Federal Trade Commission undertook an investigation of the entire system of trading posts. The young attorneys who came West to represent Native Americans had little sympathy for the old traders, who continued to take advantage of their positions of power on the reservations, to the detriment of their clients. On August 27 and 28, 1972, the Federal Trade Commission lawyers held hearings in Window Rock, Arizona, with BIA commissioner Louis Bruce and Navajo tribal chairman Peter MacDonald testifying about the financial inefficiency common in trading posts. MacDonald complained about traders holding welfare checks, charging high interest rates, selling spoiled food, and holding pawn for long periods. As a result of the inquiry, the Federal Trade Commission adopted new regulations concerning check cashing and sanitation, limited finance charges to 24 percent, and required marked prices on goods. Trading posts, once a link between two cultures, were clearly on the decline. Already by the 1960s, however, young Navajos were avoiding trading posts. They preferred shopping in supermarkets and clothing and department stores in nearby towns like Gallup, New Mexico.

By the end of the century, only a few trading posts survived, mainly in very isolated areas. One of the oldest was Two Grey Hills in New Mexico, which celebrated its one-hundredth anniversary in August 1997. For many of its remaining customers its proximity was a major factor. As Tommy Thompson, one satisfied customer, said: "My truck takes one fill-up to get to Farmington and then I have to fill it up to get back. That's a $30 trip for me. This is a regular trading post. We're still in the '40s here." Tourists also sought out the few remaining trading posts to purchase Indian-made jewelry, blankets, and rugs, and to catch a glimpse of a bygone era. But most Navajos preferred to patronize the ubiquitous Thriftway convenience stores that dotted the reservations and captured most of the former clients of the trading posts.[18]

The federal government's influence on the lives of Hispanics was also considerable, particularly on the border between the United States and Mexico. With the termination of the federal bracero program in 1962, the Mexican government faced an aggravated unemployment situation, and the United States lost a source of cheap and accessible labor. The two governments decided to approach the situation by creating a string of industrial parks along the border that were mutually advantageous to both countries. In 1962 President Gustav Díaz Ordaz of Mexico initiated and encouraged the establishment of these *maquiladoras,* at which products were assembled for American companies for export to the United States and other countries. The companies, in turn, received special tax incentives and were promised low labor costs. The wages paid by U.S. corporations in Mexico were usually less than half of those paid in the United States. The plants were also eligible for duty-free imports of the raw materials and machinery needed for the manufacture and export of assembled products. American companies were strongly attracted to the program because of the cheap labor costs, lower transportation tariffs, and closeness to major American plants. When the Border Industrial Program went into full operation in 1966, major American companies such as Motorola, Zenith, General Electric, and Levi Strauss came in large numbers to take advantage of it. Motorola, for example, moved its Phoenix assembly plant to nearby Nogales, Mexico, where wages for electronics assemblers averaged $1,060 a year, compared with $5,350 in Phoenix. In 1960 there were only 20 maquiladoras; by 1974 they had mushroomed to 476 and employed more than 53,000 people.

The Border Industrial Program led to an explosive growth of Mexican border cities. Tijuana grew almost tenfold, to 566,000, in 1980; and Nogales, Ciudad Juárez, and Nuevo Laredo boomed almost as much. As mechanization reduced the need for farm labor in Mexico by almost half between 1960 and 1973, workers seeking employment streamed into the maquiladoras on the border.[19]

A small number of Hispanics sought not jobs but a return of the lands that had been taken from them. In New Mexico a Texan field worker named Reies Lopez Tijerina formed the Alianza Federal to demand the return of lands granted by the Spanish king to settlers in the eighteenth century. These lands had been transferred to the United States under the Treaty of Guadalupe Hidalgo in 1848 and were later sold to American settlers. Tijerina demanded that the lands be returned to their original Hispanic owners. In a determined effort in 1966, he and a small band of followers seized the courthouse in Tierra Amarilla, New Mexico. He also defied Forest Service rangers on federal lands. Tijerina was captured by local sheriffs and later convicted of attacking the rangers. He went to jail and the movement collapsed.[20]

The changing federal landscape also affected Hispanics in rural areas of northern New Mexico, where some families had lived for more than six generations. Many resided in little villages such as San Cristobal, where individual farmers tilled ten acres or less, eking out a modest living. Their small tracts did not allow enough grazing room for their livestock. For many years they had been accustomed to let their animals roam on forest or mountain lands owned by the U.S. government. But by 1960 the Forest Service was actively expanding the acreage included in national forests and was restricting such grazing, and also reducing the number of grazing permits it issued each year. In San Cristobal, for example, the Forest Service issued 350 permits in 1947 but only 140 in 1967. Meanwhile, the mechanization of agriculture, requiring expensive machinery, made such small, self-sufficient homesteads less profitable. The shrinkage of available grazing lands only added to the problems of the Hispanic farmers in the region.[21]

Thus, the federal government had a pervasive influence on the world of Hispanics during these years. The abrogation of the bracero agreement in 1962 had varied consequences. By shutting off a safety valve for Mexico's unemployed, it heightened the potential for social unrest in Mexico. The Díaz government's anxiousness to avoid unrest, combined with American companies' desire for cheap labor, led to mutual Mexican-American accommodation in the creation of the maquiladora zones along the border. But such competition may have contributed to greater unrest among Chicanos in the United States, reflected in Chicano militancy in western cities, in the land grant movement in New Mexico, and in the effort by Cesar Chavez in 1962 to organize Mexican field workers. In varied ways, the changing federal landscape affected the Spanish-speaking people in the West.

❖ The years from 1960 to 1973 were as turbulent in the West as they were in the rest of the nation. In retrospect, it is clear that this was a period of transition between two economic eras. By 1960 the Kondratieff cycle that had begun in the late nineteenth century had petered out. Of course, the 1960s were also characterized by great social unrest, political protests, and bitter divisions over Vietnam and the trends of U.S. foreign policy. It was hardly surprising or accidental that the economy was also shifting in as yet unknown directions. But these economic shifts added to feelings of uncertainty and doubts about the future. The unbridled optimism of the 1950s gave way to a more guarded, pessimistic outlook between 1960 and 1973.

The federal landscape of the time revealed some of these changes. It reflected the startling transformation of the West from a sparsely populated, semirural area in 1900 to a region characterized by urban oases in the Sunbelt just a half century later. These years also saw the end of the period of intensive large-scale dam building in the West. Instead they reflected the growth of genuine concern for the environment, for wildlife, and for unpolluted clean water, air, and land, even at the cost of some economic growth. At the same time, national policies sought to improve the economic conditions of Native Americans on the reservations. And the appearance of the maquiladoras on the Mexican-American border signaled the increasing influence of Mexicans in the western economy.

These were clearly years of unsettling changes. A new wave of economic growth did not appear to be in the offing. That wave was crystallizing slowly and would appear only with the telecommunications revolution of the 1990s. But in 1973 westerners could not divine such a future because they were beset with new problems and economic instability.

A Period of Transition

U ntil 1973, westerners, like other Americans, had been preoccupied with the enormous economic growth of their region. Some of that growth was stimulated by global events, of course, including the reconstruction of war-ravaged economies in Europe and Asia, and American wars in Korea and Vietnam. The West had served as an important staging area for U.S. expansion in the Pacific and had provided the foodstuffs and the lumber to stimulate economic recovery throughout the world, especially in Germany and Japan. But by the early 1970s much of that recovery had been completed, and Germany and Japan were emerging as serious economic rivals of the United States in the world economy. As Kondratieff had prophesied, capitalist economies had a self-correcting mode. The two decades after 1973 were such a time of correction.[1]

The Era of Deindustrialization, 1973–2000

The 1970s and 1980s were a period of drift before a new economic cycle gathered momentum in the 1990s. In addition, the end of the war in Vietnam brought on an economic recession. Such recessions had occurred after every conflict in which the United States had been engaged. Other global influences also affected the West. These included the 1973 oil embargo imposed by the OPEC nations, oil producers around the globe who had organized to try to regulate the world's oil production and oil prices.

The OPEC oil embargo produced a serious energy shortage in 1973. In the West, whose inhabitants were heavily dependent on automobiles, the crisis threatened much of the economy. Meanwhile, western grain harvests between 1972 and 1975 fell below average yields. Combined with grain shortages outside the United States, that situation tended to fuel inflationary pressures. Nor did political crises such as the Watergate affair and the attempted impeachment of President Nixon bolster confidence in the economy. Many of these fears were reflected in a precipitous decline of the stock market between 1973 and 1975, which made the raising of investment capital more difficult. Regions of growth such as the West felt the lack particularly deeply. Postwar recession also led to stagnant wage levels, which affected the purchasing power of consumers. The 1965 riots in Watts had already called attention to inner-city joblessness and poverty among African Americans in Los Angeles; the economic problems of the 1970s only worsened the poverty of inner-city inhabitants. The era of unmitigated faith in unbridled economic growth seemed to be over, at least for the moment. These new conditions shook the vibrant optimism of many westerners. In previous years they had turned to the federal government to stimulate economic expansion. But Watergate and President Nixon's resignation shook their faith in a federal government that seemed to be adrift.

The energy crisis of 1973 touched most Americans. OPEC's increase of petroleum prices in 1973 further contributed to the economic environment of stagflation, with its high interest rates and slow economic growth. That situation was caused by heavy federal deficit spending for the costly Vietnam War and for expanded government programs related to President Lyndon Johnson's plans for the Great Society. In an effort to cope with the deteriorating economic situation, President Nixon imposed controversial wage and price controls between 1971 and 1973. Although he suspended the controls (with the exception of petroleum) in 1973, the policy may have encouraged artificial shortages of fuel oil and gasoline, which led to long lines of irate motorists at gasoline stations in 1973.

The oil shortage had many reverberations. It created problems in the U.S. balance-of-trade payments and heightened the inflation in the domestic economy. In 1970 U.S. oil imports totaled about $17 billion annually. Three years later the OPEC price increase raised that total to $50 billion. By then, the United States was importing about half of the oil it consumed and was thus dependent on foreign sources for its energy needs. This reliance on foreign oil supplies jeopardized national security.[2]

The policies of the Middle Eastern oil producers had a particularly important impact on the West because that region was the major domestic producer of energy in the United States. Already in 1971 President Nixon had vowed to provide an adequate supply of energy for the nation, even to try to make it self-sufficient. The OPEC action spurred him in November 1973 to proclaim Project Independence. In a widely televised speech he said: "What I have called Project Independence–1980 is a series of plans and goals set to insure that by the end of this decade Americans will not have to rely on any source of energy beyond our own. . . . The capacity for self-sufficiency is a great goal." The program affected all of the forms of energy produced in the West. It called for an expansion of about 4.7 percent of energy production each year and a concurrent reduction in the growth rate of demand for energy from 3.6 percent to 2 percent between 1974 and 1980. For the average American, this meant driving less and using smaller, more fuel-efficient cars. The program envisaged an increase of western petroleum production from 10.9 million barrels daily to 14 million. The plan also envisaged a tenfold increase in the production of nuclear power and an expansion of natural gas production from 23 trillion to 27 trillion cubic feet per year. At the same time the federal government mandated new fuel restrictions for automobile manufacturers and other industries.[3]

In an additional effort to cope with the crisis, the federal government hoped to stimulate a substantial increase in coal production. In 1973 American coal mines produced 602 million tons. Now the federal government set a goal of 962 million tons by 1980. That could be done by suspending federal clean air standards for five years and encouraging the conversion of oil-burning plants to coal with special tax incentives allowed by the Internal Revenue Service. In addition, the federal government offered to abandon all price controls on coal and to expand the leasing of federally owned coal-bearing lands. President Nixon also promised to allot at least $10 billion over a ten-year period to energy research and development.

In March 1974 the Federal Energy Administration inaugurated Project Independence. The Department of the Interior predicted that a doubling of coal production and a fivefold increase in nuclear output would be needed to achieve the project's designated goals. This was in addition to substantial increases in geothermal and hydroelectric production and a doubling in the domestic output of oil and gas. Synthetic gas would be procured from coal, and oil would be extracted from shale in the West. Interior officials estimated the total cost of the project at between $600 and $900 billion. It seemed an awesome challenge.

President Nixon also followed other alternatives by encouraging the passage of the Alaska Pipeline Act of 1973, which provided for large-scale federal investment in building a major pipeline between Alaska and other states to alleviate the oil shortage. Alaska was to play a key role in achieving America's energy independence.[4]

After he assumed office following Nixon's resignation, President Gerald Ford tried further to alleviate the oil shortage by supporting the creation of a Strategic Oil Reserve (SOR) in 1975. The SOR provided for the storage of a two- to three-year supply of oil reserves in salt formations in Louisiana and Texas at a cost of at least $16 billion. It required the federal government to purchase large amounts of domestic and Middle Eastern oil. This federal project was a boon to westerners because it maintained a strong domestic market. The initial purchase program began in 1975 and extended over a period of ten years. At first the administrators of the SOR experienced many problems—some technical, others administrative. President Jimmy Carter's secretary of energy, James Schlesinger, compounded the problems by attempting to rush the completion of the SOR in 1979 and succeeded only in impeding the program. At the time, oil prices were rapidly rising because of the Iranian revolution, and President

Carter, in a comedy of errors, slowed federal purchases of oil for the reserve. Not until oil prices declined in 1983 did the Reagan administration buy additional oil to bring the SOR to its intended level.[5]

It was not long, however, before Project Independence collapsed. From the beginning the program had encountered serious opposition from environmental groups. Coal-powered electric plants increased air pollution and ran afoul of federal clean air laws enacted just a decade earlier. Dozens of lawsuits brought by environmental groups slowed the federal program of leasing coal lands. The planned expansion of nuclear plants ran into serious problems at the same time. An accident at a nuclear facility at Three Mile Island in Pennsylvania in 1979 prompted a public outburst against nuclear plants throughout the United States even though there was no loss of life. Rightly or wrongly, public opinion was now strongly opposed to any expansion of nuclear plants. Because nuclear energy had been a vital component of Project Independence, its reduction effectively undercut much of the program.

Congressional sensitivity to environmental concerns was reflected in the passage of the Federal Coal Leasing Amendments Act of 1976, which Congress passed over President Ford's veto. The measure did much to restrict the granting of federal coal leases to private operators.[6]

As a former nuclear engineer, President Jimmy Carter was very much concerned with energy issues and with providing federal leadership to solve the nation's energy problems. As an indication of his earnestness, he asked Congress to establish a new Department of Energy. In a memorable speech in April 1977 he spoke of planning a national energy program that would be the moral equivalent of war. Along with boosting production he urged a greater emphasis on conservation, a goal that could be achieved by raising prices for energy and then levying a crude-oil equalization tax for the benefit of consumers. Carter also proposed greater reliance on coal while asking for more intensive federal regulation of coal strip mining.

To increase coal production in the West, Carter's Energy Department assigned state quotas. New Mexico was to increase its coal production fifteenfold (from 9.4 million tons yearly to 137 million tons), Wyoming tenfold, and North Dakota and Utah eightfold, with lower quotas for Colorado, Montana, and Arizona. Carter also urged less reliance on breeder reactors and reduced uranium production on federal lands in Wyoming and New Mexico. In practice this federal energy plan was extremely confusing because the Department of the Interior and the Department of Energy were making different projections and different plans, and supporting different programs.[7]

Meanwhile, environmental groups, who at first had been quite happy with Carter's emphasis on conservation, expressed increasing concern. In 1977 Secretary of the Interior Cecil D. Andrus authorized the Intermountain Power Project, the largest coal-fired power plant in the world. Then, in December 1979, Andrus gave his approval to a similar plant at Lyndyll in western Utah, on the borders of Capitol Reef National Park. Andrus allowed the Harry Allen plant to operate in Nevada, avoiding strong environmental opposition to building a plant near Zion National Park. And he granted coal-mining leases near Bryce Canyon National Park.

As confusion mounted over the direction of federal leadership, Carter unveiled his second energy plan in April 1979. In many ways it turned out to be worse than the first. He announced the deregulation of oil prices, removing price controls that the government had imposed since 1973. Almost immediately there were long lines at gasoline stations again. Another revolution in Iran affected the world oil supply and made petroleum scarcer. Carter then urged Congress to enact a windfall profits tax on energy producers. The tax would fund a federal energy security corporation that would use its revenues for ten years to finance development of synthetic fuels and coal. To achieve these goals, Carter urged close cooperation between the federal government and private corporations.[8]

The centerpiece of President Carter's energy program was a massive effort to extract oil from shales, oil-bearing rocks in Colorado. President Ford had already encouraged Congress to enact the Synfuels Act of 1976. Carter's knowledge about the West was hazy, but the idea of extracting large quantities of oil from rocks in Colorado, Wyoming, and Utah seemed very appealing. The process was costly, however, involved large amounts of water, and promised to create environmental problems. It required the processing of thousands of tons of rock using vast quantities of water in a region where water was already scarce. Even after treatment, the water used in the processing was saline and contained deposits of arsenic, ammonia, carbonic acid, and sulfates. The fact that almost all the oil shales were located on federal lands made extraction less attractive to private developers, and less profitable.

As early as 1974 Congress had proposed to grant tax credits, loans, and guaranteed purchase agreements to private corporations brave enough to try their hand at oil extraction. But private entrepreneurs did not rush in to take advantage of the offer. Nevertheless, a few major oil companies did buy some oil shale leases from the federal government for about $210 million. In his State of the Union Address in 1975, President Ford proposed that the federal government finance twenty synfuel production plants to help the program. The environmental problems caused by extracting oil from shales were monumental, however, as was evident to anyone who took the trouble to examine the process. Much of the area designated for possible extraction was a national wilderness area that required Class I air standards. Large-scale development would increase air pollution and would violate standards set by the Clean Air Act of 1970 by 600 percent. Only a few energy companies signed leases for shale development during the Ford administration.[9]

President Carter was enthusiastic about the potential of oil shales to solve the energy problem, notwithstanding the serious difficulties that would arise. With long lines of angry motorists at gasoline stations in 1979 and Iranians holding Americans hostage in the U.S. embassy in Teheran, his popularity was rapidly diminishing. Understandably, he sought to make a dramatic gesture so that he could emerge as the savior of America's energy crisis. Oil shales seemed to promise that salvation, at least in the solitude of the Oval Office in the White House. Thus, he gave his strong support to the Energy Security Act of 1980. Oil shale development, the president announced, "will dwarf the combined programs that led us to the moon and built our interstate highway system." The act provided for the establishment of a Synthetic Fuels Corporation with an appropriation of $88 billion for a ten-year period. The federal program would engage in joint ventures with private enterprises and make loans and leases for oil shale development. In a mood of euphoria, the Federal Synfuel Corporation began to step up the pace of development. The corporation was expected to produce 500,000 barrels of oil daily by 1987, a somewhat unrealistic goal.

The Era of Deindustrialization

With funds from the Federal Synthetic Fuels Corporation in 1980, the Exxon Corporation built a new company town near Rifle, Colorado, for its venture into synthetic fuels production. Exxon was expected to invest $500 billion in synthetic fuels. At the time, an economic depression was sweeping through the Midwest, and thousands of workers in the automobile, steel, and housing industries were being laid off. Many came to Colorado to work on the shale project, which offered high wages. Known as the Colony Oil Shale Project, the program produced a boom for the area and for small communities such as Silt and Parachute. As news of the project spread, more than five thousand people poured into the remote region, many with their families. Real estate values jumped tenfold as Exxon built an entire town, laying out streets and sewer lines, as well as new homes for workers, including single-family residences, apartment houses, dormitories for single men, and upscale houses for management.[10]

In July 1980 Exxon issued a white paper entitled "The Role of Synthetic Fuels in the U.S. Energy Future." Its authors declared that synthetic fuels would be the mainstay of the American petroleum industry for the next half century. Unfortunately, the article was based on wishful thinking—and perhaps on ignorance—rather than on hard facts. Exxon predicted that fifty thousand newcomers would arrive in the area annually during the coming ten to twenty years; projected 150 new shale plants to be built over a twenty-year period; and estimated a need for seven hundred new schools, shopping centers, and office buildings, and seventy-five thousand new housing units. Exxon officials shared the optimism of the Carter administration.

Very quickly, however, cost overruns and environmental problems indicated that rapid oil shale development was unrealistic. At the same time, the world oil supply situation changed dramatically. Instead of oil shortages and high prices, late in 1980 an oil surplus and falling oil prices altered the energy picture. New oil fields in the North Sea and increasing production from Alaska undercut the Carter administration's perspective of crisis. And the president's insistence on synfuel development created economic chaos. The federal government spent (or wasted) at least $1 billion on the Exxon venture and contributed to the boom-bust syndrome in Colorado.

By 1982 Exxon had decided somewhat belatedly that oil shale was a project whose time had not yet come. On April 28, 1982, Exxon's board of directors voted to stop the project immediately. Within a week, on May 2, 1982, they suspended all operations. Twenty-one hundred employees and seventy-five hundred support personnel lost their jobs. The sudden shutdown also affected the economy of the western slope of Colorado in a very harsh and unexpected manner. As the boom quickly turned into a bust, businesses failed, real estate prices plummeted, and banks closed. Denver, which had enjoyed glowing prosperity because of the energy boom in the West during the 1970s, descended into a period of economic slump in the 1980s. The value of western banks, real estate, and thousands of smaller energy companies shrank. The changing global oil economy affected the entire West and had a serious impact on Houston as well.[11]

President Ronald Reagan, with his sunny disposition, simply refused to believe that there had ever been an energy crisis. If there was one, he hoped it would go away. With his proverbial good luck, changing world conditions did dissipate the oil crisis during his tenure in the White House. Reflecting that outlook, Congress in December 1985 abolished the Federal Synthetic Fuels Corporation.

Moreover, the Reagan administration believed that government regulations impeded the development of domestic energy resources. Although President Reagan had hoped to abolish the Department of Energy, Congress did not follow his advice. But the president did succeed in persuading the lawmakers to decontrol oil and natural gas prices, and he encouraged the development of nuclear energy. After 1983, oil prices continued to decline as consumption in the United States shrank and oil prospectors found new fields around the globe. A worldwide economic recession, a reaction by consumers against the high prices demanded by OPEC, and more fuel-efficient cars were other factors. Coincidental with the abandonment of federal price controls in 1981, the erstwhile shortage turned into a glut, a glut that brought a recession to much of the energy-producing West.

It must be said, however, that the Middle Eastern nations did much to increase the wealth of the West. Between 1973 and 1982 the value of U.S.

The Era of Deindustrialization

oil reserves increased tenfold, from $100 billion to $1 trillion. That staggering sum did not include the value of coal and natural gas, for which an estimate of $50 to $500 billion might be too conservative.

During the Carter and Reagan years the federal emphasis on shifting the nation's reliance on oil to a reliance on coal met with limited success. Coal-burning power plants encountered increasing environmental problems between 1977 and 1987. The power plants in the Four Corners area (New Mexico, Utah, Colorado, and Arizona) that supplied southern California were emitting such high levels of pollution by 1977 that polluted air drifted across the West for many hundreds of miles. The Environmental Protection Agency soon required the utilities to install expensive controls, which it monitored closely. The Clean Air Act of 1970, the Federal Water Pollution Act of 1972, and the Surface Mining and Reclamation Act of 1977 imposed such rigid environmental standards on the coal industry that the cost advantages of coal over other forms of energy significantly lessened. Western states also imposed severance taxes on coal that further increased its cost. Even so, western coal supplied 36 percent of the nation's coal needs in 1983, up from 15 percent ten years earlier.[12]

All of the presidents between 1973 and 1988 had high hopes for energy self-sufficiency and the expansion of nuclear power. Federal officials on most levels of the Washington bureaucracy still believed that nuclear plants could provide the United States with clean, ample energy in the remaining years of the twentieth century. The Three Mile Island debacle and huge cost overruns dampened the public enthusiasm for nuclear power in the 1980s and created a reluctance to build new plants. As prices for labor and materials rose sharply in the inflationary environment of the 1970s, and inexperience and incompetence characterized many nuclear projects, opposition to nuclear energy crystallized. During the 1970s private utilities scrapped plans for more than one hundred planned plants. Some of the largest of these projects were to have been built in the West.

The largest nuclear project in the United States was the Washington Public Power Supply System. Since the days of the New Deal, the Pacific Northwest had been closely involved with public power. It was an important part of the federal landscape in the region, with Bonneville and Grand Coulee Dams standing as symbols of the federal commitment.

Electric rates in the region were only a fraction of what they were else-where in the United States. Although most residents of the Pacific North-west had hoped for the creation of a Columbia River Authority in the image of the Tennessee Valley Authority, Congress balked at approving such an agency in the post–World War II period. Instead, the lawmak-ers established the Bonneville Power Administration, which had limited authority. It was authorized to produce and distribute power from Bon-neville and Grand Coulee Dams, but not to build new dams under its own auspices. Nevertheless, between 1945 and 1980 the Bonneville Power Administration was the most important producer of power in the Pacific Northwest and aggressively fostered economic development of the region. By 1975 it was supplying fully half of the power in an eight-state area and was providing 80 percent of high-voltage transmission capacity there.[13]

In its efforts to increase power production in the Pacific Northwest, the Bonneville Power Administration early on embraced nuclear energy. Already in 1960 the administration was very active in promoting the building of new nuclear plants. In a special study conducted in 1968, the administration proposed the construction of twenty new nuclear plants in the Pacific Northwest. It could not build them itself, of course, but it did everything it could to promote private ventures. Over the years the Bon-neville Power Administration had been known regularly to overestimate future power needs, perhaps as a way of emphasizing its own importance. In 1966 the administration had made arrangements to distribute elec-tricity from a nuclear reactor at the federal nuclear generating plant at Hanford, Washington. In 1971 the agency encouraged and supervised the creation of a consortium of public utility districts and private com-panies to organize the Washington Public Power Supply System (WPPSS). That entity was to float the largest municipal bond issue in the nation's history to build five new nuclear plants. The Bonneville Power Adminis-tration assisted in the financing of units 1, 2, and 3 and put great pres-sure on the eighty-eight public utilities in the region, its customers, to finance units 4 and 5.

This project became one of the greatest fiascoes in the annals of Amer-ican finance and the development of nuclear plants. Construction in the 1970s was marred by corruption as well as mismanagement, cost over-

The Era of Deindustrialization

runs, and irresponsibility on the part of both the Bonneville Power Administration and the Nuclear Regulatory Commission, as well as private utility corporations, state officials in Oregon and Washington, and lawyers and brokerage houses around the nation. Bonneville Power Administration projections of the power needs of the Pacific Northwest had been utterly unrealistic. In 1983, a time of economic recession for the region, the WPPS defaulted on the bonds for units 4 and 5, creating severe financial losses not only for institutional investors, but also for tens of thousands of small investors—many of them retirees—all over the United States. The collapse of the WPPS signaled the termination of new construction of nuclear plants in the West. It was an ignominious end to the policy of energy independence that only a few years earlier President Carter had characterized as the moral equivalent of war.[14]

Federal management of the energy landscape in the West between 1973 and 1990 left a great deal to be desired. Federal price controls for oil in the 1970s had contributed to artificial shortages and had created more problems than they had solved. Most likely, they stifled intensive oil exploration in the West. Much the same could be said for federal policies governing natural gas. Intensified leasing of federal coal lands did increase western coal production but without much consideration for environmental consequences such as air and water pollution or the preservation of surface soils. The headlong frenetic rush into the oil shale program revealed a similar lack of careful planning or confrontation with the realities of the markets and the fragile western environment. And government encouragement of a large-scale nuclear power industry in the West before the adoption of federal safeguards and regulations, and before the accumulation of management expertise and experience, reflected badly on national energy policies. The missteps left economic and environmental scars on the land, wasted billions of taxpayer dollars, and brought unnecessary suffering and economic hardship to tens of thousands of people. By 1990 thoughts of energy self-sufficiency were only a distant memory. By then the United States was importing more than 50 percent of its annual petroleum needs and was more dependent than ever on foreign sources. Large oil companies found this scenario very profitable. Meanwhile, energy consumption rose sharply as Americans gave up their small, gas-efficient compacts in favor of large vans and trucks. When the federal government raised automobile speed limits, further contributing to gasoline consumption, concerns of average Americans for conserving non-renewable energy sources faded into seemingly distant historical memory.

But petroleum was not and has never been the scarcest liquid in the West. Water holds that honor. From the beginning of the century and into the 1960s, the diversion of rivers and the building of dams had taken on the dimensions of a crusade. Between 1933 and 1973 the federal government built huge dams, with the support of westerners of all political persuasions. Theirs was a profound belief that federal irrigation and reclamation programs were benevolent and would lead to a democratization of American society.

But by 1973 the Bureau of Reclamation had built on most of the desirable dam sites of the West. The costs had been enormous, amounting to many billions of dollars. Somewhat unexpectedly, the dams had promoted, not extended agriculture and the spread of self-sufficient farms, but the growth of cities. They provided the electric power first for western industry during World War II and then for the rapidly growing urban areas of the West after 1945. What these programs had not achieved was the democratization of the West as a region of small independent farmers. Of course, in the national economy of the twentieth century, agriculture took on an increasingly smaller role. That was true during the era of industrialization in the first half of the century, of course, but even more so in the postindustrial phase from 1945 to 1973, when technological, computer, and service industries rapidly grew to economic dominance.

Yet for some westerners the Jeffersonian dream of a West populated by small independent farmers never died. One such idealist was Professor Paul S. Taylor of the University of California, a leading champion of the battle to place a 160-acre limit on all federal lands offered for sale as a result of irrigation and reclamation projects. In reality, however, the western landscape in the second half of the twentieth century was primarily one of large corporate farms, heavily subsidized by federal agricultural and water subsidies. Perhaps the vision of small rural communities had been unrealistic from the beginning. But reformers such as Taylor bemoaned what they considered to be a lost opportunity.[15]

By 1973, however, congressional enthusiasm for large-scale federal water projects waned appreciably. Increasingly, most public officials—

The Era of Deindustrialization

but not all westerners—viewed them as expensive projects benefiting special interests. Often dams had negative environmental impacts, producing silting, hardships for wildlife, and wasteful evaporation of water, in addition to destroying unique scenery. Instead of the enthusiastic support typical of the first half of the century, many westerners now considered dams more critically, even negatively.

Such changing attitudes were clearly reflected during the Carter administration. Carter knew little about the West and was not very sympathetic toward the region, perhaps because in the election of 1976 he had failed to carry a single western state. He was receptive to pleas for greater protection of the natural environment, however. Much of the advice he received in this field came from environmentalist Joseph Brower, who in 1974 was the southern representative of the Audubon Society. In 1976 Brower organized the Environmental Policy Center to study water and environmental issues. He also joined the Carter campaign staff. Brower was impressed by the 1973 report of the National Water Commission, a study group initially appointed by President Johnson. That group emphasized that the nation should shift its priorities from the development of water resources to the restoration of water quality. Another study group appointed by consumer advocate Ralph Nader's Center for the Study of Progressive Law came to similar conclusions.[16]

Carter lost little time in seeking to transform changing attitudes into public policy. In February 1977 he proposed an instant moratorium on funding for fourteen major water projects, including the Central Arizona Project and a project in central Utah, and the suspension of sixty-one others. Carter believed that no new dams were necessary and that more federal funds needed to be shifted from the West to his native South and to the East, both sections still in the throes of recession. His proposals sent shock waves through Congress, where special interests were heavily entrenched, many of them representatives from western states. The result was bitter wrangling and an eventual compromise. Congress accepted only half of Carter's proposals and overrode many of his recommendations. Nevertheless, it was clear that the days of intensive dam building were over. Actually, Congress had not authorized any new major projects since 1968, when it had approved the Central Arizona Project. During the 1980s the lawmakers also severely downsized the Bureau of Reclamation and reduced appropriations for the Corps of Engineers.

The battles over dams continued into the closing years of the century. In 1997 Daniel P. Beard, a senior vice president of the Audubon Society, became one of the leaders of the movement to dismantle dams. Beard agreed that dams had contributed much to regional economies. But they had also caused environmental damage, and a great deal of money would be required to correct that damage and to overcome construction defects in the dams. "Big dam projects were conceived to meet the needs of agriculture and the mining industry," he declared. "That was acceptable so long as urban demand for water was limited, Federal money was available to build projects, and environmental values were ignored. All that has changed. There is greater competition for water between cities and farms. Federal construction money has dried up, and environmental concerns have become more urgent. . . . All it takes is political will to remove dams and give us back our beautiful canyons."[17]

But the conflicts between economic needs and environmental protection continued to dog the federal government. In 1997 the issue surfaced in a struggle between the Sierra Club and the Ute Indians in southern Utah and northern New Mexico near the Animas River. The Utes favored a federal dam and diversion project in the hope that it would alleviate some of the desperate poverty on their reservation. Senator Ben Lighthorse Campbell, the only Indian in the U.S. Senate, claimed that "the enviros have never been interested in a compromise. They just simply want to stop development and growth. And the way you do that in the West is to stop water." Other observers noted that cheap, federally subsidized water had allowed the growth of great cities and the raising of cheap food to feed the burgeoning urban populations. But the Utes had been promised federal aid since 1868 when they gave up many of their lands. They had waited for more than a century and certainly had a claim to federal funds for the improvement of the miserable farmland that the federal government, under the pressure of white settlers, had granted them. Judy Knight Frank, chairwoman of the Ute Mountain Tribe, noted bitterly in 1997 that "fish seem to have more of a right to live than I do. The environmentalists don't seem to care how we live." Most important, a reservoir would allow the Southern Utes to mine at least 400 million tons of low-sulfur coal and to transport it through a coal slurry pipeline. That was an attractive prospect to the Utes, who never did take to farming. "Why do these people keep telling us what to do?" Ms. Frank said. "We are going to be on welfare and the country is going to be taking care of us. Is that what they want?"[18]

Throughout the 1970s and during the Carter-Reagan era, the heated battle over the lifting of the 160-acre limitation on federal land sales of irrigated lands continued. Advocates of small farmers organized in an umbrella group, National Land for People, and sought to have the Department of the Interior enforce the limitation. They won some minor victories, but Democratic as well as Republican secretaries of the interior continued to sell such lands in much larger tracts to large operators and corporate farms. By the 1980s the federal landscape in the West was characterized by big rather than small farms. Then, under the Reclamation Reform Act of 1982, Congress removed the 160-acre limitation altogether. It was official. The Jeffersonian vision was dead.

The various controversies over land and water aroused a feeling throughout the West that President Carter and Congress were insensitive to western problems. The resentment flared briefly in the Sagebrush Rebellion between 1979 and 1981, a movement also fueled by anger against an expanding federal landscape in the West. One spark to the rebellion was a report by the Bureau of Land Management in 1979 that recommended that fifteen million acres of public lands be reserved for wilderness areas, thirty-six million acres for multiple land use, and eleven million acres be held for further study. That report elicited a furious retort from the legislature of Nevada. The fact that the federal government owned more than 60 percent of the total area of Nevada was further cause for resentment. In July 1979 the Nevada lawmakers passed a resolution demanding the transfer of forty-nine million acres of federal lands to state control. This action received widespread publicity in the national press, particularly in eastern media such as the *Wall Street Journal* and the *New York Times,* and *Newsweek* described the "Angry West" and used it as a cover story. Five hundred of the self-described rebels organized the League of States' Equal Rights and organized a conference in Utah at which Senators Orrin Hatch of Utah and Paul Laxalt of

Nevada openly supported John Harmer, the league's president. During 1980 Harmer addressed nine western state legislatures and stimulated much discussion.

Specifically, the leaders of the league demanded greater state rather than federal management of the public lands and argued that federal land policies stifled western economic growth. They further declared that the states had a right to the public lands within their borders. Such complaints were not new, of course; they had been made by previous generations and also by special interests who wanted the public domain in the West opened to private exploitation.

The Sagebrush Rebels hoped that state legislatures would pass resolutions demanding transfer of Bureau of Land Management lands and Forest Service lands to the states. They threatened to mount court challenges to federal land policies. And they embarked on a nationwide public relations campaign to arouse support for their cause. Despite all this activity, by 1982 the Sagebrush Rebellion had lost steam. It did succeed in making federal policies in the West more of a public issue, however, and it raised nagging questions about the balance between environmental values and economic growth.

It is difficult to know how deep an impression the Sagebrush Rebellion made on the Reagan administration. President Reagan himself hoped to improve the economy, which was in the doldrums between 1980 and 1982, by opening more federal lands to private use. Certainly his iconoclastic secretary of the interior, James Watt, sympathized with the Sagebrush Rebels and supported them by proposing new guidelines to ease coal exploitation on the public lands, even near national parks. A bipartisan coalition in the U.S. Senate blocked most such plans. Nevertheless, Watt used his administrative authority to open public lands for oil and gas development to ease energy dependence on foreign nations. Although he opposed the creation of new national parks, he succeeded, ironically, in securing increased appropriations for those already established. His strong views aroused intense hostility within and outside the Reagan administration, however, and on October 10, 1983, Watt resigned under pressure.[19]

After the end of American involvement in Vietnam in 1973, national defense budgets gradually declined over the next twenty-five years to about half of what they had been in the 1960s. President Carter was proud of having negotiated the SALT II Treaty in 1979, which reduced nuclear armaments. Nevertheless, military expenditures continued to be important to the western economy. In 1980 Carter proposed the building of new MX missiles for nuclear defense. He proposed constructing a looped track in a twenty-five-square-mile area of desert along the Utah-Nevada border to carry about two hundred missile transporters, or launchers, which could move up and down the track through twenty-three hundred horizontal shelters on each loop. He estimated the cost of the project to be about $100 billion. It would employ about twenty-three thousand people and would be a boon to the economically depressed area. If built as proposed, the missile defense system might have become an integral part of the federal landscape in the West.[20]

But the residents of southern Utah and Nevada strongly opposed the project. By the 1970s information about nuclear fallout from atomic bomb tests in the 1950s was just beginning to be revealed. It created an atmosphere of great distrust toward the federal government in this region, where residents had often been misled with lies about the supposedly benign effects of radiation and atomic testing. The project soon encountered difficulties. Engineers predicted that the MX program would require vast amounts of water in a region where water was already in short supply. Each shelter would require ten kilowatts of power and 30,000 acre-feet of water during construction and 12,000 acre-feet of water annually thereafter. Just as construction was scheduled to start in 1982, strong opposition developed in Congress. Delegations from Utah and Nevada were especially critical. At the same time, cold war tensions were lessening. By 1990 the Department of Defense had finally found a home for a greatly scaled down version of the MX system in North Dakota and the Great Plains.

Although the Reagan administration favored increasing military expenditures, it advocated a limited version of the MX system proposed by Carter. Between 1982 and 1990 the program experienced many delays and cost overruns. President Reagan scrapped the Carter plan for multiple protective shelters and instead proposed putting the new missiles in existing ICBM silos to save money. The MX project was put on hold while Reagan appointed a commission to study the subject, headed by

Brent Scowcroft, a national security expert. In 1983 the committee recommended building a smaller ICBM, placing MX missiles in existing silos, and additional negotiation of arms control agreements with the Soviet Union. Congress approved this report and directed that it be carried out after 1987 but at a reduced cost from original estimates. A 1984 estimate had been $57 billion; the revised version pared this down to $36.4 billion in 1988. In 1986 Reagan approved the building of fifty MX missiles to be placed on railroad cars. There would be two on each train, or twenty-five trains, each with seven cars. The main operating base was F. E. Warren Air Force Base in Wyoming, and the Pentagon expected to designate ten other bases in the future. The program also involved Vandenberg Air Force Base in California and Malstrom Air Force Base in Great Falls, Montana. In various ways, the MX system further expanded the federal landscape in the West.[21]

By 1990 most federal laboratories were actively engaged in technology transfer, shifting their military research and development to civilian uses. More of this transfer took place than critics such as Murray Weidenbaum had predicted in the 1960s. The Sandia Corporation in Albuquerque, Los Alamos, and the Lawrence Livermore Laboratory in California were among the leaders of this movement. They developed new manufacturing processes, ran simulations of new products, and dealt with environmental problems. "National security starts with economic security," Sandia's president, C. Paul Robinson, said in 1997, "and that means helping our industries compete."

As William Sharp, president of Goodyear Tire's global support operations, said of Sandia in 1997: "Their computer models show how a nuclear weapon will react to different conditions, so why shouldn't they show how a tire will react?" Goodyear wanted to predict, without weeks of test drives, how its tires would perform under various conditions. Similarly, a consortium of seventeen casting and forging companies asked Sandia to simplify their software so that it could be adapted to test new casting equipment. Motorola asked Sandia to conduct reliability tests on computer chips without using standard chemical cleaning agents because these chlorofluorocarbons destroy the ozone layer.

Other federal laboratories were involved with similar endeavors. Los Alamos worked with the Amoco Corporation to simulate the movement of oil under the ground. It also designed transformers that use super-conductivity technology and turned to mundane problems such as simulating stresses on concrete used in roads. The Idaho Engineering Facility became involved with the cleanup of polluted land sites and designed robots to work in dangerous environments. Lawrence Livermore was deeply involved in research on human genetic codes and the development of processes to detect carcinogens in food.

Between 1989 and 2000 the federal laboratories agreed to more than three thousand contracts for cooperative research and development with private industries. Increasingly, the costs of these projects were paid by private companies. In 1992, for example, Sandia received only $9 million from private sources; in 1997 this had grown to $35 million and was predicted to total $100 million by 2000. In part this was due to its new supercomputer, three times as powerful as the IBM Blue of chess fame. Sandia rented the computer, and a skilled staff, to prospective clients.[22]

While the federal investment in the national security establishment in the West was declining by the 1990s, government immigration policies were stimulating the fourth wave of economic expansion. The key measure was the Immigration and Naturalization Act of 1965, a rather obscure part of President Johnson's Great Society program whose importance was not realized until the 1990s. The act accounted for the influx of more than 14 million people between 1965 and 2000, or almost 40 percent of the total increase of the population. It brought a significant growth of human and investment capital in the West and represented a major milestone in American immigration policy.

Why was this measure so significant? To an unprecedented extent, it opened the United States to Asian and Latin American immigrants. Until 1965, U.S. immigration policies had favored the admission of Europeans. Thereafter, they gave preference to Asians, Latin Americans, and people of color while restricting Europeans. In the 1950s, Asians constituted 4.9 percent of immigrants; by the 1990s they constituted more than 50 percent of the newcomers. By 2000 the Asian population in the United States would number more than 10 million, with the influx still rapidly increasing in the twenty-first century. The largest contingents came from China and Taiwan, with appreciable numbers also from Korea, the Philippines, and Vietnam. Approximately half of these immigrants settled in the West, especially in Los Angeles, San Francisco, and other parts of California. Large waves of Mexicans also came to the West, although many of the settlers from South America tended to migrate to the South and Northeast, where Miami and New York City became main destinations. In many ways, the influx of such large numbers of people invigorated the western economy and helped to accelerate the computer chip revolution.[23]

Between 1965 and 2000, more than 1.5 million Filipinos came to the United States, a majority of them settling in the West. More than 40,000 entered each year, and more than two-thirds of them stayed in the Pacific coast states. In contrast to the years before World War II, this migration represented highly educated individuals; more than one-fifth were professional people and technicians. Of those over twenty-five years of age, 47 percent had college educations. The median income of their households was higher than the average for native-born Americans, but that was in part because a larger number of people in such households held paying jobs.[24]

Large-scale immigration of Koreans to the West began only after the act of 1965 opened the gates. In the 1950s immigration laws permitted only 600 Koreans to enter the United States each year; after 1965, more than 30,000 came annually. By 2000 there would be more than 1.5 million Koreans in the United States, most of them in the West. A high percentage of the newcomers were high school and college graduates. Although they tended to gravitate toward professional occupations, the Koreans, more than any other ethnic group, were highly entrepreneurial. A significant percentage established new small businesses, often in African American, Chicano, or Puerto Rican neighborhoods. They were highly successful because they brought capital and a strong work ethic with them. Koreans also entered professional management, engineering, and computer industries. Los Angeles was a major center of Korean migration.[25]

The Vietnamese immigrants had a different experience. Many were refugees who in some way were victims of the war in which American participation was prominent. Under the Indo-Chinese Refugee Act of 1975, the federal government allowed at least 300,000 Vietnamese, Cam-

The Era of Deindustrialization

bodians, and Laotians to enter the United States. A large number settled in California and other western states, although federal policy encouraged them to spread out across the nation. The Vietnamese found acculturation difficult. A considerable number lacked the education to succeed quickly in the American economy, while professional people and former high government officials found it difficult to secure equivalent positions in their new homeland. Thus, physicians were forced to become dishwashers, generals became waiters or taxi drivers, and former army colonels delivered pizza or newspapers. For many, it was a heartbreaking experience.[26]

The largest group of Asian immigrants came from China. Between 1965 and 2000 almost 2 million came to the United States, and at the millennium those numbers were still rapidly increasing. Almost half of the Chinese settled in the West. As a group, they represented a high level of education and skills. With their strong work ethic and self-discipline, the Chinese were poised to take advantage of American educational opportunities. They gravitated to managerial, professional, and technical fields and were striving for remunerative professional and technical positions within reach of the current, or perhaps the next, generation. Already by 1980 the median household income of the Chinese Americans was higher than the national average.[27]

The large-scale influx of Asians—more than 4 million between 1965 and 2000—was a distinctive development in the economic growth of the West. As a group, they were well educated and highly motivated to take advantage of economic and educational opportunities. Hardworking and disciplined, they contributed to the quality of the labor force in the West while also bringing new investment capital to the region.

❖ The years between 1973 and the end of the century provide a classic example of the functioning of long economic waves. Once one wave runs its course, a period of drift and confusion ensues. It may take ten to twenty years or more for the new technological innovations to "bunch" and begin a new wave. In this case the most important innovation was the microchip, first developed in 1971. As Schumpeter noted at midcentury, the "carriers out of new operations," the men and women who harness new technological inventions to economic growth, were engaged in developing new methods of production, new markets, new sources of supply, and new industrial organization. "The boom ends and the depression begins after the passage of the time which must elapse before the products of the new enterprise can appear on the market. And a new boom succeeds the depression when the process of resorption of the innovations is ended. The new combinations are not, as one would expect according to general principles of probability, evenly distributed through time . . . but appear, if at all, discontinuously in groups or swarms."[28]

Such swarming, Schumpeter argued, is due to the fact that the very appearance of entrepreneurs encourages others to imitate them, in ever increasing numbers. Thus there is a gradual increase in the rate of investment and the growth of capital goods industries. Schumpeter's perceptions, applied to the western economy between 1973 and 2000, do much to foster a better understanding of this period of deindustrialization, confusion, and attempted readjustments, and place them in a broader national and global context.

I n the course of a century, between 1900 and 2000, the
federal government succeeded in transforming the colonial economy of the West into a pacesetting technologically
advanced economy. In 1900 the West was a purveyor of raw
materials for the industrial areas of the Northeast. It was
rich in agriculture, minerals, and timber, but its transportation system was not fully developed and its financial institutions were weak and small. The West desperately required
more capital investment if it was to develop. It was beholden
to Wall Street and to foreign investors. Its oldest inhabitants,
Native Americans and Hispanics, were among the nation's
poorest people. Many westerners foresaw a bleak future for
this land because the vast semiarid stretches of the trans-
Mississippi area were largely unsuited for the type of farm-

Afterword

ing that had brought prosperity to the humid East and Midwest. Water, the scarcest resource in the West, held the key to population increase and economic growth. Given the diversity of unwelcoming geographic features in the West, it seemed highly unlikely that private enterprise would be able to provide the capital needed to develop the region.

In such circumstances, was it surprising that westerners turned to the federal government to secure the help they needed? Beginning with the Newlands Act of 1902, federal funds poured into the West to develop and to distribute the scarce water resources. By 1914 the newly established Reclamation Service was planning and executing dam building and reclamation projects throughout the West. By 1922 Secretary of Commerce Herbert Hoover had assumed leadership in the formation of the Colorado River interstate compact to distribute the waters of that river among the western states. Four years later Congress agreed to build what was then to be the world's largest dam, Boulder Dam near Las Vegas. Its purpose was to provide electric power for the growing metropolis of Los Angeles and to irrigate a stretch of California desert now known as the Imperial Valley.

Hoover Dam (as Boulder Dam was renamed in 1935) inaugurated a vast expansion of federal dam-building activities during the 1930s. Construction of big dams suited the philosophy of New Deal planners and also achieved the practical goal of providing needed jobs. Philosophically, multipurpose projects in the image of the Tennessee Valley Authority accomplished more than private enterprise. They provided irrigation, reclaimed agricultural land, improved river navigation, and created recreation and conservation areas, all of these meeting the economic needs of a particular region. And government could achieve all of these goals in the public interest, not for private profit. Thus, Secretary of the Interior Harold Ickes became the foremost proponent of the federal dam-building program. Under his tenure the Grand Coulee and Bonneville projects were inaugurated in the Pacific Northwest, and the Central California project and the Big Thompson in Colorado, along with hundreds of others throughout the West. These projects reflected the conventional wisdom of the day and provided much of the electric power needed by war industries in the West during World War II.

Afterword

So huge was the investment needed to develop this aspect of the West's economic infrastructure that westerners turned to the federal government as their prime banker. The Bureau of Reclamation's programs hit their stride at midcentury as the bureau and the Corps of Engineers built hundreds of dams and diversion projects throughout the region.

But by 1960 westerners' fascination with dams had begun to fade. The expense had been enormous, totaling almost $100 billion. Silting and evaporation made the dams less efficient than was originally expected. Moreover, by then the economy of the West was far less dependent on agriculture than enthusiasts and planners had envisioned half a century before. The West was developing not as a farming region but as an urban civilization in which high-tech, electronics, and service industries played a major role. And the water needs of cities were less per capita than those of farmers. In addition, the concern of Americans for the environment— for land, fish, and wildlife—also provoked increasing opposition to large dam projects. By the late 1960s many of these concerns crystallized. Although Congress approved the Central Arizona Project in 1968, that was the last of the large dam projects. Various interest groups in the West continued to advocate new projects, but Congress largely refrained from funding them.

As a matter of fact, in the 1990s environmentalists began to demand the destruction of the existing dams. Novelist Edward Abbey had first proposed such action in the 1970s. In 1997 Congress held hearings on the issue with special reference to Glen Canyon Dam. The Sierra Club unanimously advocated dismantling the structure for practical as well as aesthetic reasons. It was the beginning of a movement that is likely to attract more adherents in the twenty-first century.

At the opening of the twentieth century, when Americans gave thought to energy, they thought of coal. In 1908, President Theodore Roosevelt, an early conservationist, became one of the first chief executives to withdraw federally owned coal lands from private sale in order to preserve the nation's natural resources. Even as he acted, however, the nation's energy consumption was undergoing rapid changes. The navy was converting from coal to diesel-burning ships and became largely dependent on petroleum.

The discovery of the Spindletop gusher in east Texas in 1901 set off an era of oil wildcatting in Texas, Oklahoma, Kansas, California, and other western states to provide the needed fuel. At the same time, the proliferation of automobiles opened up vast new markets for oil in the decade before World War I. Once the United States entered that conflict, petroleum became a vital element in the national military effort. A new national motto proclaimed, "Petroleum will win the war." The navy, America's first line of defense, became dependent on the oil resources of the American West. After America entered the war in 1917, the federal government took virtual control of the oil industry through the Fuel Administration, headed by Mark Requa, a protégé of Herbert Hoover. The growing air force further fostered a close relationship between western oil producers and the American military establishment. To assure itself of sufficient supplies, the navy established its own naval oil reserves throughout the West. Although President Woodrow Wilson abolished the Fuel Administration in 1919, the navy retained its own oil reserves during the 1920s, especially after Congress in 1919 authorized the transfer of half of the navy to the West Coast and Hawaii. That move proved to be a major economic boon to the Pacific coast states and to Utah and Nevada in the interior.

During the 1920s the federal government continued to be involved in the western oil industry. After the Teapot Dome scandals of 1923, when Secretary of the Interior Albert Fall somewhat surreptitiously transferred U.S. naval oil reserves at Teapot Dome, Wyoming, and Signal Hill, California, to private oil interests, President Calvin Coolidge established the Federal Oil Conservation Board to develop national and state programs for oil conservation. Meanwhile, the State Department was seeking to negotiate agreements with Saudi Arabia and other Middle Eastern countries to secure cheap oil in the face of opposition from Britain and France, who sought to keep those reserves exclusively for themselves. But vast new discoveries of oil in Texas, California, Oklahoma, Kansas, and New Mexico in the 1920s created an oil glut that proved to be a disaster for the industry in the depression era. To prevent total collapse of the industry, the federal government imposed rigid controls between 1933 and 1935 through the Oil Code of the National Recovery Administration. Parts of

Afterword

that code continued in effect after 1935 with the Connally Act, which prohibited interstate shipment of oil produced in violation of state regulations.

Federal control over the oil industry increased during World War II. By then oil was needed not only to fuel the navy but also to feed a brand new air force totaling 300,000 planes. To assure absolute federal dominance, the Petroleum Administration for War regulated most aspects of production and refining between 1941 and 1945; then it returned the industry to private operation. Despite a spate of studies concerning the federal role, the government had not yet developed a coherent national oil policy at midcentury.

During the second half of the century the nation moved from self-sufficiency in petroleum to increasing dependence on foreign oil imports, buying 50 percent of its supply from foreign sources at the end of the 1990s. Federal policy thus shifted from regulation of the domestic industry to State Department negotiations with foreign powers, especially with OPEC in the 1970s. Some critics even charged that when President George Bush engaged the nation in the war with Iraq in 1991, his prime goal was to ensure the continued flow of Middle Eastern oil to the United States.

The federal presence in the West was also visible in the natural-gas fields. After 1945 this energy source became the most popular choice for heating and cooling. By subjecting the natural-gas industry to rigid federal regulation, the Federal Power Commission limited production. Whether regulated prices were ultimately cheaper for consumers than those produced by competition was unclear, and it became a heated issue for economists and politicians. By 1985, however, Congress had removed most federal regulations, bringing to an end a half century of government control.

The western coal mines were also a part of the federal landscape, as reflected in national policies concerning coal mining. With billions of tons of low-sulfur coal on public lands in the West, the federal government was in a prime position to affect the nature of this industry. As the OPEC nations raised the price of oil between 1971 and 1980, Congress directed a great increase in western coal mining, especially in Utah, New

Mexico, and Wyoming. By selling or leasing coal lands to private operators at attractive prices between 1970 and 2000, Congress was able to increase the production of low-sulfur coal significantly throughout the West.

Ironically, coal continued to be the nation's major source of energy at the end of the century, as it had been at the beginning. When President Bill Clinton in 1997 pledged to abide by the Kyoto global agreements on atmospheric warming and climate change, he narrowed the prospects for the nuclear industry. Other energy alternatives included natural gas, but its use declined between 1980 and 2000. By the end of the century, coal was producing 57 percent of the electrical power in the United States. An increasing amount of that coal came from Wyoming, Utah, Colorado, New Mexico, and the Dakotas, some of it from Indian lands. By 1998 engineers had developed new processes to reduce pollution, making the continued use of coal in the first decade of the twenty-first century likely.

By 1900 most of the western railroads had already been built, but the Panama Canal was still needed to link the Atlantic and Pacific Oceans and to integrate the West into national and global markets. It was clear that private enterprise was unable to provide either the capital or the managerial expertise to complete the project. The connection between the Atlantic and the Pacific was more vital than it had been in previous years because now it served the needs of national security as well as promoting the western economy. The canal would tie Hawaii closer to the East Coast and facilitate greater trade with the Pacific rim. When Theodore Roosevelt entered the White House in 1901, he had a very clear understanding of the geopolitical role of the United States and the West in a rapidly industrializing world. What he needed was a moment of opportunity. That moment came in 1903 when Roosevelt used his political wiles to make the necessary arrangements for America to build the canal. Although the process of construction was much more difficult and expensive than Roosevelt or Congress had envisaged, by 1914 a vast team of thousands of workers laboring under very difficult conditions had completed the task, laying another cornerstone in the western economy.

But the federal government's role as the architect of the West's transportation system did not end with the Panama Canal. At the same time that the government was sponsoring the building of the canal, another transportation revolution was in the works. At the turn of the century, most Americans viewed automobiles as playthings for the rich. Within a few years, however, cars had become an integral part of the American transportation network. That was particularly true in the West, where the distances to be overcome were so much greater than in the East. Even in the nineteenth century, most road construction was accomplished by the federal government. The wagon roads of the trans-Mississippi West were all built with federal funds. By the early twentieth century, federal responsibility for road building was widely accepted by Americans.

When Henry Ford and others created a mass market for automobiles in the first three decades of the twentieth century, public demand for better roads mounted. Farm groups such as the National Grange wanted improved highways to facilitate the transport of crops to railheads. At the same time, the increasing urban population, represented by such groups as the American Automobile Association, lobbied for better highways to connect cities and to link cities to the countryside, hoping to increase trade and commerce. Congress was sympathetic to the demands of these organizations, especially during the Wilson administration, which was sensitive to the needs of farmers in the South and West. Congress responded with the Highway Act of 1916, under which the federal government assumed half of the cost of road building, with the states paying the other half. A Republican Congress in 1922 was no less responsive to the demands for roads by rural and urban interests. The Highway Act of 1922 provided $1 billion for the purpose, continuing cost sharing with the states.

Meanwhile, the army was becoming concerned about the need for a national road network as between 1920 and 1950 it replaced horses with motorized equipment and moved vehicles over longer and longer distances. Captain Dwight D. Eisenhower became interested in the issue as early as 1919. When American military forces under Eisenhower's command invaded Germany in 1945 and rolled down the autobahns built by Adolph Hitler, Eisenhower became an even more convinced advocate of an American highway system.

As president he did much to procure the Highway Act of 1956, which allotted $10 billion over a ten-year period for the construction of a system that was of special importance to the West. The new highway system facilitated the growth of western cities and their suburbs. It also lessened the isolation of more remote sections of the West, such as Indian reservations, and accelerated economic growth in them. In less than two decades the system had made the West an integral part of the national marketplace. In the federal landscape, the highway system served as a connecting link tying the West into a regional economic unit.

Although historians have largely ignored airports, the federal government's active role in financing and building airports to accommodate jet transport was a major development during the second half of the century. In many localities the federal government assumed 90 percent of the cost of their construction.

Housing projects were another contributor to the infrastructure of the western economy. The federal government shaped the contours of western cities in diverse ways. With its emphasis on single-family homes, the FHA provided a foundation for suburban development in the West, in stark contrast to the older eastern cities, which private entrepreneurs had built before 1900. In addition, federal military installations affected the patterns of many urban areas in the West. Similarly, a succession of housing acts after 1949 created patterns for the renewal of downtown areas and for housing projects to serve low-income earners and subsidized housing for the aged. In subtle and often not so subtle ways, the federal government had an important influence on western cities during the period of their most rapid growth between 1940 and 2000.

In the course of the twentieth century, the federal government also became a significant promoter of tourism in the West. At the opening of the century, tourism was restricted largely to wealthy individuals and health seekers such as people with tuberculosis. Congress had created a few national parks, such as Yellowstone, but these areas were established for environmental rather than economic reasons. During the Progressive Era, Theodore Roosevelt and other conservationists advocated the withdrawal of scenic areas from public sale largely for aesthetic reasons. It is true that the federal government built El Tovar and Angel Lodges at the Grand Canyon in 1905, but its motive was to preserve the majestic scenery rather than to promote a western tourist industry. That was also the goal of Congress in creating national monuments, in 1905, and the national park system in 1916. During this same period, the promotion

152

Afterword

of tourism was largely in the hands of private individuals like the legendary Fred Harvey, who built a chain of outstanding restaurants, gift shops, and tourist attractions throughout the West. More limited in their influence than Harvey were scores of hotel owners and entrepreneurs who built luxury hotels and resorts like the Coronado in San Diego and the Broadmoor in Colorado Springs. Until 1916 the federal government was not directly involved in stimulating the tourist industry in the West.

With the establishment of the national park system, that situation began to change. After World War I more tourists traveled in automobiles than in trains. Moreover, after 1920 tourism was within the reach of the masses. Rising living standards and the availability of automobiles allowed individual wage earners more leisure to travel. The changing conditions alerted the first director of the national park system, the dynamic Steve Mather (1916–1928), to secure the appropriations from Congress needed to expand the system. It became prudent to emphasize not only the environmental but also the economic benefits of parks. During the Great Depression, when the tourist industry suffered, its importance became increasingly evident to New Deal planners. In designing their great dam projects—Hoover, Bonneville, and Grand Coulee—the planners made provisions for recreational areas such as Lake Mead at Hoover Dam to attract more tourists and thus to strengthen the economies of local areas. At the same time, the National Park Service was developing visitor areas and camping sites in national parks to attract a larger number of visitors. In the second half of the twentieth century, the tourist industry in the West exploded and the national parks became stellar attractions. In 1950 they counted 8 million visitors. In 1970 this had grown to 80 million. By 2000, 150 million people were expected to visit the national parks. Tourism has evolved into one of the important economic assets of the West.

In 1900, military installations in the West were few and far between. The U.S. Army was small, numbering fewer than 100,000 men. The forts that dotted the West were leftovers from the days of Indian warfare in the second half of the nineteenth century. By the turn of the century they were limited to serving as training centers. Congress was much more actively engaged in building up the navy, but the navy's ships, supply centers, and other installations were largely concentrated on the East

Coast. Before 1898 navy commanders had shown little interest in the Pacific. The navy maintained only the Mare Island naval shipyard and small facilities in San Francisco, Seattle, and San Diego. The military presence did not have a significant economic impact on the local economies.

The changing nature of warfare and the growing importance of the United States in international affairs soon changed the role of the West in national security policies. World War I served as a catalyst. For the first time since the Civil War, the nation mobilized millions of men, and they required military training. That led to the establishment of new training camps in the West. The navy became America's first line of defense and expanded rapidly in size. Moreover, by 1918 U.S. foreign policy included defending Hawaii and the Philippines, and maintaining a balance of power in Asia. The completion of the Panama Canal in 1914 gave the navy greater flexibility, and in 1919 new considerations of foreign policy led naval leaders to shift half of the fleet to the Pacific coast, with San Diego as the major base. This transfer was of the utmost importance for the economy of San Diego and other western cities. Between 1920 and 1940 the navy established more large installations, some in the San Francisco Bay area and others in Portland and Seattle. Suddenly these cities derived a large share of their annual income from naval expenditures—in the case of San Diego, as much as 30 percent.

The economic impact of air power was also becoming important. During World War I both the army and the navy signed contracts with airplane manufacturers in southern California and Seattle, giving rise to a new industry. The armed services also established airfields to train pilots and the accompanying support staff. As yet, air defense installations were not as important to the western economy as the army and navy bases, but the creation of airfields and test sites during this period laid the foundations for a not very distant future when air power in World War II would become a major part of the national security establishment.

In fact, World War II wrought a profound change in the federal military presence in the West. Until 1941 the influence of the armed forces on the western economy was limited except in localized areas such as San Diego. But after 1945 the United States, for the first time in its history, maintained a large standing peacetime military establishment, with a very prominent presence in the West. The contrast between the military's influence on the economy between the first and second halves of the twentieth century was stark. Along the Pacific coast the navy was a major contributor to the economic well-being of the major cities. Army camps housing hundreds of thousands of men and women proliferated in the states of the interior. And the air force established dozens of major airfields in the West, which it favored not only because of the good flying weather but also because of the availability of vast empty stretches of land suitable for training pilots and testing aircraft. As the United States became more of a Pacific power after 1945, military supply depots in the West served a major function in providing equipment for the Pacific fleet. In Utah, for example, military supply depots were the major employer between 1940 and 1960. Federally sponsored research and development of technology for military purposes provided another important source of employment, especially in places such as Los Alamos and Albuquerque in New Mexico, and Hanford in Washington.

Military expenditures to fuel western economic growth increased significantly during the second half of the twentieth century. The first great surge came with the Korean War (1950–1953) and proliferated as the cold war with the Soviet Union and other communist countries intensified in the 1950s and 1960s. As military weapons became more sophisticated, they also became more expensive. Missiles, electronic gear, and nuclear vessels cost not millions but billions of dollars. By this time the federal government was channeling vast sums not only to maintaining the network of military installations but also to funding private contractors and universities who were engaged in research and development for military purposes. These expenditures provided a major source of income for some communities. In Los Angeles, one of three employed persons worked in an activity related to the aerospace complex there.

The federal investment elsewhere in the West may not have been as great, but there was not a single western state in which federal military expenditures were not an important source of income. Although the level of such expenditures in the West varied between 1970 and 2000, they continued to be important even if in 2000 they were about half of what they had been in the 1960s. The physical reflection of this vast investment was seen in the extensive network of military installations and clusters of research and development facilities throughout the West, especially in California, Washington, Utah, Arizona, New Mexico, and Colorado, and in Alaska and Hawaii.

The federal commitment to promoting science in the interest of developing the western economy during the second half of the twentieth century was a startling departure in federal policy. Before 1945 such federal commitments were on a far more moderate scale. The U.S. Geological Survey, for example, was authorized by Congress in 1879 to promote science and to provide useful economic data for development of the trans-Mississippi West, but it operated on a very modest budget. In the 1950s and afterward the federal landscape came to embrace entire science cities and federal laboratories dedicated to nuclear research, such as Los Alamos, Lawrence Livermore National Laboratory in California, and the Nevada nuclear facility. It also included testing facilities such as Edwards Air Force Base in California and White Sands in New Mexico. By 1960 large-scale funding for places like the aerospace complex in southern California and electronics firms such as those in Colorado Springs, Silicon Valley, and Utah supported a significant percentage of technical research and development in the West. Although these activities were originally oriented to national security, by 1990 many of these laboratories and corporations were transferring their technology to nonmilitary uses as Congress reduced appropriations for defense. In diverse ways, federally financed research and development was applicable to a wide range of economic activities. The federal investment in electronics research was considerable, and it placed the West on the cutting edge of technological innovation. In 1900 the West was far behind other sections of the nation in scientific research; by 2000 federal funds had helped to transform it into a pacesetter. Federal science cities in the West still flourish, and federally financed centers of scientific research applicable to economic development have become a prominent presence in most western states.

The federal landscape in the West during the twentieth century also reflected an effort to reshape the economies of Native Americans, although that effort had only moderate success. In 1900 the Indian Service was trying to transform Indians into farmers under the Dawes Act. Understandably, most Native Americans, who did not have a heritage of stationary agriculture, resisted that effort. Furthermore, Indians had been forced to reside on some of the poorest farmland in the nation, where even experienced farmers would have had serious problems. It was not surprising, therefore, that a majority of Indians between 1900 and 1940 found themselves mired in poverty. During the New Deal, Commissioner John Collier of the Bureau of Indian Affairs attempted to reverse federal policies by emphasizing self-determination, including greater economic self-sufficiency. Despite his good intentions, he had only limited success.

World War II probably had a greater impact on western Indians than Commissioner Collier. The war opened up new domestic job opportunities in war-related industries. California shipyards, for example, provided well-paying jobs for some Indians. In addition, some of the twenty-five thousand Indian men and women in the armed forces received training that served them well in postwar civilian occupations. In the decade of the 1940s, half of those who left the reservations in wartime chose not to return. Instead, they became urban dwellers, with varying degrees of success. The BIA's attempts to accelerate the move from reservations to cities in the 1950s, however, brought chaos into the lives of many Indians, who were not prepared for such rapid changes.

By 1960 the bureau had abandoned its flawed resettlement policy and instead was focusing on improving economic life on the reservations. This effort involved an increase in job-training programs and programs designed to bring industries to the reservations. Such programs were especially popular during the administration of Lyndon Johnson. As in the New Deal, however, the programs had only modest success. The effort to entice corporations to reservations faltered within two decades. Cultural differences between Indians and corporate managers often impeded the work process. Businesses found cheap labor in Mexico and elsewhere outside the United States and were not eager to establish branches on reservations. On the other hand, growing numbers of young Indians were graduating from high schools and colleges and finding more diverse economic opportunities off the reservations, which thus lost some of their brightest youths.

In view of the experience of the 1960s, the framers of the Indian Reorganization Act of 1975 returned to the New Deal policy of encouraging greater self-determination to allow Indians more freedom to pursue economic self-sufficiency. Poverty was still a problem for most reservation dwellers, whose annual incomes were only about 20 percent of the national average. Beginning in the 1960s, tribes such as the Navajos sought to profit from rising energy prices by leasing their lands containing oil, gas, and coal. Given tribal inexperience and lack of direction from the Bureau of Indian Affairs, most tribes received only a fraction of the revenues from private business that they might have obtained.

Although income from leasing their natural resources fed tribal coffers, it did not create as many new jobs as the tribes hoped, and it still left the average reservation dweller in poverty. Profiting from their experience, many tribes in the 1980s increased their revenues from energy and invested them in a broader range of economic enterprises, especially those that provided jobs near reservations. Most important were tourism, motels, resorts, and shopping centers. The establishment of gambling casinos in the 1990s added another dimension to the equation. State restrictions on gambling usually do not apply to reservations on federal lands, and by the year 2000 Indian gambling casinos had become a noticeable feature of the federal landscape, providing jobs and income to their Indian owners. This was one more stage in the century-old struggle of Indians to overcome poverty. The economic battles of the twentieth century were no less difficult for Native Americans than the military battles of the nineteenth had been, but at least economic opportunities for Indians were more diverse in 2000 than they had been a hundred years before.

The federal landscape also came to be distinctive along the U.S.–Mexico border. At the beginning of the century, Mexico had encouraged Americans to invest in Mexican enterprises, especially petroleum. The number of Mexican emigrants to the United States was relatively small, fewer than 100,000 annually between 1900 and 1940. As the Mexican population grew very rapidly in the course of the century, however, the search for jobs led an increasing number of Mexicans to seek employment in the United States to escape the grinding poverty of their native land. Under the bracero agreement in effect from 1942 to 1962, about 200,000 Mexican guest workers entered the United States annually and became a familiar sight on western farms and railroads.

With the abrogation of the bracero agreement, the Mexican search for jobs intensified. As many as 3 million immigrants came to the United States each year between 1970 and 2000, legally or illegally. Mexico and the United States attempted to deal with their respective economic needs in these years by establishing maquiladoras along their border. These American-owned assembly plants employed Mexican workers at a fraction of the prevailing wage rates in the United States. The Mexican government also granted special tax exemptions to American companies locating in Mexico. As these enterprises proliferated between 1980 and 2000, they became a very noticeable part of the federal landscape along the border. When President Clinton secured congressional acceptance of the North American Free Trade Agreement (NAFTA) in 1995, the treaty gave a big boost to the border economy and its special economic landscape.

In fact, global commercial policies had an increasingly important economic impact on the economies of the interior states of the West. Seaports were no longer necessary for carrying on a large volume of foreign trade. In an age of air transportation, the coastal states were no longer the exclusive entry points for commerce. Of the ten states that recorded the fastest growth of export trade in the 1990s, seven—Kansas, Nebraska, New Mexico, Arizona, Colorado, Utah, and Idaho—were landlocked in the West. Arizona exported more per capita than New York State. Colorado during this decade found the value of its manufactured exports to exceed that from farms and ranches. On the Great Plains, exports of processed foods soared, and exports of such foods and computer services are expected to double in the ten-year period between 1995 and 2005. In 1988 the exports of eleven western states were about half of the national average, or $1,248 per capita. By 1996 they had grown to two-thirds of the national average, or $2,348 per capita. Greater expansion lay ahead. Idaho exported 75 percent of its production of 100 million bushels of grain. Nebraska sent state trade commissions to Taiwan, Japan, China, and Hong Kong. Japan in 1997 was the largest trading partner of Utah, Colorado, Nebraska, and Kansas. Trade has exploded because at least some manufactured goods are no longer bulky, requiring ship or rail transport. Instead, computer chips manufactured in Arizona, Utah, or New Mexico are moved by air. In short, U.S. trade policies have become a vital influence in the economic welfare of the West.[1]

In many ways, the federal government in the twentieth century played a major role in transforming an erstwhile economic colony, a colony dependent on the exploitation of its natural resources, into a trendsetter on the cutting edge of new technologies. By providing much-needed capital, the government achieved what private enterprise would have found much more difficult to accomplish in the time span of a century. To understand the contribution of the federal government, one must first realize that designating the American economy as "capitalist" is meaningless. Such a term is a verbal construct and nothing more. Adam Smith would not have recognized the U.S. economy as such. Rather, the American—and the western—economy is the result of an intricate mix of government and private enterprise. In the crazy-quilt pattern that developed during the course of the twentieth century, it is difficult to discern where the functions of one began and the other ended. Certain it is that the influence of the federal government in the western economy grew enormously during this period and left an indelible stamp on the landscape of the trans-Mississippi West.

The builders of this landscape worked within two of the waves of global technological innovation perceived by Nicolae Kondratieff and Joseph Schumpeter. The first wave gathered force in the late nineteenth century and was stimulated by inventions in chemicals, by automobiles, and by electricity. It had mostly run its course by midcentury. The second wave was fostered by transistors, computer chips, and telecommunications in the later twentieth century and was still in force in the year 2000. As the youngest region in the United States, the West was fully caught up in the whirlwind of the new technology. It had lagged behind the rest of the nation between 1900 and 1940, but it increasingly became a leader during the remainder of the century. The history of the West would have been very different had these national and global trends not engulfed the region.

These waves of economic change were not the product of impersonal or mechanistic forces. They were deliberate results of the efforts of men and women who valued entrepreneurial innovation and who were the key element in producing economic change. In that sense, the Schumpeterian analysis is still instructive. By encouraging fiscal and monetary policies conducive to generating economic change, the innovators were able to introduce a dynamism into American economic development that was lacking in other nations. But more was needed. These innovators also

Afterword

adapted the political and institutional framework to accommodate economic change and to integrate the waves of technological development with fluctuations in price levels. This is not to say that their efforts were an unbounded success; not at all. Major problems in the western economy at the end of the twentieth century indicated that much remained to be done. The gap in income between rich and poor was worrisome, erratic rates of economic growth were disruptive, fluctuations in employment patterns were often alarming, and social inequalities and environmental desecration were glaring problems. These are only a few of the major issues that await imaginative responses in the twenty-first century.

In 2000 the West entered the new century as a federal landscape. Everywhere the imprint of the federal government was writ large. It could be seen in the dams that produced energy. It was evident in the shape of western cities and in the network of national highways and airports that bound them together. It was evident in the extensive network of national defense installations and the research-and-development clusters so visible in many areas of the West. It was evident on Indian reservations and in the ubiquitous national park system, which became a part of the human landscape as surely as that created by nature. If the nineteenth-century West was the product of individuals interacting with the environment, so in the twentieth century, to a considerable extent, the West was the creature of the federal government.

Notes

Preface

1. Peter Hall and Paschal Preston, *The Carrier Wave: New Information Technology and the Geography of Innovation, 1846–2003* (London: Unwin Hyman, 1980), 3–22; Joshua S. Goldstein, *Long Cycles: Prosperity and War in the Modern Age* (New Haven: Yale University Press, 1988), provides an excellent survey of theories in the field. The West in this book refers to the area west of the Mississippi River, excluding Texas.

2. Nicolae Kondratieff, "The Long Waves in Economic Life," *Review of Economic Statistics* 17 (April 1935): 105–15; see also the translation of his book, *The Long Wave Cycle* (New York: Richardson and Snyder, 1984).

3. Among Joseph Schumpeter's best-known works are *Business Cycles* (New York: McGraw-Hill, 1939), and *Capitalism, Socialism and Democracy* (New York: Harper and Brothers, 1942); the quotation is from his *History of Economic Analysis* (New York: Oxford University Press, 1954), 213, 223.

4. Jacob J. von Duijn, *The Long Wave in Economic Life* (London: Allen and Unwin, 1983); Ernest Mandel, *Long Waves of Capitalist Development* (Cambridge: Cambridge University Press, 1980); and Gerhard Mensch, *Stalemate in Technology* (Cambridge, Mass.: Ballinger, 1979), are fine introductions to the subject. See also N. Rosenberg and C. Fritschtak, "Technological Innovation and Long Waves," *Cambridge Journal of Economics* 8 (March 1984): 17–24.

5. Carlota Perez, "Structural Change and the Assimilation of New Technologies in the Economic and Social Systems," *Futures* 15 (October 1983): 357–75. Stephen F. Cox, "Talking, Reading and Writing Western History," *Journal of the Southwest* 29 (Winter 1987): 377, emphasizes the federal role; whereas Donald J. Pisani, "Federalism and the American West, 1900–1940," in *Essays in Honor of Martin Ridge,* ed. Robert C. Ritchie and Paul A. Hutton (Albuquerque: University of New Mexico Press, 1997), 83–108, focuses on the role of state and local governments. I believe that a distinction needs to be made between policy and administration. Although the federal government set many policies, as this volume will demonstrate, at the same time, state and local governments retained some authority in determining their administration.

6. David Hackett Fischer, *The Great Wave: Price Revolutions and the Rhythms of History* (New York: Oxford University Press, 1996), 3–10, 181–202.

Chapter 1. A Colonial Landscape, 1900–1929

1. Frederick Jackson Turner, "Contributions of the West to American Democracy," in *The Frontier in American History* (New York: Harper and Brothers, 1920), 258.

4

Notes to Pages xi–2

2. David McCullough, *The Path between the Seas: The Creation of the Panama Canal* (New York: Simon and Schuster, 1978). An older work by John H. Kemble, *The Panama Route, 1848–1869* (Berkeley: University of California Press, 1943), is still useful.

3. On the impact of the canal on the West, see G. Allen Greb, "Opening a New Frontier: San Francisco, Los Angeles and the Panama Canal, 1900–1914," *Pacific Historical Review* 47 (August 1978): 405–24. A brief account of the expositions is in *Historical Dictionary of World's Fairs and Expositions, 1851–1988,* ed. John E. Findling (Westport, Conn.: Greenwood Press, 1990), 219–26, 227–30.

4. See John B. Rae, *The American Automobile Industry* (Boston: Twayne, 1984); and Rae's earlier book, *The Road and the Car in American Life* (Cambridge: MIT Press, 1971).

5. Drake Hokanson, *The Lincoln Highway: Main Street across America* (Iowa City: University of Iowa Press, 1988); Bruce E. Seely, *Building the American Highway System: Engineers as Policy Makers* (Philadelphia: Temple University Press, 1987); John E. Wickman, "Ike and the Great Truck Train–1919," *Kansas History* 13 (Autumn 1990): 139–48. For an example of local conditions, see William P. Corbett, "Men, Mud, and Mules: The Good Roads Movement in Oklahoma, 1900–1910," *Chronicles of Oklahoma* 58 (Summer 1980): 133–50.

6. Donald Worster, *Rivers of Empire: Water, Aridity and the Growth of the American West* (New York: Pantheon Books, 1986); Donald J. Pisani, *From the Family Farm to Agribusiness, 1850–1931* (Berkeley: University of California Press, 1984); Arthur E. Morgan, *Dams and Other Disasters: A Century of the Army Corps of Engineers in Civil Works* (Boston: Porter Sargent, 1971); an older, but still useful work is Arthur Maas, *Muddy Waters: The Army Engineers and the Nation's Rivers* (Cambridge: Harvard University Press, 1951).

7. On tourism, see Earl Pomeroy, *In Search of the Golden West: The Tourist in Western America* (New York: Knopf, 1957); and Hal K. Rothman, *Preserving Different Pasts: The American National Monuments* (Urbana: University of Illinois Press, 1989); Alfred Runte, *National Parks: The American Experience* (Lincoln: University of Nebraska Press, 1987). A local example is discussed in Ann Hyde, "From Stagecoach to Packard Twin Six: Yosemite and the Changing Face of Tourism, 1880–1930," *California History* 69 (Summer 1990): 154–69, 224–25.

8. The best discussion is Roger N. Lotchin, *Fortress California, 1910–1961: From Warfare to Welfare* (New York: Oxford University Press, 1992), 23–41; William R. Braisted, *The U.S. Navy in the Pacific, 1909–1922* (Austin: University of Texas Press, 1971), 473–82, 535–48; Richard F. Pourade, *The Rising Tide,* vol. 6 of *The History of San Diego* (San Diego: Union Publishing Company, 1967), 1–26.

9. There is no good comprehensive history of the West in World War I. For brief surveys, see Michael P. Malone and Richard W. Etulain, *The American West* (Lincoln: University of Nebraska Press, 1989), 17–19; and Gerald D. Nash, *The American West in the Twentieth Century* (Albuquerque: University of New Mexico Press, 1977), 63–71.

10. Philip Taft, "The Bisbee Deportation," *Labor History* 13 (Winter 1972): 3–40; Taft, "The Federal Trials of the IWW," *Labor History* 3 (Winter 1962): 57–91; Melvyn Dubofsky, *We Shall Be All: A History of the Industrial Workers of the World* (Chicago: Quadrangle Books, 1969), 342–43, 350–58, 376–78; Benjamin Rader, "The Montana Lumber Strike of 1917," *Pacific Historical Review* 36 (May 1967): 189–207; Harold M. Hyman, *Soldiers and Spruce: Origins of the Loyal Legion of Loggers and Lumbermen* (Los Angeles: University of California Institute of Industrial Relations, 1963).

11. On oil, see Ralph Andreano, "The Structure of the California Petroleum Industry," *Pacific Historical Review* 39 (May 1970): 171–92; Joe S. Bain, *The Economics of the Pacific Coast Petroleum Industry,* 3 vols. (Westport, Conn.: Greenwood Press, 1969); and Kenny Franks, *The Oklahoma Petroleum Industry* (Norman: University of Oklahoma Press, 1980). On shipping, consult Wytze Gorter, *The Pacific Coast Maritime Shipping Industry, 1930–1948,* 2 vols. (Berkeley: University of California Press, 1952–54).

12. Roger Bilstein, "Aviation and the Changing West," *Journal of the West* 30 (January 1991): 5–17; Joseph J. Corn, *The Winged Gospel: America's Romance with Aviation, 1900–1950* (New York: Oxford University Press, 1983); John B. Rae, *Climb to Greatness: The American Aircraft Industry, 1920–1960* (Cambridge: MIT Press, 1968); Ann Markusen, Peter Hall, Scott Campbell, and Sabrina Deitrich, *The Rise of the Gunbelt* (New York: Oxford University Press, 1991), 51–81.

13. Bernard De Voto, "The West: A Plundered Province," *Harper's* 169 (August 1934): 358.

14. A detailed account of farm conditions is in James H. Shideler, *Farm Crisis, 1919–1923* (Berkeley: University of California Press, 1957).

15. See Norris Hundley, *Water and the West: The Colorado River Compact and the Politics of Water in the American West* (Berkeley: University of California Press, 1975); and Hundley's comprehensive *The Great Thirst: California and Water, 1770s–1990s* (Berkeley: University of California Press, 1992). On Hoover Dam, see Joseph E. Stevens, *Hoover Dam: An American Adventure* (Norman: University of Oklahoma Press, 1988); and Beverly Moeller, *Phil Swing and Boulder Dam* (Berkeley: University of California Press, 1971).

16. See Seely, *Building the American Highway System,* 71–99, 141–64.

Chapter 2. Changing the Federal Landscape in the Great Depression, 1929–1940

1. *Congressional Record,* 74th Cong., 1st sess., 865–66, January 24, 1935, quoted in Richard Lowitt, *The New Deal and the West* (Bloomington: Indiana University Press, 1984), 205.

2. Harold Ickes, in 77th Cong., 1st sess., Senate, Subcommittee of the Committee on Public Lands and Surveys, *Hearings Pursuant to Senate Resolution #53* (Washington, D.C.: Government Printing Office, 1942), 5, 6, 15.

3. In addition to Lowitt, *New Deal and the West,* see Jean Christie, "New Deal Resources Planning: The Proposals of Morris L. Cooke," *Agricultural History* 53 (July 1979): 597–606; Theodore Saloutos, "The New Deal and Farm Policy in the Great Plains," *Agricultural History* 43 (July 1969): 345–55; and Richard S. Kirkendall, *Social Scientists and Farm Politics in the Age of Roosevelt* (Columbia: University of Missouri Press, 1966); on water, see Richard L. Berkman and W. Kip Viscusi, *Damming the West* (New York: Grossman, 1973).

4. The strong, pungent language of Ickes is reflected in Harold Ickes, "Thought for the Morrow," *Colliers* 94 (December 8, 1934): 21; see also Donald C. Swain, "The Bureau of Reclamation and the New Deal, 1933–1940," *Pacific Northwest Quarterly* 61 (July 1970): 137–46; Norris Hundley, "The Great American Desert Transformed: Aridity, Exploitation, and Imperialism in the Making of the Modern American West," in *Water and Arid Lands of the Western United States,* ed. M. T. El-Ashry and D. C. Gibbons (New York: Cambridge University Press, 1988), 21–88.

5. Lowitt, *New Deal and the West,* 84–85; Nash, *The American West in the Twentieth Century,* 155–69.

6. Oliver Knight, "Correcting Nature's Error: The Colorado–Big Thompson Project," *Reclamation Era* 30 (September 1949): 267–69; Donald B. Cole, "Transmountain Water Diversion in Colorado," *Colorado Magazine* 25 (March 1948): 49–64, and 25 (May 1948): 118–35.

7. Michael L. Lawson, *Damned Indians: The Pick-Sloan Plan and the Missouri River Sioux, 1944–1980* (Norman: University of Oklahoma Press, 1982).

8. Robert de Roos, *Thirsty Land: The Story of the Central Valley Project* (Stanford: Stanford University Press, 1948); Clayton R. Koppes, "Public Water, Private Land: Origins of the Acreage Limitation Controversy, 1933–1953," *Pacific Historical Review* 47 (November 1978): 607–38; Lawrence B. Lee, "California Water Politics: Depression Genesis of the Central Valley Project, 1933–1944," *Journal of the West* 24 (October 1985): 63–81; a more detailed account is in Charles E. Coate, "Water, Power, and Politics in the Central Valley Project, 1933–1967" (Ph.D. diss., University of California, Berkeley, 1969).

A suggestive analysis is Norris Hundley, "California's Original Waterscape: Harmony and Manipulation," *California History* 66 (March 1987): 2–11, 69–70.

9. Stewart H. Holbrook, *The Columbia River* (New York: Holt, Rinehart and Winston, 1965).

10. Charles McKinley, *Uncle Sam in the Pacific Northwest* (Berkeley: University of California Press, 1952), is still useful. Also see Philip J. Funigiello, *Toward a National Power Policy: The New Deal and the Electric Utility Industry, 1933–1941* (Pittsburgh: University of Pittsburgh Press, 1974); and Funigiello's article, "The Bonneville Power Administration and the New Deal," *Prologue* 5 (Summer 1973): 89–97. Roosevelt is quoted in Lowitt, *New Deal and the West,* 162.

11. The Roosevelt quote is in *Franklin D. Roosevelt and Conservation, 1911–1945,* 2 vols., ed. Edgar B. Nixon (Hyde Park, N.Y.: Franklin D. Roosevelt Library, 1957), 2:19–20. For three different perspectives on the Dust Bowl, see R. Douglas Hurt, *Dust Bowl* (Chicago: Nelson Hall, 1981); Paul Bonnifield, *The Dust Bowl* (Albuquerque: University of New Mexico Press, 1979); and Donald Worster, *The Dust Bowl* (New York: Oxford University Press, 1979).

12. Farm programs of the New Deal are summarized in Lowitt, *New Deal and the West,* 8–80. Mary W. M. Hargreaves, *Dry Farming in the Northern Great Plains: Years of Readjustment, 1920–1990* (Lawrence: University Press of Kansas, 1993), places the New Deal policies in broad perspective.

13. Douglas Helms, "Conserving the Plains: The Soil Conservation Service in the Great Plains," *Agricultural History* 64 (Spring 1990): 58–73.

14. The quote from Powell is in Lowitt, *New Deal and the West,* 62; also see Henry A. Wallace, *New Frontiers* (New York: Reynal and Hitchcock, 1934), 16, 32.

15. Nixon, ed., *Roosevelt and Conservation,* 1:608–9, 2:3–5, 19–20; William H. Droze, *Trees, Prairies, and People: A History of Tree Planting in the Plains States* (Denton: Texas Women's University Press, 1977).

16. Harold Ickes, "The National Domain and the New Deal," *Saturday Evening Post,* December 23, 1933, 10; Phillip O. Foss, *Politics and Grass: The Administration of Grazing on the Public Domain* (Seattle: University of Washington Press, 1960); Wesley Carr Caleff, *Private Grazing and Public Lands* (Chicago: University of Chicago Press, 1960). Stegner quote in T. H. Watkins and Charles S. Watson Jr., *The Land No One Knows: America and the Public Domain* (San Francisco: Sierra Club, 1975), 115; also quoted in Lowitt, *New Deal and the West,* 71.

17. John A. Brennan, *Silver and the First New Deal* (Reno: University of Nevada Press, 1969); John M. Blum, *From the Morgenthau Diaries: Years of Crisis, 1928–1938* (Boston: Houghton Mifflin, 1959), 188–99.

18. McKinley, *Uncle Sam,* 459–67; Elmo R. Richardson, "Olympic National Park: Twenty Years of Controversy," *Forest History* 12 (April 1968): 6–15; and Richardson's more detailed account in *BLM's Billion-Dollar Checkerboard: Managing the O & C Lands* (Washington, D.C.: Government Printing Office, 1980). A broader survey is William G. Robbins, *Lumberjacks and Legislators: Political Economy of the U.S. Lumber Industry, 1890–1941* (College Station: Texas A&M University Press, 1982).

19. Donald G. Parman, *The Navajos and the New Deal* (New Haven: Yale University Press, 1976); Lawrence C. Kelly, *The Assault on Assimilation: John Collier and the Origins of Indian Policy Reform* (Albuquerque: University of New Mexico Press, 1983); Peter Iverson, *Carlos Montezuma and the Changing World of American Indians* (Albuquerque: University of New Mexico Press, 1982).

20. Suzanne Forrest, *The Preservation of the Village: New Mexico's Hispanics and the New Deal* (Albuquerque: University of New Mexico Press, 1989); David Dinwoodie, "Indians, Hispanics, and Land Reform: A New Deal Struggle in New Mexico," *Western Historical Quarterly* 17 (July 1986): 291–323.

21. Leonard J. Arrington, "The New Deal in the West: A Preliminary Statistical Inquiry," *Pacific Historical Review* 38 (August 1969): 311–16; and Arrington, "The Sagebrush Insurrection: New Deal Expenditures in the Western States, 1933–1939," *Pacific Historical Review* 52 (February 1983): 1–16, are the best short analyses.

Chapter 3. Expanding the Federal Landscape in World War II, 1940–1945

1. General overviews include Harold G. Vatter, *The U.S. Economy in World War II* (Irvington, N.Y.: Columbia University Press, 1988); and Simon J. Kuznets, *National Product in Wartime* (New York: National Bureau of Economic Research, 1945). On California, see Sterling J. Brubaker, "The Impact of the Federal Government Activities on California's Economic Growth, 1930–1956" (Ph.D. diss, University of California, Berkeley, 1959), 6–7, 47–51, 155–68. On the federal government and the Bank of America, see Gerald D. Nash, *A. P. Giannini and the Bank of America* (Norman: University of Oklahoma Press, 1992), 129–37; Felice A. Bonadio, *A. P. Giannini: Banker of America* (Berkeley: University of California Press, 1994), 274–84; and Lynne Pierson Doti and Larry Schweikart, *Banking in the American West* (Norman: University of Oklahoma Press, 1991), 148–57.

2. An overview is Gerald D. Nash, *World War II and the West: Reshaping the Economy* (Lincoln: University of Nebraska Press, 1990). On African Americans, see Quintard Taylor, *In Search of the Racial Frontier: African Americans in the American West, 1528–1990* (New York: Norton, 1998), 251–77.

3. Frederick C. Lane, *Ships for Victory: A History of Shipbuilding under the U.S. Maritime Commission in World War II* (Baltimore: Johns Hopkins University Press, 1951). Also see Mark S. Foster, *Henry J. Kaiser: Builder in the Modern American West* (Austin: University of Texas Press, 1989); and Foster's suggestive "Giant of the West: Henry J. Kaiser and Regional Industrialization, 1930–1959," *Business History Review* 59 (Spring 1985): 1–23.

4. Michael S. Sherry, *The Rise of American Air Power: The Creation of Armageddon* (New Haven: Yale University Press, 1987); Robert J. Serling, *Legend and Legacy: The Story of Boeing and Its People* (New York: St. Martin's Press, 1992). Still useful for California is William J. Cunningham, *The Aircraft Industry: A Study in Industrial Location* (Los Angeles: L. L. Morrison, 1951).

5. Leonard J. Arrington and Anthony T. Cluff, *Federally Financed Industrial Plants Constructed in Utah during World War II* (Logan: Utah State University Press, 1969), 36–38; Richard A. Lauderbaugh, *American Steelmakers and the Coming of the Second World War* (Ann Arbor: University of Michigan Research Press, 1980), 3, 20–22; see also Foster, "Giant of the West," 7–8.

6. Charlotte F. Muller, *The Light Metals Monopoly* (New York: Columbia University Press, 1947), 24–43, 50–67; Arrington and Cluff, *Industrial Plants,* 17–32; and Nash, *World War II and the West,* 91–121.

7. "Magnesium by the Ton," *Fortune* 29 (March 1944): 184–87, 194–96; Muller, *Light Metals Monopoly,* 150–95; Nash, *World War II and the West,* 122–30.

8. On braceros, see Richard B. Craig, *The Bracero Program* (Austin: University of Texas Press, 1971); Erasmo Gamboa, *Mexican Labor and World War II: Braceros in the Pacific Northwest, 1942–1947* (Austin: University of Texas Press, 1990); and Ellis W. Hawley, "The Politics of the Mexican Labor Issue, 1950–1965," *Agricultural History* 40 (July 1966): 157–76. On cattle, see Nash, *The American West in the Twentieth Century,* 203; and John T. Schlebecker, *Cattle Raising on the Plains, 1900–1961* (Lincoln: University of Nebraska Press, 1963), 169–85.

9. Robert F. Campbell, *The History of Basic Metals Price Control* (New York: Columbia University Press, 1948), 67–70; Thomas R. Navin, *Copper Mining and Management* (Tucson: University of Arizona Press, 1978), 130–45.

10. Richard L. Neuberger, "The Great Canol Disaster," *American Mercury* 66 (April 1949): 229–41; John G. Clark, *Energy and the Federal Government: Fossil Fuel Policies, 1900–1946* (Urbana: University of Illinois Press, 1987), 316–87; Kenneth Coates, ed., *The Alaska Highway* (Vancouver: University of British Columbia Press, 1985); Heath Twichell, *Northwest Epic: The Building of the Alaska Highway* (New York: St. Martin's Press, 1992).

11. Markusen et al., *Gunbelt,* 3, 64–65, 68, 86–87, 92–93, 236–37; Irving B. Holley, *Buying Aircraft: Materiel Procurement for the Army Air Forces* (Washington, D.C.: Government Printing Office, 1964); Benjamin S. Kelsey, *The Dragon's Teeth: The Creation of United States Air Power for World War II* (Washington, D.C.: Smithsonian Institution Press, 1982).

12. Roger Lotchin, "The Metropolitan-Military Complex in Comparative Perspective: San Francisco, Los Angeles, and San Diego, 1919–1941," *Journal of the West* 18 (July 1979): 19–30; Clayton Koppes, *JPL and the American Space Program: The Jet Propulsion Laboratory, 1936–1976* (New Haven: Yale University Press, 1982); Richard G. Hewlett and Oscar Anderson, *The New World, 1939–1946,* vol. 1: *History of the Atomic Energy Commission* (University Park: Pennsylvania State University Press, 1962).

Chapter 4. Reconverting the West, 1945–1960

1. Stephen K. Bailey, *Congress Makes a Law: The Story of the Employment Act of 1946* (New York: Columbia University Press, 1950), 30–32; Roland Young, *Congressional Politics in the Second World War* (New York: Columbia University Press, 1956), 200; U.S. Surplus Property Board, *Aluminum Plants and Facilities* (Washington, D.C.: Government Printing Office, 1945), 40–46; Donald E. Spritzer, *The New Dealer from Montana: The Senate Career of James E. Murray* (New York: Garland, 1986), 193–209, 216–59, 305–38.

2. Frank Trippett, "The Great American Cooling Machine," *Time* 114 (August 13, 1979): 75; Raymond Arsenault, "The End of the Long Hot Summer: The Air Conditioner and Southern Culture," in *Searching for the Sunbelt,* ed. Raymond Mohl (Knoxville: University of Tennessee Press, 1990), 176–211; W. R. Baron, "Retrieving American Climate History: A Bibliographic Essay," *Agricultural History* 63 (Spring 1989): 7–35. David H. Fischer, "Climate and History: Priorities for Research," *Journal of Interdisciplinary History* 10 (Spring 1980): 821–30, raises broader questions on the subject. On the impact of refrigerator cars, see the delightful work of John H. White, *The Great Yellow Fleet: A History of American Railroad Refrigerator Cars* (San Marino, Calif.: Golden West Books, 1986).

3. Rayner Banham, *The Architecture of a Well Tempered Environment* (London: Architectural Press, 1969), 51–54, 176–77; Wade Greene, "Air Conditioning," *New York Times Magazine,* July 14, 1974, 12, 16, 18.

4. Trippett, "The Great American Cooling Machine," 75; "Air Conditioned Cars," *Newsweek* 40 (September 1, 1952): 54; "Measuring the Misery," *Newsweek* 53 (June 15, 1959): 29; "Now It's the Weather Bureau in a Storm Center," *U.S. News and World Report* 46 (June 22, 1959): 98–99; Robert Friedman, "The Air Conditioned Century," *American Heritage* 35 (August–September 1984): 20–22.

5. Gail A. Cooper, *Air Conditioning America: Engineers and the Controlled Environment, 1900–1960* (Baltimore: Johns Hopkins University Press, 1998). See also *New York Times,* September 6, 1970; and John Reese, "The Air Conditioning Revolution," *Saturday Evening Post,* July 9, 1960, 100.

6. U.S. Bureau of the Census, *Statistical Abstract of the United States: 1970* (Washington, D.C.: Government Printing Office, 1970), 7–12, 14–15, 17–21, 25, 37.

7. On the rise of western cities, see Carl Abbott, *The New Urban America: Growth and Politics in Sunbelt Cities,* rev. ed. (Chapel Hill: University of North Carolina Press, 1987); and also Abbott, *The Metropolitan Frontier: Cities in the Modern American West* (Tucson: University of Arizona Press, 1993).

8. Mark S. Foster, "Prosperity's Prophet: Henry J. Kaiser and the Consumer Urban Culture, 1930–1950," *Western Historical Quarterly* 17 (April 1986): 165–84; see also Mark S. Foster, "Urbanization in the Wide Open Spaces: Recent Historiography on Sunbelt Cities," *Journal of the West* 33 (Spring 1991): 68–85.

9. Larry Schweikart and Lynn Doti, "Financing the Postwar Housing Boom in Phoenix and Los Angeles, 1945–1960," *Pacific Historical Review* 58 (May 1989): 173–94; and Doti and Schweikart, *Banking in the American West: From the Gold Rush to Deregulation* (Norman: University of Oklahoma Press, 1991), 146–58.

10. This discussion is informed by Nash, *The American West in the Twentieth Century,* 228–42; and John M. Findlay, *Magic Lands: Western Cityscapes and American Culture after 1940* (Berkeley: University of California Press, 1992), 160–213. See also John Findlay, "Far Western Cityscapes and American Culture since 1940," *Western Historical Quarterly* 22 (February 1991): 19–43.

11. Findlay, "Far Western Cityscapes," 19–43; Doti and Schweikart, *Banking in the American West*; Schweikart and Doti, "Financing the Post-war Housing Boom."

12. Everett M. Rogers and Judith K. Larsen, *Silicon Valley Fever* (New York: Basic Books, 1984); and Peter Hall and Ann Markusen, eds., *Silicon Landscapes* (Boston: Allen and Unwin, 1985), provide good introductions to the subject. See also Rebecca Sue Lowen, "Exploiting a Wonderful Opportunity: Stanford University, Industry, and the Federal Government, 1937–1965" (Ph.D. diss., Stanford University, 1990), chap. 1.

13. Richard O. Davies, *The Age of Asphalt: The Automobile, the Freeway and the Condition of Metropolitan America* (Philadelphia: Lippincott, 1975); Mark H. Rose, *Interstate: Express Highway Politics, 1941–1956* (Lawrence: Regents Press of Kansas, 1979).

14. Quoted in Arthur R. Gomez, *Quest for the Golden Circle: The Four Corners and the Metropolitan West, 1945–1970* (Albuquerque: University of New Mexico Press, 1994), 116–17.

15. Gomez, *Four Corners*, 21–29; Duane A. Smith, *Rocky Mountain Boom Town: A History of Durango* (Albuquerque: University of New Mexico Press, 1980), 153–71; Raye C. Ringholz, *Uranium Frenzy: Boom and Bust on the Colorado Plateau* (New York: Norton, 1989), 28–32; Gary Lee Shumway, "A History of the Uranium Industry on the Colorado Plateau" (Ph.D. diss., University of Southern California, 1970), 99–118.

16. Petroleum issues are discussed in Gomez, *Four Corners*, 33–41, 58–64; Martin Melosi, *Coping with Abundance: Energy and Environment in Industrial America* (Philadelphia: Temple University Press, 1985), 241–76; and Gerald D. Nash, *United States Oil Policy, 1890–1964* (Pittsburgh: University of Pittsburgh Press, 1968), 180–208. A suggestive essay that provides context is William L. Lang, "Using and Abusing Abundance: The Western Resource Economy and the Environment," in *Historians and the American West,* ed. Michael Malone (Lincoln: University of Nebraska Press, 1983), 270–99.

17. Ernest R. Bartley, *The Tidelands Oil Controversy: A Legal and Historical Analysis* (Austin: University of Texas Press, 1953).

18. Eisenhower is quoted in Elmo R. Richardson, *Dams, Parks and Politics: Resource Development and Preservation in the Truman-Eisenhower Era* (Lexington: University of Kentucky Press, 1973), 74; see also 116–18, 144–45, 161–62, and 192–94. Hal K. Rothman, *Preserving Different Pasts: The American National Monuments* (Urbana: University of Illinois Press, 1989), is helpful; a former director of the national parks records his experiences in Conrad L. Wirth, *Parks, Politics, and the People* (Norman: University of Oklahoma Press, 1980).

19. On Hell's Canyon, see Richardson, *Dams,* 116–20, 123–26.

20. Ibid., 42–45, 79–80, 107, for a discussion of the Olympic Park controversy.

21. On Dinosaur National Monument, see Richardson, *Dams,* 59; see also ibid., 129–53, 194–97; Wallace Stegner, ed., *This Is Dinosaur* (New York: Knopf, 1956); and Clinton P. Anderson, *Outsider in the Senate* (New York: World, 1970), 238–42. Context is provided by Samuel P. Hays, *Beauty, Health, and Permanence: Environmental Politics in the United States, 1955–1985* (New York: Cambridge University Press, 1987).

22. On McKay, see Richardson, *Dams,* 83–90, 105–13, 114–28, 129–52.

23. Brower is quoted in *New York Times,* September 22, 1997; see also John C. Freemuth, *Islands under Siege: National Parks and the Politics of External Threats* (Lawrence: University Press of Kansas, 1991).

24. *New York Times,* September 22, 1997.

25. *Albuquerque Journal,* July 27, 1997.

26. Quote is in ibid.; see also *New York Times,* September 20, 22, 1997.

Chapter 5. The Military-Industrial Complex in the Cold War, 1945–1960

1. James R. Killian Jr., *Sputnik, Scientists, and Eisenhower* (Cambridge: Harvard University Press, 1977), 247.

2. See "What Is the Military-Industrial Complex?" *Time* 93 (April 11, 1969): 23.

3. James L. Clayton, "Defense Spending: Key to California's Growth," *Western Political Quarterly* 15 (June 1962): 285; 86th Cong., 1st sess., Subcommittee for Special Investigation of the Committee on Armed Services, "Employment of Retired Commissioned Officers by Department of Defense Contractors" (Washington, D.C., 1968), is informative.

4. Eisenhower's speech is from *The Economic Impact of the Cold War,* ed. James L. Clayton (New York: Harcourt Brace, 1970), 242–43; Jack Raymond, "The Growing Threat of Our Military-Industrial Complex," *Harvard Business Review* 51 (May–June 1968): 56–64, is typical of dozens of articles with a similar theme. The definitive analysis of the problem for these years is Roger Bolton, *Defense Purchases and Regional Growth* (Washington, D.C.: Brookings Institution, 1966).

5. Markusen et al., *Gunbelt,* 50, 174–210; relevant also is Ann Markusen, *Regions: The Economics and Politics of Territory* (Totowa, N.J.: Rowman and Littlefield, 1987), especially chap. 9.

6. Markusen et al., *Gunbelt,* 174–76, 181–83, 187, 191–92.

7. Quotation in Fort Carson, Public Affairs Office, *A Tradition of Victory* (Fort Carson, Colo.: Public Affairs Office, 1986), 38–39.

8. Markusen et al., *Gunbelt,* 176–83; Clayton, "Defense Spending: Key to California's Growth," 280–93; David Henry and Richard Oliver, "The Defense Buildup, 1977–1985: Effects on Production and Employment," *Monthly Labor Review* (August 1987): 3–11.

9. Leonard Arrington and George Jensen, *The Defense Industry of Utah* (Logan: Utah State University Press, 1965); Thomas G. Alexander, "Utah War Industry during World War II: A Human Impact Analysis," *Utah Historical Quarterly* 51 (Winter 1983): 72–92; James L. Clayton, "Impact of the Cold War on the Economies of California and Utah, 1946–1965," *Pacific Historical Review* 36 (November 1967): 449–73.

10. Lotchin, *Fortress California,* is a cogent analysis.

11. H. L. Nieburg, *In the Name of Science* (Chicago: Quadrangle Books, 1966), reprinted in Clayton, ed., *Economic Impact of the Cold War,* 130, 164.

12. Rogers and Larsen, *Silicon Valley Fever,* 230–51.

13. Martin J. Schiesl, "Airplanes to Aerospace: Defense Spending and Economic Growth in the Los Angeles Region, 1945–60," in *The Martial Metropolis,* ed. Roger W. Lotchin (New York: Praeger, 1984), 135–50, 181–88; G. R. Simonson, "The Demand for Aircraft and the Aircraft Industry, 1907–1958," *Journal of Economic History* 20 (September 1960): 361–82.

14. Harold Mansfield, *Vision: A Saga of the Sky* (New York: Duell, Sloan, and Pearce, 1956), 316–25; Gerald B. Nelson, *The Life and Times of an American City* (New York: Knopf, 1977), 39–42; William A. Schoeneberger, *California Wings: A History of Aviation in the Golden State* (Woodland Hills, Calif.: Windsor, 1984).

15. Mansfield, *Vision,* 183, 263–64, 314–15, 342; Markusen et al., *Gunbelt,* 165, 168–71, on Wichita; and Leonard Arrington and Jon G. Perry, "Utah's Spectacular Missiles Industry: Its History and Impact," *Utah Historical Quarterly* 30 (Winter 1962): 3–39.

16. On Colorado Springs, see Marshall Sprague, *Newport in the Rockies* (Chicago: Swallow Press, 1971); Amanda Ellis, *The Colorado Springs Story,* 9th rev. ed. (Colorado Springs: House of San Juan, 1977); and Markusen et al., *Gunbelt,* 174–210.

17. Patrick Moynihan, "State vs. Academe," *Harper's* 261 (December 1980): 31–36.

18. Stuart W. Leslie, *The Cold War and American Science: The Military-Industrial-Academic Complex at MIT and Stanford* (New York: Columbia University Press, 1993); Roger L. Geiger, *Research and Relevant Knowledge: American Research Universities since World War II* (New York: Oxford University Press, 1993).

19. Bolton, *Defense Purchases,* 117–24; Clayton, "Defense Spending: Key to California's Growth," 280, 289–91.

20. Robert S. McNamara, "Decision Making in the Defense Department," *Vital Speeches of the Day* 29 (June 1, 1963): 508–12.

21. Murray Weidenbaum, "The Transferability of Defense Industry Resources to Civilian Uses," in *Convertability of Space and Defense Resources to Civilian Needs: A Search for New Employment Potentials,* 89th Cong., 2d sess., Senate Committee on Labor and Public Welfare, Subcommittee on Employment and Manpower (Washington, D.C.: Government Printing Office, 1964), 848–55; Seymour Melman, *Our Depleted Society* (New York: Holt, Rinehart and Winston, 1965).

22. Robert A. Solo, "Gearing Military R & D to Economic Growth," *Harvard Business Review* 40 (November–December, 1962): 49–54; John H. Rubel, "Military R & D: The Most Fruitful Source of Long Term Growth," in Clayton, ed., *Economic Impact,* 147–57.

23. See Clayton, "Impact of the Cold War on the Economies of California and Utah."

Chapter 6. A Period of Transition, 1960–1973

1. The term *Sunbelt* was first used by Kevin Phillips, *The Emerging Republican Majority* (New Rochelle, N.Y.: Arlington House, 1969); quotation is from *New York Times,* February 8, 1976; see also Kirkpatrick Sale, *Power Shift: The Rise of the Southern Rim and Its Challenge to the Eastern Establishment* (New York: Random House, 1975); Carl Abbott, "New West, New South, New Region: The Discovery of the Sunbelt," in *Searching for the Sunbelt,* ed. Raymond Mohl (Knoxville: University of Tennessee Press, 1990), 7–24.

2. Abbott, *Metropolitan Frontier* (Tucson: University of Arizona Press, 1993), 57–78.

3. Mel Scott, *The San Francisco Bay Area: A Metropolis in Perspective* (Berkeley: University of California Press, 1959), 261; Abbott, *Metropolitan Frontier,* 46–47.

4. Rogers and Larsen, *Silicon Valley Fever,* 25–26, 37–38, 103–21.

5. Critics include Paul S. Taylor, *Essays on Land, Water and the Law in California* (New York: Arno Press, 1979); Edward Abbey, "Even the Bad Guys Wear White Hats: Cowboys, Ranchers, and the Ruin of the West," *Harper's* 272 (January 1986): 51–55; and Peggy F. Bartlett, *American Dreams, Rural Realities: Family Farms in Crisis* (Chapel Hill: University of North Carolina Press, 1993).

6. Philip Fradkin, *A River No More: The Colorado River and the West* (New York: Knopf, 1981); Harrison C. Dunning, "Dam Fights and Water Policy in California," *Journal of the West* 29 (July 1990): 14–27; Berkman and Viscusi, *Damming the West,* passim.

7. Wallace Stegner, "Myths of the Western Dams: The Disadvantages Often Outweigh the Benefits," *Saturday Review of Literature* 48 (October 23, 1965): 29–31.

8. Melosi, *Coping with Abundance,* 268–69; *New York Times,* January 30, 1969.

9. Melosi, *Coping with Abundance,* 301–4; Gomez, *Four Corners,* 48–49; Richard H. K. Vietor, *Environmental Politics and the Coal Coalition* (College Station: Texas A&M University Press, 1980). Wilbur Jacobs in *On Turner's Trail: 100 Years of Writing Western History* (Lawrence: University Press of Kansas, 1994), 316–17, n. 4, suggests that federal intimidation of Indians in the Four Corners area led them to sign coal leases.

10. William S. Bryans, "Coal Mining in Twentieth Century Wyoming: A Brief History," *Journal of the West* 21 (October 1982): 24–35; A. Dudley Gardner and Verla R. Flores, *Forgotten Frontier: A History of Wyoming Coal Mining* (Boulder: Westview Press, 1989); see also Lynton R. Hayes, *Energy, Economic Growth, and Regionalism in the West* (Albuquerque: University of New Mexico Press, 1980).

11. Marjane Ambler, *Breaking the Iron Bonds: Indian Control of Energy Development* (Lawrence: University Press of Kansas, 1990); Phil Reno, "Planning Indian Economic Development," in *Economic Development in American Indian Reservations,* University of New Mexico, Native American Studies Development Series 1 (Albuquerque: Native American Studies, 1979); C. Mathew Snipp, ed., *Public Policy Impacts on American Indian Economic Development* (Albuquerque: Native American Studies, 1988), 1–22.

12. Allen V. Kneese and F. Lee Brown, *The Southwest under Stress: National Resource Development Issues in a Regional Setting* (Baltimore: Johns Hopkins University Press, 1981), 183–208, a study performed under the aegis of Resources for the Future.

13. Larry W. Burt, "Western Tribes and Balance Sheets: Business Development Programs in the 1960s and 1970s," *Western Historical Quarterly* 23 (November 1992): 475–95; Keith La Verne Fay, "Industrial Development and Its Impact on American Indian Reservation Economic Policies" (Ph.D. diss., American University, 1973), 1–105.

14. Individual company histories, compiled from BIA records, are summarized in Fay, "Industrial Development," 268–371; quotation is from 237.

15. Kneese and Brown, *Southwest under Stress,* 209–32; Fay, "Industrial Development," 239–48.

16. On timber, see Fay, "Industrial Development," 232, 294–96; Snipp, ed., *Public Policy Impacts,* 7; and Sar A. Levitan and William B. Johnston, *Indian Giving: Federal Programs for Native Americans* (Baltimore: Johns Hopkins University Press, 1975), for the broader context.

17. Kneese and Brown, *Southwest under Stress,* 7–24, 209–29.

18. Willow Roberts, *Stokes Carson: Twentieth Century Trading on the Navajo Reservation* (Albuquerque: University of New Mexico Press, 1987); *Albuquerque Journal,* August 3, 1997.

19. Niles Hansen, *The Border Economy: Regional Development in the Southwest* (Austin: University of Texas Press, 1981), 77, 97–100, 156–57, 161, 183; Robert B. South, "Transnational Maquiladora Location," *Annals of the Association of American Geographers* 80 (December 1990): 549–70; Lawrence A. Herzog, *Where North Meets South: Cities, Space, and Politics on the United States–Mexico Border* (Austin: University of Texas Press, 1990).

20. Peter Nabokov, *Tijerina and the Courthouse Raid* (Berkeley: Ramparts Press, 1970); Richard Gardner, *Grito! Reies Tijerina and the New Mexico Land Grant War of 1967* (Indianapolis: Bobbs Merrill, 1970).

21. The problems are discussed in Paul Kutsche and John R. Van Ness, *Cañones: Values Crisis and Survival in a Northern New Mexico Village* (Albuquerque: University of New Mexico Press, 1981).

Chapter 7. The Era of Deindustrialization, 1973–2000

1. Lloyd Rodwin, "Deindustrialization and Regeneration," in *Deindustrialization and Regional Economic Transformation: The Experience of the United States,* ed. Lloyd Rodwin and Hidehiko Sazanami (Boston: Unwin Hyman, 1989), 15.

2. Franklin Tugwell, *The Energy Crisis and the American Political Economy* (Palo Alto: Stanford University Press, 1988), 39–59, 97–107; Thomas C. Schelling, *Thinking Through the Energy Problem* (Washington, D.C.: Committee for Economic Development, 1979), 14–15; see also John Blair, *The Control of Oil* (New York: Random House, 1976), chap. 11; and Dankwart Rustow, *Oil and Turmoil: America Faces OPEC and the Middle East* (New York: Norton, 1982), chap. 5.

3. Tugwell, *Energy Crisis,* 101, 104, 168, 196; Les Gapay, "Elusive Goal: U.S. Self Sufficiency in Energy Is Unlikely, Experts Say," *Wall Street Journal,* July 22, 1974; quote in Hayes, *Energy,* 26–27; *The National Energy Plan* (Washington, D.C.: Government Printing Office, 1977).

4. Tugwell, *Energy Crisis,* 23–38, 103, 140; Hayes, *Energy,* 13–15, 20–27. An example of the impact of economic waves on institutions is Lynton K. Caldwell, "Environmental Policy as a Catalyst of Institutional Change," *American Behavioral Scientist* (May–June 1974): 711–30.

5. An excellent detailed account of the program is David Leo Weimer, *The Strategic Petroleum Reserve* (Westport, Conn.: Greenwood Press, 1982).

6. Thadis W. Box, *Rehabilitation Potentials of Western Coal Lands* (Cambridge, Mass.: Ballinger, 1974), 22; S. David Freeman, *Energy: The New Era* (New York: Vintage Books, 1974), 77; see also Frederick J. Athearn, "Black Diamonds: A History of Federal Coal Policy in the Western United States, 1862–1981," *Journal of the West* 21 (October 1982): 44–50.

7. Jimmy Carter, *Keeping Faith: Memoirs of a President* (New York: Bantam Books, 1982), 91–124; see also Cranford Goodwin, *Energy Policy in Perspective: Today's Problems, Yesterday's Solutions* (Washington, D.C.: Brookings Institution, 1981).

8. Ann Pelham, *Energy Policy,* 2d ed. (Washington, D.C.: Congressional Quarterly Press, 1981), 208, 221–25; Tugwell, *Energy Crisis,* 121–27, 136; Carter, *Memoirs,* 114; Hayes, *Energy,* 175.

9. Andrew Gulliford, *Boomtown Blues: Colorado Oil Shale, 1885–1985* (Niwot: University Press of Colorado, 1989), 1–44; quote is from Jimmy Carter, "The Nation's Economy," *Vital Speeches of the Day* 46 (March 14, 1980): 354–57.

10. The story is well told in Gulliford, *Boomtown Blues,* 85–118; see also Paul L. Russell, *History of Western Oil Shale* (East Brunswick, N.J.: Center for Professional Advancement, 1980).

11. On Exxon, see Gulliford, *Boomtown Blues,* 119–94; Kathy Kellogg Peterson, ed., *Oil Shale: The Environmental Challenges* (Golden: Colorado School of Mines Press, 1981); James L. Regens, Robert W. Rycroft, and Gregory A. Daneke, eds., *Energy and the Western United States* (New York: Praeger, 1982), 49–67. See also Eleanor Johnson Tracy, "Exxon's Abrupt Exit from Shale," *Fortune,* May 31, 1982, 106; *New York Times,* May 3, 9, 1982.

12. Don E. Kash and Robert W. Rycroft, *U.S. Energy Policy: Crisis and Complacency* (Norman: University of Oklahoma Press, 1984); Hayes, *Energy,* 75–122, 175.

13. James Leighland and Robert Land, *WP$$: Who Is to Blame for the WPPSS Disaster?* (Cambridge, Mass.: Ballinger, 1986), 1–22; see also Kai N. Lee, Donna Lee Klemka, and Marion E. Marts, *Electric Power and the Future of the Pacific Northwest* (Seattle: University of Washington Press, 1980); and David Myhra, *Whoops/WPPSS: Washington Public Power Supply System Nuclear Plants* (Jefferson, N.C.: McFarland, 1984).

14. Leighland and Land, *WP$$,* 23–230, provides an excellent account of the complexities. Also see "The Fallout from Whoops," *Business Week,* July 11,1983, 80–87; Michael C. Blumm, "The Northwest's Hydroelectric Heritage: Prologue to the Pacific Northwest Power Planning and Conservation Act," *Washington Law Review* 58 (April 1983): 175–244.

15. Michael C. Robinson, *Water for the West: The Bureau of Reclamation, 1902–1977* (Chicago: Public Works Historical Society, 1979); Taylor, *Land, Water,* passim; Worster, *Rivers of Empire,* 301–8.

16. Peter Wiley and Robert Gottlieb, *Empires in the Sun: The Rise of the New American West* (New York: Putnam, 1982), 54–64; Richard D. Lamm and G. Michael McCarthy, *The Angry West: A Vulnerable Land and Its Future* (Boston: Houghton Mifflin, 1982); Paul W. Gates, "The Intermountain West against Itself," *Arizona and the West* 27 (Autumn 1985): 205–36.

17. *New York Times,* October 6, 1997.

18. *New York Times,* September 20, 1997.

19. The Sagebrush Rebellion is covered in detail by C. Brant Short, *Ronald Reagan and the Public Lands: America's Conservation Debate, 1979–1984* (College Station: Texas A&M University Press, 1989). See also Paul W. Gates, "Pressure Groups and Recent Land Policies," *Agricultural History* 55 (April 1981): 103–27; and William L. Graf, *Wilderness Preservation and the Sagebrush Rebellions* (Savage, Md.: Rowman and Littlefield, 1990).

20. Edmund Beard, *Developing the ICBM: A Study in Bureaucratic Politics* (New York: Columbia University Press, 1976); Jack Manno, *Arming the Heavens: The Hidden Military Agenda for Space* (New York: Dodd, Mead, 1984); Peter Hall, "The Creation of the American Aerospace Complex, 1955–65: A Study in

Industrial Inertia," in *Defence Expenditures and Regional Development,* ed. Michael Breheny (London: Mansell, 1988), 102–20; and Peter Galison and Bruce Hevly, eds., *Big Science: The Growth of Large-Scale Research* (Stanford: Stanford University Press, 1992), are only a few of the books in the large literature dealing with the subject.

21. 100th Cong., 1st sess., House Committee on Armed Services, Report of the Subcommittee on Research and Development and Subcommittee on Procurement and Military Nuclear Systems, *MX Rail Garrison and Small ICBM: A Program Review,* Committee Print no. 18 (Washington, D.C.: Government Printing Office, 1988), 1–17; *New York Times,* December 15, 1997.

22. *New York Times,* August 25, 1997; for earlier period, see Necah Stewart Furman, *Sandia National Laboratories: The Postwar Decade* (Albuquerque: University of New Mexico Press, 1990).

23. For general background, see H. Brett Melendy, *Asians in America: Filipinos, Koreans, and East Indians* (Boston: Twayne, 1977).

24. Ibid., 95–110; Luciano Mangiafico, *Contemporary American Immigrants: Patterns of Filipino, Korean, and Chinese Settlement in the United States* (New York: Praeger, 1988), 41–76.

25. Mangiafico, *Contemporary American Immigrants,* 77–110, 149–94.

26. Gail Paradise Kelly, *From Vietnam to America* (Boulder: Westview Press, 1977), 39–60, 163–206; Darrel Montero, *Vietnamese Americans: Patterns of Resettlement and Socioeconomic Adaptation in the United States* (Boulder: Westview Press, 1979): 21–72.

27. Shih-Shan Henry Tsai, *The Chinese Experience in America* (Bloomington: Indiana University Press, 1986), 151–71; Ivan Light, *Ethnic Enterprise in America* (Berkeley: University of California Press, 1972), 1–18, 45–100.

28. Joseph A. Schumpeter, *The Theory of Economic Development* (New York: Oxford University Press, 1961), 213, 223; first published in 1911.

Afterword

1. *New York Times,* May 28, 1997.

The economic history of the twentieth-century West still has many gaps, although the existing literature is extensive. An excellent bibliographic guide is Richard W. Etulain, comp., *The American West in the Twentieth Century: A Bibliography* (Norman: University of Oklahoma Press, 1994), which has an informative section on business and economic history. A glimpse of topics that deserve more attention is provided by my essay in Gerald D. Nash and Richard W. Etulain, eds., *Researching Western History* (Albuquerque: University of New Mexico Press, 1997). Useful bibliographical references are also provided in Gene Gressley, "Colonialism: A Western Complaint," *Pacific Northwest Quarterly* 54 (January 1963): 1–8; and William G. Robbins, "'The Plundered

Bibliographic Essay

Province' Thesis and the Recent Historiography of the American West," *Pacific Historical Review* 55 (November 1986): 577–97.

Journalists have had much more interest than historians in the broad themes of western economic history. Although they have not focused exclusively on the economy, they have tried to assess it in a broader social and cultural context. Their works include Neil Morgan, *Westward Tilt: The American West Today* (New York: Random House, 1963); Kirkpatrick Sale, *Power Shift: The Rise of the Southern Rim and Its Challenge to the Eastern Establishment* (New York: Random House, 1975); and Peter Wiley and Robert Gottlieb, *Empires in the Sun: The Rise of the New American West* (New York: Putnam, 1982). An outstanding collection of essays has been gathered by R. Douglas Hurt, ed., *The Rural West since World War II* (Lawrence: University Press of Kansas, 1998). Many of the contributions deal with economic issues, especially agriculture. Brief summaries of economic trends can be found in Michael Malone and Richard W. Etulain, *The American West: A Twentieth Century History* (Lincoln: University of Nebraska Press, 1989); and Gerald D. Nash, *The American West in the Twentieth Century* (Albuquerque: University of New Mexico Press, 1977). Suggestive essays are also found in Gerald D. Nash and Richard W. Etulain, eds., *The Twentieth Century West: Historical Interpretations* (Albuquerque: University of New Mexico Press, 1989).

Chapter 1. A Colonial Landscape, 1900–1929

The economic development of the West during the first three decades of the twentieth century must be pieced together from a variety of writings. An overview that provides economic analysis is Kerry Ann Odell, "The Integration of Regional and Interregional Capital Markets: Evidence from the Pacific Coast States, 1883–1913," *Journal of Economic History* 49 (June 1989): 297–310. On the influence of the Panama Canal on the western economy, see G. Allen Greb, "Opening a New Frontier: San Francisco, Los Angeles, and the Panama Canal, 1900–1914," *Pacific Historical Review* 47 (August 1978): 405–24. General works touching on the canal include David McCullough, *The Path between the Seas: The Creation of the Panama Canal* (New York: Simon and Schuster, 1978), which places the waterway in the broad context of western development. Still useful is the older work of John H. Kemble, *The Panama Route,*

1848–1869 (Berkeley: University of California Press, 1943), because it places the enthusiasm of westerners for the canal at the opening of the twentieth century in historical perspective. That enthusiasm was strongly reflected in the expositions held by San Diego and San Francisco to celebrate the completion of the waterway in 1915 and 1916. The most concise brief accounts of these fairs are in John Findling, ed., *Historical Dictionary of World's Fairs and Expositions, 1851–1988* (Westport, Conn.: Greenwood Press, 1990), 42–53, 301–303. See also Richard Reinhart, "The Other Fair," *American Heritage* 40 (May–June 1989): 42–53.

183

Although the automobile and airplane have had a revolutionary effect on the twentieth-century West, the literature concerning their influence is not extensive. Their impact is touched on in John B. Rae, *The Road and the Car in American Life* (Cambridge: MIT Press, 1971); and in Rae's later work, *The American Automobile Industry* (Boston: Twayne, 1984). The important influence of engineers in developing the western road system is highlighted in Bruce Seely, *Building the American Highway System: Engineers as Policy Makers* (Philadelphia: Temple University Press, 1987). The dramatic role of the Lincoln Highway movement in raising western consciousness about automobiles is highlighted in Drake Hokanson, *The Lincoln Highway: Main Street across America* (Iowa City: University of Iowa Press, 1988). State historical journals in the trans-Mississippi West contain many articles about local conditions in the beginning of the automobile age. See William P. Corbett, "Men, Mud, and Mules: The Good Roads Movement in Oklahoma, 1900–1910," *Chronicles of Oklahoma* 58 (Summer 1980): 133–50; and Charles E. Dickson, "Prosperity Rides on Rubber Tires: The Impact of the Automobile on Minot during the 1920s," *North Dakota History* 53 (Summer 1986): 14–23. Relevant also is Mark S. Foster, *From Streetcar to Superhighway: American City Planners and Urban Transportation, 1900–1940* (Philadelphia: Temple University Press, 1981), which, while it does not focus on the West, contains material of interest. Less has been written on the role of airplanes in the West. Consult "Aviation in the West," a special issue of the *Journal of the West* 30 (January 1991); and Arlene Elliott, "The Rise of Aeronautics in California, 1849–1940," *Southern California Quarterly* 52 (March 1970): 1–32. Of broader scope is Joseph Corn, *The Winged Gospel: America's Romance with Aviation, 1900–1950* (New York: Oxford University Press, 1983).

More has been written about water in the West during these years. Donald J. Pisani, *From the Family Farm to Agribusiness: The Irrigation Crusade in California and the West, 1850–1931* (Berkeley: University of California Press, 1984), provides excellent coverage of that subject. In "State vs. Nation: Federal Reclamation and Water Rights in the Progressive Era," *Pacific Historical Review* 51 (August 1982): 265–82, Pisani argues for the importance of state water policies, in contrast to Donald Worster, who in *Rivers of Empire: Water, Aridity, and the Growth of the American West* (New York: Pantheon Books, 1986) makes claims for the primacy of federal legislation. An exhaustive study of water in one state is Ira G. Clark, *Water in New Mexico: A History of Its Management and Use* (Albuquerque: University of New Mexico Press, 1987). The significance of the broad impact of water on economic development is detailed in F. Lee Brown et al., *Water and Poverty in the Southwest* (Tucson: University of Arizona Press, 1987).

Much of the story of industries in the West during the Progressive Era (1900–17) still needs to be told. One of the pioneers in emphasizing the importance of tourism is Earl Pomeroy, *In Search of the Golden West: The Tourist in Western America* (New York: Knopf, 1957). For these years Al Runte, *National Parks: The American Experience* (Lincoln: University of Nebraska Press, 1987), provides a good introduction; as does Hal K. Rothman, *Preserving Different Pasts: The American National Monuments* (Urbana: University of Illinois Press, 1989), both of which consider the economic as well as environmental influences of national parks and monuments. An eloquent statement about the appeal of such sites is Wallace Stegner, *The American West as Living Space* (Ann Arbor: University of Michigan Press, 1987). The impact of the military establishment on the western economy is impressively documented by Roger Lotchin in *Fortress California, 1910–1961: From Warfare to Welfare* (New York: Oxford University Press, 1992), especially in reference to naval expansion and air power. The oil industry can be followed in various works such as Kenny A. Franks, *The Oklahoma Petroleum Industry* (Norman: University of Oklahoma Press, 1980); and the still useful work by Carl Coke Rister, *Oil! Titan of the Southwest* (Norman: University of Oklahoma Press, 1949). For California, the history of this period can be gleaned in exhaustive detail from Gerald T. White, *Formative Years in the Far West: A History of*

Standard Oil of California and Predecessors through 1919 (New York: Appleton-Century-Crofts, 1962).

The impact of World War I on the western economy has attracted relatively little attention. Its influence on major industries of the time, such as agriculture, cattle, lumbering, shipbuilding and aircraft manufactures, must be pieced together from scattered studies. Informative are Mansel G. Blackford, *The Politics of Business in California, 1890–1920* (Columbus: Ohio State University Press, 1977); and Frank L. Kidner, *California Business Cycles* (Berkeley: University of California Press, 1946). A suggestive piece is Peter Neuschul, "Seaweed for War: California's World War I Kelp Industry," *Technology and Culture* 30 (July 1989): 561–83. Some discussion of the aircraft industry in the West during the war years is in Edwin H. Rutkowski, *The Politics of Military Aviation Procurement, 1926–1934* (Columbus: Ohio State University Press, 1966); and Jacob A. Vander Meulen, *Building an American Military Industry* (Lawrence: University Press of Kansas, 1991). Informative on agriculture is Joan Jensen, "Canning Comes to New Mexico: Women and the Agricultural Extension Service, 1914–1919," *New Mexico Historical Review* 57 (October 1982): 361–86. Labor disputes in wartime have attracted attention from historians including Melvyn Dubofsky, *We Shall Be All: A History of the Industrial Workers of the World* (Chicago: Quadrangle Books, 1969), which covers the wartime strikes in the copper mines of Arizona. Philip Taft, "The Bisbee Deportation," *Labor History* 13 (Winter 1972): 3–40, provides an additional analysis of that event. Also see Benjamin G. Rader, "The Montana Lumber Strike of 1917," *Pacific Historical Review* 36 (May 1967): 189–207. David M. Emmons, *The Butte Irish: Class and Ethnicity in an American Town, 1875–1925* (Urbana: University of Illinois Press, 1989), provides a fuller context. On lumber strikes in the Pacific Northwest, Harold M. Hyman, *Soldiers and Spruce: Origins of the Loyal Legion of Loggers and Lumbermen* (Los Angeles: University of California Institute of Industrial Relations, 1963); and Robert L. Tyler, *Rebels of the Woods: The I.W.W. in the Pacific Northwest* (Eugene: University of Oregon Books, 1967), are informative. But the economic history of the West in the 1920s is spotty. Much can be learned from biographies of entrepreneurs; for example, William B. Friedricks, "A Metropolitan Entrepreneur par Excellence: Henry E. Huntington and the Growth of

Southern California, 1898–1927," *Business History Review* 63 (Summer 1989): 329–55; Felice A. Bonadio, *A. P. Giannini* (Berkeley: University of California Press, 1994); and the broader account in Gerald D. Nash, *A. P. Giannini and the Bank of America* (Norman: University of Oklahoma Press, 1992). Water development has received some attention, notably from Norris Hundley in *Water and the West: The Colorado River Compact and the Politics of Water in the American West* (Berkeley: University of California Press, 1975); Beverly Moeller, *Phil Swing and Boulder Dam* (Berkeley: University of California Press, 1971); and Joseph E. Stevens, *Hoover Dam: An American Adventure* (Norman: University of Oklahoma Press, 1988).

The influence of women in the western economy of the 1920s is an intriguing subject. During that decade the economy throughout the United States underwent what one observer has described as feminization. The growth of service industries, financial services, and health care offered greater job opportunities for women than the heavy-goods industries had provided a generation or two earlier. Some of the writings on this theme include Paula M. Bauman, "Single Women Homesteaders in Wyoming, 1880–1930," *Annals of Wyoming* 58 (Spring 1986): 39–53; Grace Dobler, "Oil Field Camp Wives and Mothers," *Kansas History* 10 (Spring 1987): 10–42; Cornelia Butler Flora and Jan L. Flora, "Structure of Agriculture and Women's Culture in the Great Plains," *Great Plains Quarterly* 8 (Fall 1988): 195–205. Articles about women in other states include Mary W. M. Hargreaves, "Women in the Agricultural Settlement of the Northern Great Plains," *Agricultural History* 50 (January 1976): 179–89; and Joan M. Jensen, "I've Worked, I'm Not Afraid of Work: Farm Women in New Mexico, 1920–1940," *New Mexico Historical Review* 61 (January 1986): 27–52.

Chapter 2. Changing the Federal Landscape in the Great Depression, 1929–1940

The most useful general introduction to the West in the 1930s is Richard Lowitt, *The New Deal and the West* (Bloomington: Indiana University Press, 1984), which focuses mainly on federal policy affecting natural resources. Those interested in other aspects of western history during this period need to consult specialized studies and works detailing the federal impact on the states. These include Michael Malone, *C. Ben Ross and the New Deal in Idaho* (Seattle: University of Washington Press, 1970); a special issue of the *Pacific Historical Review*, vol. 38 (August 1969); and James F. Wickens, *Colorado in the Great Depression* (New York: Garland, 1979). A regional approach is taken by three excellent studies of the Dust Bowl: Donald Worster, *Dust Bowl* (New York: Oxford University Press, 1979); Paul Bonnifield, *The Dust Bowl* (Albuquerque: University of New Mexico Press, 1979); and R. Douglas Hurt, *The Dust Bowl* (Chicago: Nelson-Hall, 1981).

On New Deal farm programs in the West, Richard S. Kirkendall, *Social Scientists and Farm Politics in the Age of Roosevelt* (Columbia: University of Missouri Press, 1966), is helpful. Gilbert Fite, *George N. Peek and the Fight for Farm Parity* (Norman: University of Oklahoma Press, 1954), explains many of the complexities of the western farm dilemma. An outstanding brief summary is Theodore Saloutos, "The New Deal and Farm Policy in the Great Plains," *Agricultural History* 43 (July 1969): 344–55. The administration of the Taylor Grazing Act is the prime concern of Phillip O. Foss, *Politics and Grass* (Seattle: University of Washington Press, 1960). Very critical of federal policies is William Voigt Jr., *Grazing Lands and Misuse by Industry and Government* (New Brunswick: Rutgers University Press, 1976). Douglas Helms, "Conserving the Plains: The Soil Conservation Service in the Great Plains," *Agricultural History* 64 (Spring 1990): 58–73, provides a concise summary; while C. Roger Lambert, "The Drought Cattle Purchase 1934–1935: Problems and Complaints," *Agricultural History* 45 (April, 1971): 85–93, analyzes that program satisfactorily. William H. Droze, *Trees, Prairies and People: A History of Tree Planting in the Plains States* (Denton: Texas Women's University Press, 1977), discusses the varied aspects of one of President Roosevelt's favorite programs.

The literature on water and power is more developed. A brief summary is provided by Donald C. Swain, "The Bureau of Reclamation and the New Deal, 1933–1940," *Pacific Northwest Quarterly* 61 (July 1970): 137–46. On the Big Thompson project, Oliver Knight, "Correcting Nature's Error: The Colorado–Big Thompson Project," *Reclamation Era* 30 (September 1949): 267–69, is a good brief statement. The best recent study is Daniel Tyler, *The Last Water Hole in the West: The Colorado Big Thompson Project and the Northern Colorado River Conservancy District* (Niwot: University Press of Colorado, 1992). The Columbia River projects are ably described by Charles McKinley in *Uncle Sam in the Pacific Northwest* (Berkeley: University of California Press, 1952); while Philip Funigiello, "The Bonneville Power Administration and the New Deal," *Prologue* 5 (Summer 1973): 89–97, skillfully summarizes main trends. See also Philip Funigiello, *Toward a National Power Policy: The New Deal and the Electric Utility Industry, 1933–1941* (Pittsburgh: University of Pittsburgh Press, 1974). A well-written popular account is Stewart H. Holbrook, *The Columbia River* (New York: Holt, Rinehart and Winston, 1965); the broad context is discussed in Richard White, *The Organic Machine: The Changing World of Indians and Whites, Salmon, and Energy on the Columbia River* (New York: Hill and Wang, 1995). On the Grand Coulee Dam, Paul C. Pitzer, *Harnessing a Dream* (Pullman: Washington State University Press, 1994), is informative. On dams in the Missouri basin, Marion E. Ridgway, *The Missouri Basin's Pick-Sloan Plan* (Urbana: University of Illinois Press, 1955); and Michael L. Lawson, *Damned Indians: The Pick-Sloan Plan and the Missouri River Sioux, 1944–1980* (Norman: University of Oklahoma Press, 1982), are helpful. The Central Valley project has attracted much attention. An older but still useful book is Robert de Roos, *Thirsty Land: The Story of the Central Valley Project* (Stanford: Stanford University Press, 1948). A more detailed work that carries the story forward is Charles E. Coate, "Water, Power, and Politics in the Central Valley Project, 1933–1967" (Ph.D. diss., University of California, Berkeley, 1969). Lawrence Lee details the political fallout from the project in "California Water Politics: Opposition to the CVP, 1944–1980," *Agricultural History* 54 (July 1980): 402–23. Also see Clayton R. Koppes, "Public Water, Private Land: Origins of the Acreage Limitation Controversy, 1933–1953," *Pacific Historical Review* 47 (November 1978): 607–36. The project is evaluated in its broader historical context by Norris Hundley Jr. in "California's Original Waterscape: Harmony and Manipulation," *California History* 66 (March 1987), 2–11, 69–70. Natural resources policies in the 1930s are discussed in scattered studies. Joe S. Bain, *The Economics of the Pacific Coast Petroleum Industry* (Berkeley: University of California Press, 1945), pt. 2, provides useful statistical data about the industry; Gerald D. Nash, *U.S. Oil Policy, 1890–1964: Business and Government in Twentieth Century America* (Pittsburgh: University of Pittsburgh Press, 1968), discusses the impact of federal policies on western states. Informative on federal policies in the lumber industry are William G. Robbins, *Lumberjacks and Legislators: Political Economy of the U.S. Lumber Industry, 1890–1941* (College Station: Texas A&M University Press, 1982); and Robbins, "The Great Experiment in Industrial Self-Government: The Lumber Industry and the National Recovery Administration," *Journal of Forest History* 25 (July 1981): 128–43. The controversies in the Pacific Northwest are best described in Elmo R. Richardson, *BLM's Billion-Dollar Checkerboard: Managing the O & C Lands* (Santa Cruz: Forest History Society, 1980); and in "Olympic National Park: Twenty Years of Controversy," *Forest History* 12 (April 1968): 6–15. The impact of the Forest Service is competently assessed in Harold K. Steen, *The U.S. Forest Service: A History* (Seattle: University of Washington Press, 1976).

The history of business in the West during the 1930s is an underdeveloped area. Indispensable are Leonard J. Arrington, "The New Deal in the West: A Preliminary Statistical Inquiry," *Pacific Historical Review* 38 (August 1969): 311–16; and Lynn P. Doti and Larry Schweikart, *Banking in the American West: From the Gold Rush to Deregulation* (Norman: University of Oklahoma Press, 1991). The latter work includes an excellent chapter on this period.

The economic role of minorities is scrutinized in various works. A succinct analysis of Hispanics in New Mexico is provided in David Dinwoodie, "Indians, Hispanics, and Land Reform: A New Deal Struggle in New Mexico," *Western Historical Quarterly* 17 (July 1986): 291–323; and in the brilliant study by Suzanne Forrest, *The Preservation of the Village: New Mexico's Hispanics and the New Deal* (Albuquerque: University of New Mexico Press, 1989). The older work by Paul S. Taylor, *Mexican Labor in the United States,* 3 vols. (Berkeley: University of California Press, 1928–1934), is still informative. The economic tribulations of western Indians can be followed in Donald Parman, *The Navajos and the New Deal* (New Haven: Yale University Press, 1976); and Lawrence C. Kelly, *The Assault on Assimilation: John Collier and the Origins of Indian Policy Reform* (Albuquerque: University of New Mexico Press, 1983). The experience of

African Americans is ably described in Quintard Taylor, *In Search of the Racial Frontier: African Americans in the American West, 1528–1990* (New York: Norton, 1998). Other relevant works include Albert Broussard, *Black San Francisco: The Struggle for Racial Equality in the West, 1900–1954* (Lawrence: University Press of Kansas, 1993). A work that has some economic relevance is Olen Cole Jr., "Black Youth in the Program of the Civilian Conservation Corps for California, 1933–1942" (Ph.D. diss., University of North Carolina, 1986); also see Dennis Mihelich, "The Lincoln Urban League: The Travail of Depression and War," *Nebraska History* 70 (Winter 1989): 303–16. The activities of a remarkable African American business entrepreneur are detailed in Jonathan D. Greenberg, *Staking a Claim: Jake Simmons and the Making of an African American Oil Dynasty* (New York: Atheneum, 1990). Most Asian Americans lived on the Pacific coast during this period. Some aspects of their economic status are revealed in John Modell, *The Economics and Politics of Racial Accommodation: The Japanese of Los Angeles, 1900–1942* (Urbana: University of Illinois Press, 1977); and Roger Daniels, "Japanese America, 1930–1941: An Ethnic Community in the Great Depression," *Journal of the West* 24 (October 1985): 35–49. Robert Higgs, "Landless by Law: Japanese Immigrants in California Agriculture to 1941," *Journal of Economic History* 38 (March 1978): 205–25, provides additional perspective.

The literature on women in the western workforce is scattered. See Sheilah Kishler Bennett and Glen H. Elder Jr., "Women's Work in the Family Economy: A Study of Depression Hardship in Women's Lives," *Journal of Family History* 4 (Summer 1979): 153–76. Books with special reference to the West include Sarah Deutsch, *No Separate Refuge: Culture, Class, and Gender on an Anglo-Hispanic Frontier in the American Southwest, 1880–1940* (New York: Oxford University Press, 1987); Vicky L. Ruiz, *Cannery Women, Cannery Lives: Mexican Women, Unionization, and the California Food Processing Industry, 1930–1950* (Albuquerque: University of New Mexico Press, 1987); and Ruiz, *From out of the Shadows: Mexican Women in Twentieth Century America* (New York: Oxford University Press, 1998), stressing social conditions. Laurie K. Mercier, "Women's Economic Role in Montana Agriculture: You Had to Make Every Minute Count," *Montana: The Magazine of Western History* 38 (Autumn 1988): 50–61; Dorothy Schwieder, "South Dakota Farm Women in the Great

Depression," *Journal of the West* 24 (October 1985): 6–18; Schwieder and Deborah Fink, "Plains Women Rural Life in the 1930s," *Great Plains Quarterly* 8 (Spring 1988): 79–88; and Miriam B. Murphy, "Women in the Utah Work Force from Statehood to World War II," *Utah Historical Quarterly* 50 (Spring 1982): 139–59, help to fill in the broader picture of the role of women in the workforce during the 1930s.

Chapter 3. Expanding the Federal Landscape in World War II, 1940–1945

The importance of World War II in transforming the West is emphasized in Gerald D. Nash, *The American West Transformed: The Impact of World War II* (Bloomington: Indiana University Press, 1985); and Nash, *World War II and the West: Reshaping the Economy* (Lincoln: University of Nebraska Press, 1990). This thesis is challenged by Roger Lotchin, "California Cities and the Hurricane of Change: World War II in the San Francisco, Los Angeles, and San Diego Metropolitan Areas," 410–24; Paul Rhode, "The Nash Thesis Revisited: An Economic Historian's View," 363–92; and Martin Schiesl, "Fortress California at War: San Francisco, Los Angeles, Oakland, and San Diego, 1941–45," 277–87, all in *Pacific Historical Review* 63. All three maintain that the influence of the war on the economy was not particularly significant. Some insights about the West can be gained from general studies such as Simon J. Kuznets, *National Product in Wartime* (New York: National Bureau of Economic Research, 1945); and Harold G. Vatter, *The U.S. Economy in World War II* (New York: Columbia University Press, 1988).

More specialized works deal with particular industries. Shipbuilding in the West is included in Frederick C. Lane, *Ships for Victory: A History of Shipbuilding under the U.S. Maritime Commission in World War II* (Baltimore: Johns Hopkins University Press, 1951). A wonderful account of Henry J. Kaiser's activities is in Mark S. Foster, *Henry J. Kaiser: Builder in the Modern American West* (Austin: University of Texas Press, 1989), which also covers steel, public works, and housing enterprises. Foster summarizes Kaiser's impact in "Giant of the West: Henry J. Kaiser and Regional Industrialization, 1930–1950," *Business History Review* 59 (Spring 1985): 1–23. Ewald T. Grether, *The Steel and Steel Using Industries of California* (Berkeley: University of California Press, 1946), provides much useful data. No one has explicitly studied the western oil industry in wartime, but helpful works include Harold F. Williamson et al., *The American Petroleum Industry,* 2 vols. (Evanston: Northwestern University Press, 1959–63); and John W. Frey and Chandler Ide, *The Petroleum Administration for War, 1941–1945* (Washington, D.C.: Government Printing Office, 1946). Federal policies toward western copper producers are treated in Robert F. Campbell, *The History of Basic Metals Price Control* (New York: Columbia University Press, 1948), particularly the Premium Price Plan. Although not focused on the West, Roland Young, *Congressional Politics in the Second World War* (New York: Columbia University Press, 1956), explains the formulation of economic policies. Federal aluminum policies are thoroughly covered in Charles M. Wiltse, *Aluminum Policies of the War Production Board and Predecessor Agencies, May 1940 to November 1945* (Washington, D.C.: Civilian Production Administration, 1946); and Charlotte F. Muller, *The Light Metals Monopoly* (New York: Columbia University Press, 1947). References to the West can be found in Tom Lilley et al., *Problems of Accelerating Aircraft Production in World War II* (Boston: Harvard Graduate School of Business Administration, 1946). See also Martin J. Schiesl, "Airplanes to Aerospace: Defense Spending and Economic Growth in the Los Angeles Region, 1945–1960," in *The Martial Metropolis,* ed. Roger Lotchin (New York: Praeger, 1984), 135–50, which briefly touches on the World War II experience. Robert J. Serling, *Legend and Legacy: The Story of Boeing and Its People* (New York: St. Martin's Press, 1992), is informative.

The economic impact of the military has been detailed for Utah more than any other state, largely due to the efforts of Leonard J. Arrington. Among his publications in this sphere are Leonard J. Arrington and Archer L. Durham, "Anchors Aweigh in Utah: The U.S. Naval Supply Depot at Clearfield, 1942–1962," *Utah Historical Society Quarterly* 31 (Spring 1963), 109–26; Arrington and Thomas G. Alexander, "Sentinels on the Desert: The Dugway Proving Ground (1942–1963) and Deseret Chemical Depot (1942–1955)," *Utah Historical Society Quarterly* 32 (Winter 1964): 32–43; Arrington and Thomas G. Alexander, "Supply Hub of the West: Defense Depot Ogden, 1941–1964," *Utah Historical Society*

Quarterly 32 (Spring 1964): 99–121; and Arrington and A. Erb Jr., "Utah's Biggest Business: Ogden Air Materiel Area at Hill Air Force Base, 1938–1965," *Utah Historical Society Quarterly* 33 (Winter 1965): 9–33. Good summaries can be found in Arrington and George Jensen, *The Defense Industry of Utah* (Logan: Utah State University Press, 1965); Arrington and Anthony T. Cluff, *Federally Financed Industrial Plants Constructed in Utah during World War II* (Logan: Utah State University Press, 1969); and Thomas G. Alexander, "Utah War Industry during World War II: A Human Impact Analysis," *Utah Historical Quarterly* 51 (Winter 1983): 72–92.

The literature on atomic energy is extensive. A good start is provided by James W. Kunetka, *City of Fire: Los Alamos and the Atomic Age, 1943–1945,* rev. ed. (Albuquerque: University of New Mexico Press, 1979); and the official history of the Atomic Energy Commission, Richard G. Hewlett and Oscar Anderson, *The New World, 1939–1946* (University Park: Pennsylvania State University Press, 1967).

Historians have given some attention to the wartime workforce. Braceros are discussed in Richard B. Craig, *The Bracero Program* (Austin: University of Texas Press, 1971); Ernesto Galarza, *Merchants of Labor: The Mexican Bracero Story* (Santa Barbara: McNally and Loftin, 1964); and Erasmo Gamboa, *Mexican Labor and World War II: Braceros in the Pacific Northwest, 1942–1947* (Austin: University of Texas Press, 1990). Also see Otey M. Scruggs, "Evolution of the Mexican Farm Labor Agreement of 1942," *Agricultural History* 34 (July 1960): 140–49. Some discussion of the economic impact of the war on Indians can be found in Alison Bernstein, *American Indians and World War II: Toward a New Era in Indian Affairs* (Norman: University of Oklahoma Press, 1991). On African Americans, two fine articles by Quintard Taylor are instructive: "The Great Migration: The Afro-American Communities of Seattle and Portland during the 1940s," *Arizona and the West* 23 (Summer 1981), 109–26; and Alonzo N. Smith and Quintard Taylor, "Racial Discrimination in the Work Place: A Study of Two West Coast Cities in the 1940s," *Journal of Ethnic History* (Spring 1980): 35–54. Alonzo Smith also wrote an informative dissertation, "Black Employment in the Los Angeles Area, 1938–1948" (Ph.D. diss., UCLA, 1978). Marilynn Johnson, *Conscripted*

193

Bibliographic Essay

Cities: World War II and San Francisco's East Bay (Berkeley: University of California Press, 1994), contains valuable information about blacks in Oakland and Richmond.

An introduction to women in the workplace is provided by Susan M. Hartman, *The Home Front and Beyond: American Women in the 1940s* (Boston: Twayne, 1982). D'Ann Campbell raises an important question in "Was the West Different? Values and Attitudes of Young Women in 1943," *Pacific Historical Review* 47 (August 1978): 453–63. Excellent accounts are in Sheila T. Lichtman, "Women at Work, 1941–45: Wartime Employment in the San Francisco Bay Area" (Ph.D. diss., University of California, Davis, 1981); and Amy V. Kesselman, *Fleeting Opportunities: Women Shipyard Workers in Portland and Vancouver during World War II and Reconversion* (Albany: State University of New York Press, 1990). On the other hand, Shernah Gluck, *Rosie the Riveter Revisited: Women, the War, and Social Change* (Boston: Twayne, 1987), is pedestrian and superficial.

Chapter 4. Reconverting the West, 1945–1960

One of the best short accounts of western cities in the context of postwar economic growth is Carl Abbott, *The Metropolitan Frontier* (Tucson: University of Arizona Press, 1993). Also helpful are Larry Schweikart and Lynn Doti, "Financing the Postwar Housing Boom in Phoenix and Los Angeles, 1945–1960," *Pacific Historical Review* 58 (May 1989): 173–94; and Mark S. Foster, "Prosperity's Prophet: Henry J. Kaiser and the Consumer Urban Culture, 1930–1950," *Western Historical Quarterly* 17 (April 1986): 165–84. Further references on the subject are provided in Mark S. Foster, "Urbanization in the Wide Open Spaces: Recent Historiography on Sunbelt Cities," *Journal of the West* 33 (Spring 1991): 68–85. Gilbert Guinn, "A Different Frontier: Aviation, the Army Air Forces and the Evolution of the Sunshine Belt," *Aerospace Historian* 29 (March 1982): 32–45, gives a brief glimpse of the military influence on the economic growth of the Sunbelt.

Historians of the West have not devoted much attention to the impact of air-conditioning on the course of the region's development. The most comprehensive effort is by Gail Cooper, *Air Conditioning America: Engi-*

neers and the Controlled Environment, 1900–1960 (Baltimore: Johns Hopkins University Press, 1998). Informative also are Frank Trippett, "The Great American Cooling Machine," *Time* 114 (August 13, 1979): 75; and Robert Friedman, "The Air Conditioned Century," *American Heritage* 35 (August–September 1984): 20–22. The history of swamp coolers is even more obscure, but see Bob Cunningham, "The Box That Broke the Barrier: The Swamp Cooler Comes to Southern Arizona," *Journal of Arizona History* 26 (Summer 1985): 163–74.

In addition to the references on housing cited above, useful discussions include Don Parsons, "The Development of Redevelopment: Public Housing and Urban Renewal in Los Angeles," *International Journal of Urban and Regional Research* 6 (September 1982): 393–413; and Thomas S. Hines, "Housing, Baseball, and Creeping Socialism: The Battle of Chavez Ravine, 1949–1959," *Journal of Urban History* 8 (February 1982): 123–43.

The best account of industrial parks is Everett M. Rogers and Judith K. Larsen, *Silicon Valley Fever* (New York: Basic Books, 1984), a work that is used by John Findlay in *Magic Lands: Western Cityscapes and American Culture after 1940* (Berkeley: University of California Press, 1992). The most detailed analysis of the Stanford Industrial Park is Rebecca Sue Lowen, "Exploiting a Wonderful Opportunity: Stanford University, Industry, and the Federal Government, 1937–1965" (Ph.D. diss., Stanford University, 1990). The outstanding authority in this field is Ann Markusen, whose many books and articles provide the best introduction to the subject. These include Peter Hall and Ann Markusen, eds., *Silicon Landscapes* (Boston: Allen and Unwin, 1985); Markusen, *Profit Cycles, Oligopoly, and Regional Development* (Cambridge: MIT Press, 1985); Markusen, *Regions: The Economics and Politics of Territory* (Totowa, N.J.: Rowman and Littlefield, 1987); and Markusen, *The Cold War Economy* (New York: Basic Books, 1992).

On highways in the 1950s, see Mark Rose, *Interstate: Express Highway Politics, 1941–1956* (Lawrence: University Press of Kansas, 1979); and Richard O. Davies, *The Age of Asphalt: The Automobile, the Freeway, and the Condition of Metropolitan America* (Philadelphia: Lippincott, 1975). The impact of roads on sparsely settled areas in the West is skillfully analyzed in Arthur R. Gomez, *Quest for the Golden Circle: The Four Corners and the*

Metropolitan West, 1945–1970 (Albuquerque: University of New Mexico Press, 1994).

The uranium boom of the 1950s has attracted a number of scholars. One of the most thorough is Gary Lee Shumway, "A History of the Uranium Industry on the Colorado Plateau" (Ph.D. diss., University of Southern California, 1970); also see Duane A. Smith, *Rocky Mountain Boom Town: A History of Durango* (Albuquerque: University of New Mexico Press, 1980); and Raye C. Ringholz, *Uranium Frenzy: Boom and Bust on the Colorado Plateau* (New York: Norton, 1989). Other energy sources are competently surveyed in Martin Melosi, *Coping with Abundance: Energy and Environment in Industrial America* (Philadelphia: Temple University Press, 1985). Despite the passage of years, Ernest R. Bartley, *The Tidelands Oil Controversy: A Legal and Historical Analysis* (Austin: University of Texas Press, 1953), still provides the most reliable guidance on this issue. On the manifold effects of the Alaska pipeline, see Mim Dixon, *What Happened to Fairbanks: The Effects of the Trans Alaska Oil Pipeline on the Community of Fairbanks, Alaska* (Boulder: Westview Press, 1978). Coal is the focus of Richard H. K. Vietor, *Environmental Politics and the Coal Coalition* (College Station: Texas A&M University Press, 1980).

One of the pioneers in tracing the interaction of economic and environmental policies is Elmo R. Richardson, *Dams, Parks and Politics: Resource Development and Preservation in the Truman-Eisenhower Era* (Lexington: University of Kentucky Press, 1973). In addition to works cited earlier in regard to dams and electric power, see Russell Martin, *A Story That Stands Like a Dam: Glen Canyon and the Struggle for the Soul of the West* (New York: Henry Holt, 1987); and Mark Harvey, *A Symbol of Wilderness: Echo Park and the American Conservation Movement* (Albuquerque: University of New Mexico Press, 1994).

Chapter 5. The Military-Industrial Complex in the Cold War, 1945–1960

The historical influence of the military establishment on the western economy deserves a full-length study. Until such a work appears, a wide range of books and scattered articles provide some guidance. These include Gerald D. Nash, "The West and the Military-Industrial Complex," *Mon-*

tana: *The Magazine of Western History* 49 (Winter 1990): 72–75. James L. Clayton, ed., *The Economic Impact of the Cold War* (New York: Harcourt Brace, 1970), does not focus on the West, but provides some national perspective. Roger Bolton, *Defense Purchases and Regional Growth* (Washington, D.C.: Brookings Institution, 1966), is an outstanding work that includes much material relating to the West. Ann Markusen, Peter Hall, Scott Campbell, and Sabrina Deitrick, *The Rise of the Gunbelt: The Military Remapping of Industrial America* (New York: Oxford University Press, 1991), is an excellent starting place for analysis of the subject. For California, the best work is Roger Lotchin, *Fortress California: From Warfare to Welfare, 1910–1961* (New York: Oxford University Press, 1992). Useful articles include James L. Clayton, "Defense Spending: Key to California's Growth," *Western Political Quarterly* 15 (June 1962): 280–93; and Clayton, "Impact of the Cold War on the Economies of California and Utah, 1946–1965," *Pacific Historical Review* 36 (November 1967): 449–73. More recent studies include Arthur C. Verge, "The Impact of the Second World War on Los Angeles," *Pacific Historical Review* 63 (August 1994): 289–314; and Marilynn S. Johnson, "War as a Watershed: The East Bay and World War II," *Pacific Historical Review* 63 (August 1994): 315–31. David L. Clark, "Improbable Los Angeles," in *Sunbelt Cities: Politics and Government since World War II,* ed. Richard Bernard and Bradley Rice (Austin: University of Texas Press, 1983), 268–308, is a broad essay focusing mainly on politics.

For other western states, the works of Leonard J. Arrington and associates already cited are essential. See also Leonard J. Arrington and Jon G. Perry, "Utah's Spectacular Missiles Industry: Its History and Impact," *Utah Historical Quarterly* 30 (Winter 1962): 3–39; and Edward Malaki, "Federal R&D Spending in the U.S.A.: Some Impacts on Metropolitan Economies," *Regional Studies* 16 (February 1982): 19–35. The role of western universities is skillfully detailed in Stuart W. Leslie, *The Cold War and American Science: The Military-Industrial-Academic Complex at MIT and Stanford* (New York: Columbia University Press, 1993); and Peter Galison and Bruce Healy, eds., *Big Science: The Growth of Large-Scale Research* (Stanford: Stanford University Press, 1992). Many works on missiles contain considerable material on the West. These include Ernest G. Schwiebert, ed., *A History of the U.S. Air Force Ballistic Missiles* (New

York: Praeger, 1965); Edmund Beard, *Developing the ICBM: A Study in Bureaucratic Politics* (New York: Columbia University Press, 1976); and a related work by Michael H. Armacost, *The Politics of Weapon Innovation: The Thor-Jupiter Controversy* (New York: Columbia University Press, 1969). Also see Jack Manno, *Arming the Heavens: The Hidden Military Agenda for Space* (New York: Dodd, Mead, 1984). A suggestive essay on economic implications of the military-industrial complex is Peter Hall, "The Creation of the American Aerospace Complex, 1955–1965: A Study in Industrial Inertia," in *Defence Expenditures and Regional Development,* ed. Michael Breheny (London: Mansell, 1988). Interest in the military-industrial complex in the 1960s inspired an extensive literature. A detailed bibliography can be found in Charles Moskos Jr., "The Concept of the Military-Industrial Complex: Radical Critique or Liberal Bogey?" *Social Problems* 21 (April 1977): 498–512. Also see Seymour Melman, *Our Depleted Society* (New York: Holt, Rinehart and Winston, 1965); John K. Galbraith, *Economics and the Public Purpose* (Boston: Houghton Mifflin, 1973); and Daniel Yergin, *Shattered Peace: The Origins of the Cold War and the National Security State* (Boston: Houghton Mifflin, 1973). Works that focus mainly on disarmament include Emile Benoit and Kenneth Boulding, eds., *Disarmament and the Economy* (New York: Harper and Row, 1963); and John J. Clark, *The Economics of Defense* (New York: Random House, 1963).

Chapter 6. A Period of Transition, 1960–1973

The economic growth and development of Sunbelt cities are treated in Carl Abbott, *The Metropolitan Frontier: Cities in the Modern American West* (Tucson: University of Arizona Press, 1993); Kirkpatrick Sale, *Power Shift: The Rise of the Southern Rim and Its Challenge to the Eastern Establishment* (New York: Random House, 1975); and other works cited in the previous chapters. Rural areas are discussed in Peggy F. Bartlett, *American Dreams, Rural Realities: Family Farms in Crisis* (Chapel Hill: University of North Carolina Press, 1993); and, more directly oriented to the West, in R. Douglas Hurt, ed., *The Rural West since 1945* (Lawrence: University Press of Kansas, 1998).

A rising concern about dams in the West was reflected at the time in a succession of articles and books. Wallace Stegner, "Myths of the Western Dams: The Disadvantages Often Outweigh the Benefits," *Saturday Review of Literature* 48 (October 23, 1965): 29–31, was one of the first to sound the alarm. Richard L. Berkman and W. Kip Viscusi, *Damming the West* (New York: Grossman, 1973), presents a brief against overbuilding. After that a number of books took up the issue, including Philip Fradkin, *A River No More* (New York: Knopf, 1981); Peter Wiley and Robert Gottlieb, *Empires in the Sun: The Rise of the New American West* (New York: Putnam, 1982); Donald Worster, *Rivers of Empire: Water, Aridity, and the Growth of the American West* (New York: Pantheon, 1986); and Marc Reisner, *Cadillac Desert: The American West and Its Disappearing Water* (New York: Viking Press, 1986).

The literature about the economic development of Indians is growing. An excellent introduction is Marjane Ambler, *Breaking the Iron Bonds: Indian Control of Energy Development* (Lawrence: University Press of Kansas, 1990). Sharply focused is Allen V. Kneese and F. Lee Brown, *The Southwest under Stress: National Resource Development Issues in a Regional Setting* (Baltimore: Johns Hopkins University Press, 1981). Also see Phil Reno, *Mother Earth, Father Sky and Economic Development: Navajo Resources and Their Use* (Albuquerque: University of New Mexico Press, 1981). A very distinguished collection of essays is *Public Policy Impacts on American Indian Economic Development,* ed. C. Mathew Snipp (Albuquerque: Native American Studies, University of New Mexico, 1988). One of the most thorough studies in this sphere is Keith LaVerne Fay, "Industrial Development and Its Impact on American Indian Reservation Economic Conditions" (Ph.D. diss., American University, 1973), which also contains brief summaries of individual business firms on Indian reservations. A sober appraisal is Larry W. Burt, "Western Tribes and Balance Sheets: Business Development Programs in the 1960s and 1970s," *Western Historical Quarterly* 23 (November 1992): 475–95, which also has helpful bibliographical references. A firsthand account of economic changes on the Navajo reservation by a trader is by Willow Roberts, *Stokes Carson: Twentieth Century Trading on the Navajo Reservation* (Albuquerque: University of New Mexico Press, 1987).

An excellent introduction to the United States–Mexico border economy is Niles Hansen, *The Border Economy: Regional Development in the Southwest* (Austin: University of Texas Press, 1981); see also Lawrence A. Herzog, *Where North Meets South: Cities, Space, and Politics on the United States–Mexico Border* (Austin: University of Texas Press, 1990); Philip Garcia and Aida Hurtado, "Joblessness among Hispanic Youth, 1973–1981," *Aztlan* 15 (Fall 1984): 243–61. Other minority groups are discussed in Ivan Light, *Ethnic Enterprise in America: Business and Welfare among Chinese, Japanese and Blacks* (Berkeley: University of California Press, 1972); Edna Bonacich and John Modell, *The Economic Basis of Ethnic Solidarity: Small Business in the Japanese-American Community* (Berkeley: University of California Press, 1980). Also consult Edna Bonacich, Ivan Light, and Charles Wong, "Koreans in Small Business," *Society* (September–October 1977): 54–59; and Ivan Light and Edna Bonacich, *Immigrant Entrepreneurs: Koreans in Los Angeles, 1965–1982* (Berkeley: University of California Press, 1988). A major problem of African Americans is discussed in Andrew J. Kliman, "Rising Joblessness among Black Male Youth, 1950–1980: A Regional Analysis" (Ph.D. diss., University of Utah, 1988); and Susan M. Strom, "Black Community Organizations and the Role of the Black Press in Resource Mobilization in Los Angeles from 1940 to 1980" (Ph.D. diss., University of Minnesota, 1989).

An imaginative analysis of women in the western workforce is Louise Lamphere et al., *Sunbelt Working Mothers: Reconciling Family and Factory* (Ithaca: Cornell University Press, 1993). A regional study is Charlene J. Allison, Sue-Ellen Jacobs, and Mary A. Porter, *Winds of Change: Women in Northwest Commercial Fishing* (Seattle: University of Washington Press, 1989). Also see Lea Ybarra, "When Wives Work: The Impact on the Chicano Family," *Journal of Marriage and the Family* 44 (February 1982): 169–78. An interesting article on women entrepreneurs is Gloria Ricci Lothrop, "A Trio of Mermaids: Their Impact upon the Southern California Sportswear Industry," *Journal of the West* 25 (January 1986), 73–82.

Chapter 7. The Era of Deindustrialization, 1973–2000

The energy crisis of the 1970s generated an extensive literature. Some of these writings relate specifically to the West, such as Lynton R. Hayes, *Energy, Economic Growth, and Regionalism in the West* (Albuquerque: University of New Mexico Press, 1980); and James L. Regens, Robert W. Rycroft, and Gregory N. Daneke, eds., *Energy and the Western United States* (New York: Praeger, 1982). Also see Franklin Tugwell, *The Energy Crisis and the American Political Economy* (Palo Alto: Stanford University Press, 1988). An excellent work is David Leo Weimer, *The Strategic Petroleum Reserve* (Westport, Conn.: Greenwood Press, 1982). On coal, Thadis W. Box, *Rehabilitation Potentials of Western Coal Lands* (Cambridge, Mass.: Ballinger, 1974), introduces the subject. A very thorough analysis of an important aspect of western coal exploitation is Brian J. Morton, "Coal Leasing in the Fourth World: Hopi and Navajo Coal Leasing, 1954–1977" (Ph.D. diss., University of California, Berkeley, 1985). Coal mining in Wyoming is covered in A. Dudley Gardner and Verla R. Flores, *Forgotten Frontier: A History of Wyoming Coal Mining* (Boulder: Westview Press, 1989). The best study of the oil shale debacle is Andrew Gulliford, *Boomtown Blues: Colorado Oil Shale, 1885–1985* (Niwot: University Press of Colorado, 1989).

The concern about nuclear energy in the Pacific Northwest is best described in James Leighland and Robert Land, *WP$$: Who Is to Blame for the WPPSS Disaster?* (Cambridge, Mass.: Ballinger, 1986); and the more argumentative volume by David Myhra, *Whoops/WPPSS: Washington Public Power Supply System Nuclear Plants* (Jefferson, N.C.: McFarland, 1984). A more sober appraisal of the historical and legal background is Michael C. Blumm, "The Northwest's Hydroelectric Heritage: Prologue to the Pacific Northwest Power Planning and Conservation Act," *Washington Law Review* 58 (April 1983): 175–244. On the increasing alarm over nuclear issues, see Michele S. Gerber, *On the Home Front: The Cold War Legacy of the Hanford Site* (Lincoln: University of Nebraska Press, 1992).

Western land problems are critically discussed in Paul S. Taylor, *Essays on Land, Water, and the Law in California* (New York: Arno Press, 1979). Two outstanding articles by Paul W. Gates, a preeminent authority, deserve close examination: "Pressure Groups and Recent Land Policies," *Agricultural History* 55 (April 1981): 103–27; and "The Intermountain West against Itself," *Arizona and the West* 27 (Autumn 1985): 205–36. Ellen Liebman, *California Farmland: A History of Large Agricultural Landholding* (Totowa, N.J.: Roman and Allanheld, 1983); Will Voigt Jr., *Grazing Lands: Use and Misuse by Industry and Government* (New

Brunswick: Rutgers University Press, 1976); and Mark Friedberger, *Shakeout: Iowa Farm Families in the 1980s* (Lexington: University Press of Kentucky, 1989), all deal with the decline of agricultural communities. The Sagebrush Rebellion is well covered in C. Brant Short, *Ronald Reagan and the Public Lands: America's Conservation Debate, 1979–1984* (College Station: Texas A&M University Press, 1989); and R. McGregor Cawley, *Federal Land, Western Anger: The Sagebrush Rebellion and Environmental Politics* (Lawrence: University Press of Kansas, 1993).

General works that touch on economic experiences of Asian Americans include H. Brett Melendy, *Asians in America: Filipinos, Koreans and East Indians* (Boston: Twayne, 1977). Harry L. Kitano and Roger Daniels, *Asian Americans: Emerging Minorities* (Englewood Cliffs, N.J.: Prentice-Hall, 1988), is informative; and Bill Ong Hing, *Making and Remaking Asian America through Immigration Policy, 1850–1990* (Stanford: Stanford University Press, 1990), is valuable for understanding the relationship between federal policies and economic impact. Sucheng Chan, *The Asian Americans: An Interpretive History* (Boston: G. K. Hall/Twayne, 1994), integrates social and economic influences. The economic adjustments of Filipinos after 1965 are best described in Luciano Mangiafico, *Contemporary American Immigrants: Patterns of Filipino, Korean, and Chinese Settlement in the United States* (New York: Praeger, 1988). Business activities of Koreans are touched on in this work and also in Philip P. Choy, *Koreans in America* (Chicago: Nelson Hall, 1979); and in Edna Bonacich, *Immigrant Entrepreneurs: Koreans in Los Angeles, 1965–1982* (Berkeley: University of California Press, 1988). The literature on economic adjustments of Vietnamese is large. A good introduction is Gail Paradise Kelly, *From Vietnam to America: A Chronicle of the Vietnamese Immigration to the United States* (Boulder: Westview Press, 1977). Darrel Montero, *Vietnamese Americans: Patterns of Resettlement and Socioeconomic Adaptation in the United States* (Boulder: Westview Press, 1979), provides useful economic data. Case studies of individual experiences are found in Paul J. Strand and Woodrow Jones Jr., *Indochinese Refugees in America: Problems of Adaptation and Assimilation* (Durham: Duke University Press, 1985); and James A. Freeman, *Hearts of Sorrow: Vietnamese American Lives* (Stanford: Stanford University Press, 1989).

A broad survey of economic adjustments of Chinese immigrants is included in Shih-shan Henry Tsai, *The Chinese Experience in America* (Bloomington: Indiana University Press, 1986). Older works include Stanford Lyman, *Chinese Americans* (New York: Random House, 1974); Francis L. K. Hsu, *The Challenge of the American Dream: The Chinese in the United States* (Belmont, Calif.: Wadsworth, 1971); and Ivan H. Light, *Ethnic Enterprise in America: Business and Welfare among Chinese, Japanese, and Blacks* (Berkeley: University of California Press, 1972).

203

Index

C

California, 11, 12; aerospace industry in, 95; agribusiness in, 106; Asian immigration to, 142; and Boulder Dam, 24, 146; and Central Valley Project, 26; food production in World War I, 14–15; military installations in, 78, 81, 98, 156; and MX missile system, 139; oil in, 148; Silicon Valley, 104–5; in World War II, 42, 44, 46; Camp (Fort) Carson, 82, 84, 92

Campbell, Ben Lighthorse, 135

Carrier, Willis H., 58, 59

Carter, Jimmy: and coal, 130; energy plan of, 125–26, 128, 132; land policy of, 136; and MX missiles, 138; and Strategic Oil Reserve, 124; and West, 134

cattle industry, 14–15, 48

Central Arizona Project, 107, 134, 147

Central Valley Project (Calif.), 26, 146

Chaffee, George, 8, 9

Chandler, Harry, 89

Chapman, Oscar, 71

Chavez, Cesar, 118

Chavez, Dennis, 38

Chinese and Taiwanese immigrants, 140, 142

Civilian Conservation Corps (CCC): and Dinosaur National Monument, 70; and Native Americans, 35–36, 37, 38; in New Deal era, 18–29, 34

Clean Air Act of 1970, 127, 130

Clinton, Bill, 73, 150

coal industry, 73, 109–11, 112, 114, 115, 123–26, 130, 147, 149–50

Cold War, 60, 98

Collier, John, 35–36, 157

colonialism and the West, 3–4, 20, 21–22, 145–46

Colorado: agribusiness in, 106; and Big Thompson Project, 25; coal in, 125; and global economy, 156, 159; military installations in, 81, 87, 98, 156; oil shales in, 126, 128, 129; silver in, 33; uranium in, 65; in World War I, 15

Colorado Fuel and Iron Company, 46

Colorado River, 24, 25, 108

Colorado Springs, 82–85, 87, 91–92, 156

Columbia River, 26–27

Commodity Credit Corporation, 29

computer chips, 101, 104

Cooke, Morris L., 31

copper industry, 14, 15, 49

Council of Energy Resources, 111

D

dams: in New Deal era, 23–27, 39, 146; in 1950s, 60, 68; 1960–73, 102, 106–7; 1973–2000, 133, 134, 147;

Defense Plant Corporation, 44, 45, 46, 47, 57

Denver, 44, 61, 101, 109, 129

Department of Agriculture (U.S.): and Hispanics in 1930s, 37–38; policies in New Deal, 28–29

Department of Defense (U.S.): expenditures by, 64, 78, 92, 97; and MX missiles, 138; R&D contracts, 78, 92, 97

Department of Energy (U.S.), 125, 129

Grazing Service (U.S.), 24

Great Plains: agribusiness in, 106; and global economy, 159; Native American businesses in, 113; during New Deal, 27, 29–31; in World War I, 14–15

Great Plains Drought Area Committee, 31

H

Hanford (Wash.), 51–52, 92, 155

harbors, 13

Hatch, Carl, 38

Hatch, Orrin, 136

Hawaii, 12, 150; military expenditures in, 81, 98, 148, 154, 156

Hell's Canyon (Idaho), 68

Hewlett-Packard, 92

High-tech industries, 63–64, 87, 92

highway acts: 1916, 7; 1921, 19; 1956, 64–65, 151

Hill Air Force Base, 85

Hispanics: and civil rights movement, 102; and U.S.–Mexican border, 117, 158–59; during 1930s, 35–38; and New Mexico land grants, 11, 117–18

Hoover, Herbert: and Colorado River Compact (1922), 19, 146; and New Deal, 24, 41; and World War I, 14–15, 27, 148

Hoover Dam. See Boulder Dam

Housing Act of 1949, 63, 152

I

Ickes, Harold: and western colonialism, 21–23, 146; and forests in 1930s, 34; and oil in World War II, 49; and tidelands (offshore), 67–68

Idaho, 12, 33; forests in, 34; and global economy, 159; military installations in, 78; scientific research in, 140

Immigration and Naturalization Act of 1965, 140

Indian Reorganization Act of 1975, 157–58

Indians. See Native Americans

Indian Service. See Bureau of Indian Affairs

industrial parks, 63–64

Industrial Workers of the World, 16

Intercontinental Ballistic Missile (ICBM), 94

Intermountain Power Project, 126

Interstate Highway Act of 1956, 64–65, 151

irrigation, 8, 9, 23, 26

J

Jackson Hole National Monument, 69–70

Jet Propulsion Laboratory, 51, 93

Johnson, Lyndon B., 105, 110, 122, 140, 157

K

Kaiser, Henry J., 45, 57, 61–62

Kansas, 159

Kettner, William D., 13, 14

Keynes, John Maynard, xii, 41, 56

Killian, James, 78

Kindelberger, Dutch, 88

Kondratieff, Nicolae, xi–xiii, 4, 41, 52, 74, 80, 101, 119, 121, 160

Koreans, 140, 141

National Park Service: and Dinosaur National Monument, 70–71; during New Deal, 24, 28, 34; in 1950s, 74

National Resources Planning Board, 41

Native Americans, 11, 145; economic development and businesses, 110–16, 156–57; in 1930s, 35–36; and roads, 65; in World War II, 48

natural gas, 66–67, 111, 123, 132, 149

Navajos: and coal leases, 114; and economic development, 111–16, 158; and Lake Powell, 72, 73; and New Deal, 36–37; and roads in 1950s, 65

Navy (U.S.), 11–12, 13, 16

Nebraska, 85, 159

Nelson, Donald, 49

Nevada, 12; air-conditioning in, 59; mining in, 33; MX missiles in, 138, 139; and U.S. Navy, 12, 148; and Sagebrush Rebellion, 136–37; Nevada Test Site (nuclear), 156

New Deal: agriculture and, 27–31, 39; investment, 21; and Native Americans, 110, 157; and World War I, 18; and World War II, 41

Newlands Act, 9–10, 19, 146

New Mexico: coal in, 109–10, 125, 150; energy in 1970s, 126; and global economy, 159; Hispanic villages in, 118; military installations in, 78, 81, 87, 98; Native American businesses, 112, 113; natural gas in, 66; uranium in 1950s, 65–66

Nieburg, H. L., 86–87

Nixon, Richard, 107, 122, 123, 124

North American Air Defense Command (NORAD), 82, 83, 85, 92

North American Free Trade Agreement (NAFTA), 159

North Dakota: coal in, 125, 150; farm crisis of 1930s in, 29; military installations in, 78, 81; MX missiles in, 138, 139; and World War II, 44

Northrop, Jack, 88

nuclear energy, 123, 125, 130–32

nuclear power plants, 130, 132

O

Office of Economic Opportunity (OEO), 113, 116

Office of Indian Affairs. *See* Bureau of Indian Affairs

Office of Price Administration (OPA), 48–49

oil industry, 67–68, 108–9, 111, 123, 132; before World War I, 6, 148; in World War I, 16; in World War II, 49, 50, 149

oil shales, 126–29

Oklahoma, 66, 81, 148

Olympic National Park, 35, 70, 72

OPEC, 121, 122, 123, 149

Oppenheimer, J. Robert, 51

Oregon, 12, 34, 44

Oregon and California Railroad lands, 34–35

P

Pacific Northwest: and aerospace industry, 91; and aluminum, 47; dam building in, 26–27, 146; and forests in 1930s, 34–35; nuclear power in, 130–32; timber issues in, 70; in World War I, 15, 16

Index

About the Author

Gerald D. Nash is Distinguished Professor of History at the University of New Mexico. He received a B.A. from New York University, an M.A. in history from Columbia University, and a Ph.D. in history from the University of California, Berkeley. He has served as a postdoctoral fellow at Harvard University and has taught at the University of California, Stanford University, and, for the last thirty years, at the University of New Mexico. He has been a Fellow of the Newberry Library, the Huntington Library, and the National Endowment for the Humanities. During 1990–91 he served as George Bancroft Professor of American History at the University of Göttingen in Germany. He served as president of the Western History Association in 1990–91. He is the author of many books, including *The American West in the Twentieth Century, The American West Transformed: The Impact of World War II, Creating the West,* and *A. P. Giannini and the Bank of America.* His most recent book is *Researching Western History* (1997), which he edited with Richard W. Etulain. He is currently engaged in studies of the military influence on the western economy.